The
TONYA
TAPES

The Tonya Harding Story

In Her Own Voice

Lynda D. Prouse

Foreword by Michael Rosenberg

aU
Di
en
CE

audience artist group

First published in USA in 2008
by World Audience

ISBN 978-1-934209-80-6

10-digit ISBN 1-93420980-5

$18.99

© 2008, World Audience, Inc.

303 Park Avenue South, #1440
New York, NY 10010-3657
USA

Photos Courtesy of Tonya Harding and Linda Lewis.

Photo on front cover courtesy of Al Harding.

Photo of Author on back cover courtesy of David M. Szabo.

Edited by Kyle David Torke.

Book Design by Matthew Ward (Mockfrog Design).

World Audience (www.worldaudience.org) is a global consortium of
artists and writers, producing quality books, the literary journal *Audience*,
and *The Audience Review*. Our periodicals and books are edited by
M. Stefan Strozier and assistant editors. Submit stories, poems,
paintings, photography, or artwork: submissions@worldaudience.org.
Inquire about being a reviewer: theatre@worldaudience.org. Thank you.

New York (NY, USA).

Newcastle (NSW, Australia).

In loving memory of my parents, Bob and Vera Prouse,
and to my husband, David Szabo,
whose steadfast belief in me made this book possible.

Lynda D. Prouse

To all those who have suffered abuse and haven't been heard.

Tonya Harding

Contents

Acknowledgments

Thanks to my dear friend and manger Michael Rosenberg, who has gone far beyond the call of duty in order to see this book published. For his deep belief in 'The Tonya Tapes', his encouragement when others failed to 'get it', his excellent writing and editing skills, I am profoundly grateful. Thanks also to Linda Lewis for her support and tireless efforts in gathering many of the photographs for this book, and to those at World Audience, especially publisher Mike Strozier for his enthusiasm and patience, Matthew Ward for his thoughtful and creative book design, and of course, editor 'extraordinaire' Kyle Torke. I am also very grateful to publicist Nicole Goesseringer, who has become such an integral part of our team.

And to my friends and family, especially brothers Terry and Bob, and sister Marlene, thank you for your support and for the time spent listening to me as I worked through this project. I love you all dearly.

Finally, thank you Tonya for trusting me with your story. The journey we took together has truly touched my heart.

—Lynda D. Prouse

My love and thanks to Michael Rosenberg, Lynda Prouse, Linda and Greg Lewis, and to all those others who have been so supportive in helping me to regain my life.

—Tonya Harding

Foreword

by **Michael A. Rosenberg**

Tonya Harding's First-and-Only Figure Skating Manager

What may surprise you is that Tonya Harding is nice … very nice.

If you went to a dinner party and around the table were seated champi-on athletes from several sports, at the end of the evening Tonya would most likely be one of your favorite guests. She is quick-witted, interesting, charm-ing, funny … and, as I said, nice.

Her delightful social presence is amazing when you consider she was raised by an alcoholic and abusive mother and a weak father, sexually molested by her half-brother, forced by her parents to move to different homes (which for the most part were trailers parked in relatives' driveways) at least twice per school year, lived in truly dirt poor conditions, and was never really taught by anyone the 'niceties' of social interaction.

Admittedly, she can also be unpolished, tough, coarse, and more com-fortable in a pool hall with a cigarette in one hand and a beer in the other – or working on a carburetor under the hood of a car – than practicing a choreographed skating program on the ice. Unlike most women in figure skating, Tonya's image is definitely not the 'girl-next-door' (which irked the United States Figure Skating Association to no end), and that dichotomy of personality has always made her a magnet for the press.

But somehow, some way, Tonya Harding wakes up each morning with a positive attitude and deep faith that eventually her life will all work out. She doesn't look back on her tribulations in a negative way; instead, she always seems to be optimistic and cheerful. And she's been jailed, on pro-bation, despised, made the object of jokes on national TV, fined all of the money she had (and more), and ended up broke – while watching many of her fellow skaters make millions of dollars due primarily to the upsurge of the sport she unwittingly brought to a spectacularly popular level.

I first met Tonya in 1991 after she won the first of her two National Figure Skating Championships; I signed her as a client with the expectation that she would be a serious contender for the Gold Medal at one of the two upcoming Olympics.

She was the most athletic female skater I had ever seen (and I have represented over 100 National, World, or Olympic Figure Skating Champions during my 25-year career*); she was the first American woman to complete successfully the legendary (and only once previously performed by anyone) triple-Axel, the 3½-revolution difficult jump that immediately brought her international fame.

I decided to fire her as a client in the fall of 1993, three months before the "whack on the knee" scandal, because her former husband, Jeff Gillooly, was constantly interfering in our relationship and advising her to demand more money for her skating appearances than I could negotiate for her. He was a rude, obnoxious, and arrogant man, and his influence over her was much greater than mine.

Terminating our relationship turned out, of course, to be one of the luckiest decisions in my life; otherwise, I would have been in front of the Portland grand jury stating that "I knew nothing of the plot against Nancy Kerrigan," and I would have appeared as either a liar or at the least a very poor manager.

Instead, I watched all of the legal drama play out in the press, and I occasionally gave interviews (as her former manager) stating that I believed Tonya when she said that "she had nothing to do with conspiring against Nancy" – who had been her roommate several times and who she considered to be a friend. I believed then, and believe to this day, that Tonya wasn't afraid to compete against Nancy: Tonya had beaten Nancy several times and was certain that she would again. The only skater Tonya 'feared' was the 15-year-old Ukrainian, Oksana Baiul, the reigning World Champion. Tonya was cocky – but she wasn't a criminal.

The next time I saw Tonya was in Lillehamer at the Olympic Games as she answered questions from world reporters at the biggest press conference in Olympic history; and I saw her again when she had a security guard at the arena bring me backstage and she begged me on her knees to take her back as a client. Although I truly liked Tonya and believed in her innocence, I declined to re-sign her, mostly because I then represented her rival, Oksana Baiul, and considered my current obligations to Oksana to be an obvious conflict of interest.

When Tonya returned to the U.S. following a melodramatic and disappointing performance at the Olympics (in front of the 5th highest-rated television audience of all time), awaiting her were the FBI and assorted prosecutors who wanted to question her about the assault on Nancy. No one knew at that time that she had been terrorized, intimidated, and ultimately gang-raped as a 'final warning' not to testify against Jeff and his cohorts. She has never admitted to these violent and tragic experiences out of an inappropriate and undeserved sense of shame until this book.

So, she didn't openly testify against the people who brutalized her, and they ended up plea-bargaining shorter jail sentences for themselves. As for Tonya, she was found guilty only of "hindering the prosecution" because she "had found out after-the-fact that those men had conspired and then assaulted Nancy and then failed to tell the authorities."

We should all recognize that neither the prosecutors nor the judge brought conspiracy charges against her, and that she was not found guilty of conspiracy – and she insisted all along that she would never play any part in hurting Nancy. Furthermore, no evidence or proof was ever presented that would have led to a conclusion of guilt on that charge.

Regardless, she was placed on three years of probation, fined $160,000.00, and compelled to perform 500 hours of community service. The sentence of the court, in my subjective opinion, was totally overboard in punishing her for "hindering the prosecution," and I believe her punishment resulted from a judiciary bowing to public opinion and the conventional wisdom of the day. And the legal and emotional consequences almost killed her.

Several years later, I attempted to help Tonya make a professional comeback by inviting her to skate in the 'World Cup Skating Championship,' which I produced for ESPN. Until that time, no one else had helped her at all because she had been banned from amateur skating by the sanctimonious United States Figure Skating Association – and boycotted from performing by the professional producers, ice shows, and promoters.

She accepted my invitation – then trained and practised hard – and skated wonderfully. A sold-out crowd gave her a standing ovation, the television audience was huge, and she won the Silver Medal. She was back.

But Tonya's stars always seemed to be crossed, and before she could accept any of the many offers that came to her following the competition and her highly-rated appearance on 'Larry King Live,' the heavily publicized 'hubcap incident' occurred, and all of her opportunities disappeared overnight.

Again, years went by before Tonya called me regarding an invitation she had gotten from Fox TV to fight on a new show entitled 'Celebrity Boxing.'

They had offered her $5,000, which she correctly felt was unfair, and she asked that I try to negotiate a better fee for her participation. I agreed, and after much give-and-take with Fox and the show's sponsors, she earned $150,000 for that night.

As it turned out, the ratings were astronomical, and she should have received even more money – but both of us celebrated her victory over Paula Jones in the ring – and more importantly, we celebrated the fact that she was solvent again, at least for the moment.

After the boxing match, we again went our separate ways; she continued boxing with mixed success, and I sold my management firm to a large corporation and semi-retired. Only when Lynda Prouse, a superb writer I had worked with before on several other clients' books, called me regarding *The Tonya Tapes* did my most infamous ex-client come back into my life.

When you read her story and hear her side – in her own words – I firmly believe that you will see the fine line between 'extraordinary talent' and 'extraordinary trouble.' I believe you will understand much better why she did what she did, and you will finally admire her unimaginably strong spirit. Her magnificent spirit has helped her survive what would have broken most of us.

The most universally recognized figure skater in history is not 'broken' ... she stands tall (for 5'1"), defiant, contagiously optimistic ... and she has most of us rooting for her to 'make it' in life. I certainly do.

—Michael Rosenberg

* Former manager of Dorothy Hamill, Oksana Baiul, Victor Petrenko, Rudy Galindo, Alexei Urmanov, Tai Babilonia & Randy Gardner, Elizabeth Manley, Linda Fratianne, Klimova & Ponamarenko, Punsalan & Swallow, Jill Trenary, Gritschuk & Platov, Caryn Kadavy, Jozef Sabovcik, and Tonya Harding, among others. Also partially represented Katarina Witt in the United States and promoted Elvis Stojko tours in Canada.

In the music world, managed Peggy Lee and Johnny Rivers and promoted nationally Stevie Wonder, Aretha Franklin, Smokey Robinson, Quincy Jones, and other soul superstars.

Introduction

by **Lynda D. Prouse**

Tonya Harding is arguably the most tarnished woman in the history of sport, and the scandal that surrounded her in the winter of 1994 exposed a shockingly dark side to the seemingly pristine world of competitive figure skating.

Her infamy began prior to the Olympic Games when rumors circulated of Tonya's involvement with the attack on her teammate, Nancy Kerrigan, who had been clubbed on the knee at the U.S. National Figure Skating Championships. Nancy was forced to withdraw from the competition while Tonya went on to win the event, ensuring a coveted placement on the Olympic and World team.

Considered to be one of the best skaters of her time, Tonya was the only American woman to complete a triple Axle jump in competition; however, her rough image and lifestyle left much to be desired in the eyes of those who controlled the sport. She had already won a National title in 1991 over Kristi Yamaguchi and Nancy Kerrigan, and went on to place second at the World Championships that same year – behind Kristi, but above Nancy. The following year, Tonya came fourth at the Olympics where Kristi was crowned Champion and Nancy claimed Bronze. When Kristi retired from amateur competition, it became clear to many that a media-inspired rivalry between Tonya and Nancy was fast unfolding. Tonya had the jumps and athleticism while Nancy had the look and artistry.

At the 1993 National Championships, Nancy won the title and Tonya placed fourth, losing her chance to compete at the World Championships where Nancy would skate, but only place fifth. Then came the 1994 Nationals and the scandalous assault. The story was immediately picked up by the international media and would dominate television and the press for months.

While Tonya declared her innocence, intense investigations began, and soon after authorities began making inquiries, one of those involved implied that Jeff Gillooly, Tonya's ex-husband, had master-minded the plot. Speculation followed that Tonya would be pulled from the Olympic team; however, her lawyers stepped in and threatened the United States Figure

Skating Association (USFSA) with a lawsuit. Until her guilt was proven in court, she would not be banned from skating.

Nancy recovered from her injury in time to compete at the Olympics, and her appearance on the same ice as Tonya, amid a massive media frenzy, became one of the most watched television events in history. One hundred and twenty seven million viewers worldwide tuned in for the short program alone, which ultimately led to an incredible rise in the popularity of the sport, creating untold future opportunities for figures skaters and those involved in the industry. Nancy would capture the Silver Medal from the Olympics and go on to a successful professional career while Tonya placed a dismal eighth and would soon find her life in shatters.

Pleading guilty to a charge of 'hindering the prosecution', Tonya admitted to learning after she arrived home from Nationals that her ex-husband and his cronies (Shawn, Derrick, Shane – see Author's Note regarding the use of some last names) were allegedly involved in the attack. The reason she didn't come forward as soon as she discovered who had instigated the assault was never fully explained until the writing of this book. And, until now, no one has explained the reason she went back to her husband in the first place, who, she maintained, beat and belittled her.

As punishment for her (however tangential) participation in Nancy Kerrigan's assault, Tonya was stripped of her National title, put on probation, and served with huge monetary fines and hundreds of hours of community service. As the final reprimand, she was officially banned from sanctioned competition for life and unofficially shunned by the figure skating world in general. Although no rulings had been made that would prevent her from skating professionally, few skaters wanted to associate with Tonya for fear their own careers would be in jeopardy. Allowing the public to see inside a sport that had worked hard to manufacture an image of 'ice princesses with fairy-tale lives' had been a great embarrassment to the figure skating hierarchy, and it mattered not that this unrealistic image often drove young women to eating disorders, drug and alcohol abuse, and a tremendous amount of emotional instability. Meanwhile, the players in the sport took advantage of the constant media attention; and through television specials, shows, and professional competitions, they generated millions of dollars in revenues.

Tonya's expulsion from the skating community was devastating. Her very existence evolved around the sport, and skating was the only area of her life where she shone. According to Tonya, any measure of true self-worth she felt came from her skating ability. Growing up in poverty and dominated by an alcoholic mother, she was constantly berated, and the verbal abuse she received from her mother in public would cause several people to call Social Services. In private, Tonya says, the beatings she took were frequent and harsh and the sexual molestation she suffered at the hands of an older half-brother, which began when she was five and continued into her teens, served to further harden her spirit.

Without skating to earn an income, Tonya found herself in dire financial straits. While her mother, ex-husband, friends, and others apparently cashed in on her downfall, she was now heavily in debt and maintains it took several years before she was able to pay off legal bills incurred as a result of the scandal. She remarried, but was separated from her new husband within just a few months.

After a couple of years, the media circus that surrounded Tonya began to subside; however, after saving an elderly woman's life, she was soon in the headlines again. A few months later, interest in Tonya reached another fever-pitch when she reported to the police that she was the victim of a kidnapping attempt. Jokes were made about the incident; but according to Tonya, people didn't realize that since 1994 she had been continually hounded and followed by obsessive strangers. Some left love notes at her door while others left death threats.

Although Tonya had publicly expressed her regret to Nancy Kerrigan several times, Tonya's sentiments had always been conveyed through the media. So, in 1997, she agreed to meet Nancy face-to-face on national television and apologize again. Tonya asserts that although Nancy said she would never appear with her, the enticement of a large fee must have been a strong incentive. While Tonya was also paid for her appearance, she says she didn't realize that a skating show, in which Nancy was starring, was to immediately follow the 'apology' and be broadcast in its entirety. Again, the television ratings for the so-called 'apology show' went through the roof.

In the spring of 1999, Tonya was re-signed by the skating management firm she had been associated with during her more successful years. Owned by Michael Rosenberg, the organization represented a large stable of Olympic and World Champions but had been forced to sever Tonya's relationship when her then-husband caused constant conflict by repeatedly interfering with her career. With the firm's renewed backing, she made several appearances on national talk shows, expressing her desire to compete and perform as a professional skater, believing she had "more-than paid her dues for past mistakes." Then, in the fall of 1999, she was invited by the firm to participate in its ESPN Skating Professional Competition, featuring past Olympic and World Champions, where she incredibly placed second behind an Olympic Silver Medalist. After the event concluded, the firm was flooded with requests for Tonya interviews and appearances. The highest rated were 'Larry King Live,' 'Rivera Live,' and 'Maury Povich'; and she was featured prominently in 'TV Guide.' Business offers also poured in; she was asked to host a nationally syndicated radio talk show, star in American produced skating shows in Asia, Europe, and Australia, and to tour North America as the featured skater in a revitalized Ice Capades.

Prior to the ESPN event, Michael Rosenberg asked if I would consider authoring Tonya's autobiography based on my extensive experience with elite skaters and on the articles and best-selling books I had written about them. I suppose that I, too, had inadvertently taken advantage of the surge in the popularity of the sport caused by 'Tonya-Nancy.' However, I was somewhat wary of this latest offer, having formed my own generally negative opinion of Tonya Harding.

I reluctantly agreed to meet Tonya at the ESPN event in Huntington, West Virginia, and was immediately struck by her diminutive appearance and courteous manner. Where was the larger-than-life woman with the brusque attitude that I, like millions of others, had come to expect? Was I being duped into falling for a first-rate acting job, or had the media's portrayal of Tonya Harding been hugely blown out of proportion? Either way, I assumed, the interviews I agreed to conduct with her could be very, very interesting.

Over the course of the next few months, I telephoned Tonya at arranged times and interviewed her in the same manner I had done with many other celebrity figure skaters. The sessions were taped, with her consent, and what she provided would give me the basis for the autobiography I intended to write. As in past experiences, I would glean as much information as possible, create the manuscript in Tonya's voice, and be credited on the cover with an "As Told To." Upon completion, the plan was to publish and market the new book as one of the 'great comeback tales' of the century.

I spent many hours interviewing Tonya, and, to say the least, I was not disappointed with her story. In fact, at times, I was so saddened or shaken

I would have to stop the interview. Much of her story I found riveting, some of the events appalled me, and many of our discussions left me drained, but I was always drawn back for more. When the answers to some of my questions didn't seem to make sense, I would ask again and again until I was satisfied with her response – or just simply realized that I couldn't get anything else from her. During the interviews, neither of us thought the tapes would be used for anything more than the information I sought to write the autobiography; and as such, Tonya, especially, was probably freer in her words than she would have been had she thought otherwise.

We were close to finishing the interviews when a series of events would bring Tonya's comeback, and the original book, to an abrupt halt. In early January, 2000 – exactly six years after the attack on Nancy Kerrigan – Tonya was driving to a coaching job and lost control of her vehicle. Although she was not charged in the mishap, she suffered some painful injuries and was prescribed various medications that she took along with the anti-depressant she had been on since 1996. According to Tonya, she was never properly warned about the potentially serious impact of taking such a combination of drugs nor of the possible effects alcohol mixed with these drugs might have on her system.

In late February, after taking her pills and consuming what Tonya says was only a small amount of alcohol, she got into a quarrel with her then-boyfriend that escalated into what would become known as the 'hubcap incident..' This resulted in her arrest and guilty plea to disorderly conduct and malicious mischief. Another media whirlwind ensued, and her boyfriend sold his side of the story to a tabloid (that Tonya later proved had doctored the photographs of his injured face). Consequently, she served three days in jail, 80 hours of community service, and attended anger management classes. Shortly after the incident, she again appeared on 'Larry King Live' to try and set the record straight about the tabloid and to state her desire to "turn her life around."

While Tonya and her boyfriend took up separate residences, she amazingly continued to see him; and even during our (by then) sporadic interviews and informal conversations, she remained loyal to him, telling me he must have sold the story during a "moment of weakness." They would split up for good a few months later.

Not as surprisingly, all business offers were withdrawn pending a resolution to Tonya's latest episode. Because the book was to be marketed as a 'comeback story,' we decided we needed to completely rewrite the proposal. More interviews followed; however, after reviewing the project, her manager and I had misgivings about the autobiographical theme of the book, and we decided to shelve the project for the time-being. I stopped work on the manuscript and filed the tapes away.

Tonya went on to make further headlines a couple of years later for driving under the influence and then by taking up the life of a pro boxer. One of the 'celebrity' matches – Fox's 'Celebrity Boxing,' pitting her against an alleged paramour of President Clinton – Paula Jones – again sent the television ratings to record highs. Then during the 2006 Winter Olympics, Tonya appeared on 'Entertainment Tonight,' commenting on the Olympics and the newest reality show, 'Skating with Celebrities.' During one of these interviews, a television reporter asked Tonya if she would ever tell her whole story. I watched the show and thought, She has already told it – to me. I also realized I was sitting on part of sports history in the form of those taped interviews. Would others be as fascinated, surprised, and interested as I was if they had a chance to listen to the tapes?

Not quite certain what to do, I contacted a literary lawyer. As I suspected, I was informed I owned the tapes and began to formulate an idea. I would not proceed, however, until I had Tonya's permission. After all, I may own the tapes, but they contained her story.

I had some difficulty tracking Tonya down because she had moved yet again and, this time, to another state. After exchanging a few pleasantries, I began to explain what I wanted to do with the tapes before I was abruptly interrupted.

"I'll sue you," she yelled into the phone, obviously upset. She was later to explain she was "sick and tired of everyone else taking advantage of her name." Tonya's tirade was quieted, however, when she realized that this wasn't something I was going to do without her consent, and that I was willing to share any profits with her that may come as a result of my plan.

My idea was to publish the interviews very much as they were spoken with some interjection by me if an explanation was necessary or if I wanted to let the reader know Tonya's mood at the time of the interview. Other than this, and the points outlined below in the Author's Note, Tonya's answers to my questions would not be substantively cut or edited and would read as I heard them at the time of the sessions. I was to prepare the entire manuscript, and she would later provide an additional interview intended as an update since the earlier sessions.

Initially, Tonya insisted I not release a certain section of the tapes that she found especially degrading and embarrassing. She had confided details to me that explained why she did not come forward when she first learned of her ex-husband's involvement in the attack, and she thought those circumstances should be portrayed in a delicate manner (when we had intended on releasing the book as an autobiography). According to Tonya, I was only one of a few people to whom she had revealed the unsavory truth regarding her silence.

While I understood Tonya's qualms, upon listening to the tapes again, I realized that for this book to go forward as intended, she would have to allow the complete story to be told. Nothing could be left out. After much discussion, Tonya acquiesced. I could release everything she had told me, leading up to the occurrence in question – and everything after, but she requested I delete the graphic details (which were not more than a paragraph in length) and substitute my words for hers. She was still very much humiliated and ashamed by what had happened to her.

What you are about to read may shock you. Some of the details you may find difficult to believe, and you may wonder how the abuse Tonya suffered was able to repeat itself for as long as it did. Like me, you may feel sadness for the little girl she was and whose life could have been so different had she been raised in a more stable household. Whatever your reaction to her story, and whether you have liked or disliked Tonya Harding, you will gain a rare insight into her world and, by extension, the cloistered milieu of the figure skating community and competitive sports in general. Hopefully, you will come away with a better understanding of the woman who once stood on the edge of greatness in her sport only to have it all go so horribly wrong.

Author's Note

Although I have attempted to transcribe the tapes as accurately as possible, I have taken the liberty of correcting some grammar and removing certain colloquial language, especially if the utterances became too repetitive or interfered with the flow of words. Ultimately, I wanted a finished book that was easy to read. I purposely did not significantly modify Tonya's responses to my questions, 'clean-up' her language, or try to make her sound like someone she is not. For the reader to know the real Tonya Harding, it was essential to leave her words as close to spoken as possible.

As Tonya and I became more comfortable with each other, some of our sessions would veer away from the interviewing process, and we would become engrossed in conversation that may have nothing to do with what I had originally intended to include in the autobiography. If I believed these conversations were pertinent to her story, or would allow the reader a better understanding of Tonya, I included some of the conversation or at least made a reference to those discussions. If I did not deem them to be relevant, I deleted them.

For the most part, my questions to Tonya are as they are written in this book; however, at times, I may have shortened or somewhat revised them to make them more concise and readable. Interjections I may have made to keep the interview moving may have also been deleted if I believed they were not necessary to include. Other comments I may have made that were not pertinent to Tonya's response to a question may also have been deleted, as were her remarks, if any, to those comments.

While I endeavored to present the interviews in the order I conducted them, at times, maintaining strict chronology was impossible because it is my usual method to re-question a subject after I have transcribed a tape if certain points were not made clear to me or if I required further information. For the most part, I have included the additional questions and answers in the applicable interview for the sake of chronological coherency. Accordingly, if Tonya presented further information at a later date regarding an earlier interview, I added the information to the chapter in question. Also, during the course of the interviewing process, Tonya would sometimes recall an incident or begin talking about an event that was out of the chronological order I originally planned for the particular interview. In certain cases, I have left them as she spoke them. To re-situate her words and the questions that her revelations inspired me to ask would have interfered with the conversation as it took place. However, if I could move those discussions without interrupting the conversational flow, I relocated them to a more appropriate chapter. Furthermore, if any questions or answers were repetitious, I deleted or moved them, in part, to a more suitable section.

I conducted all the interviews, with the exception of three, between 1999 and 2001. The exceptions were the sessions regarding the update and the 1994 Olympics that I had not fully covered during our original interviews. I believed, to tell her story fully, I needed to re-interview Tonya and glean more information about the 1994 Olympics. I made both of those tapes in January, 2007. The final interview, which took place in May, 2007, was conducted after I completed the first draft of the book. It was during the editing process that Michael Rosenberg and I noticed areas that required clarification in order to complete the story. I inserted Tonya's answers to these further questions in corresponding sections.

To differentiate between Tonya's words and mine, I have presented my questions and explanations in bold type. If I included a prologue to the chapter, or if I felt the need to clarify certain points, the type is also in italics and sometimes parenthesized. If I am clarifying Tonya's words, the type is italicized and in parentheses.

I have chosen not to use the last names of some of the people mentioned in *The Tonya Tapes*, especially those convicted for the assault on Nancy Kerrigan and whose names are on public and court records. The exception, of course, is the use of Jeff Gillooly's name because he was so personally involved with Tonya.

Lastly, Tonya was worried that she may not have remembered certain events and dates exactly as they happened. She didn't want to "get into trouble" for inadvertently providing me with incorrect information. My response to her was, "I will be on the watch *(during the editing)* for anything, but as far as you saying something *(untruthful)* – I don't know – unless there were times that you weren't telling me the truth." She answered, "No. I always told you the truth … It *(the book)* is my version of my life."

"I want people to understand me and not make decisions … rash decisions on who I am and what I am, based on what they hear. I want to set the story straight about my life, about who I am, and it is a closure for me. I am closing the door from my past life."

• • •

"If I can help one person through life – don't make the same mistakes that I have made – you're human, you're going to make mistakes, but think before you make your mistakes. Don't go the same route that I did. And if I help somebody out, I guess it's all worth it."

Tonya Harding – from Chapter 12

(1)

The Comeback

*"When somebody takes your whole, entire life away from you ...
it's like you are lost."*

After Tonya was charged with 'hindering the prosecution,' following the
attack on Nancy Kerrigan, she was stripped of her U.S. National titles
and banned from amateur competition for life by the United States
Figure Skating Association. Furthermore, she was unofficially barred
from professional competition and shows. Ironically, these same professional events became much more popular because of the 1994 scandal
and would go on to make many people wealthy – especially the figure
skaters who either agreed with the ban or refused to skate in the same
events as Tonya. Prior to the scandal, those world-class figure skaters
who retired from amateur competition usually managed to make much
less of a living by coaching or touring with ice shows.

Enjoying a popularity without precedent, the figure skating boom
would continue for the next four years, but by the spring of 1999, interest in the sport was on the decline, and many assumed Tonya was invited to the nationally televised ESPN professional competition in October
of that same year to give figure skating a much-needed 'shot in the arm.'
Indeed, upon attending the high security event in Huntington, West
Virginia, I witnessed the intense media coverage where some 48 news
agencies had sent reporters to cover the competition. Vying with each
other for interviews and photographs of Tonya were the usual tabloid
media, including 'Hard Copy' and 'Entertainment Tonight' along with
the more established press such as 'The New York Times,' 'The
Washington Post,' 'USA Today,' and 'CNN.' Even Europe had dis-
patched people to report on the notorious skater's return to the ice.

Tonya's competitors included Elizabeth Manley, Canadian, World,
and Olympic Silver Medalist; Rory Flack, U.S. Professional Champion;
Tonia Kwiatkowski, U.S. Silver Medalist; and Surya Bonaly, French
and European Champion and World Silver Medalist. Tonya placed second (in a tie with Flack), behind Bonaly, and after her performance,
which showed an unusually artistic side, she was the only skater to
receive a standing ovation from the audience.

Following is my first interview with Tonya, which took place in November, 1999, after she had skated in the event and prior to the infamous hubcap episode when her life would again begin to unravel.

• • •

How did you feel when you first learned you had been invited to the ESPN competition?
Well, when Michael *(Rosenberg – Tonya's manager for much of her amateur career, her 'come-back' into skating in 1999, and for this book)* called me in the afternoon – I was getting ready to go and teach, and when he called me, I was just ecstatic. I mean, I was in tears; I was crying. I couldn't believe that after all this time, it was really going to happen for me. And, I don't know, even to this day – it is still a whirlwind – it's just like, I can't believe that I got the opportunity, and I got through it, and I proved to myself that I could actually do it.

This was your dream – right?
It was a dream, yes. To be able to come back and to be able to skate again, but in a different way – no pressures, just going out and skating and having a good time. Being in amateur skating, where you are training to win or to place, or to have a position to go to a next event, but this, even though it was a pro competition – first place, second place, fifth place didn't matter because I just wanted to go out and skate and have a good time and see all my friends and skate for my fans and friends and family.

Were you worried about how you would be accepted by the other skaters?
I was very nervous going to this, preparing for it and everything. Having four weeks to prepare and not knowing how I would be accepted by the other skaters …

Had you seen any of the other skaters *(prior to the event)*?
I had seen a couple of skaters over the past few years when they came to town for tours and things like that. And I took a trip to Sun Valley and skated *(practised)* there for a couple of days and saw some people up there, and they were very nice to me. And, so, I knew a few of them would be nice to me, but I didn't know how all of them would be and whether or not they would try to stay away from me or be scared of me. When I got there,

everybody was very nice and giving me hugs and kisses on the cheek. It was really nice to be welcomed back. Then the first day of competition, going to the rink and seeing all the media there – it was a very emotional time – from that point until I got through with that night … and it was, I don't know.

It affected you. How could it not?
I was crying during the afternoon. It was hard keeping the tears back seeing everybody and having people coming up and welcoming me back and saying, "I'm so glad that you're back" and "It's going to be great to skate" and "You will have fun."

It must have been more than relief. Did you feel that was where you were supposed to be?
I have always loved to skate, and that is all I wanted to do. Having my whole, entire career taken away from me by somebody else – not losing it myself – I do have blame, but when somebody takes your whole, entire life away from you, and you don't know what to do, it's like you're lost.

Who are you referring to? Are you referring to Jeff *(Gillooly – Tonya's first husband)?*
Yes, and all his goons.

If somebody told me I couldn't write anymore, what would I do? It *(your chosen career)* **defines your life, doesn't it?**
Exactly. Exactly.

You worked hard to get there, didn't you? You knew four weeks ahead of time, but you had really been working on your skating every day, right? Isn't this something that you had just continued to do *(since the ban)?*
Well, off and on for the last five and a half years. I always kept myself in shape and went through a program of some kind, always making sure I had my jumps and spins. I was trying to make myself a more graceful skater. I've always been noted for my jumps and spins, but nothing in between. When I went here *(to ESPN)* – on the first night, even though I fell, my artistic impression marks were higher than what my technical marks were, and it has never been that way, except for a couple of times.

You reminded me of one of the Russian or European skaters – you know – the deep knees and the edges; I was really surprised. It looked as if you had been training in Europe.
Yeah.

It was beautiful to watch – the artistry.
I worked on that really a lot over the last five and a half years. Basically, just keeping myself in shape and teaching myself new artistic moves on the ice and working on choreography. I had just finished a program, but when I got doing the program, I was changing things here and there until I felt exactly what I wanted – videotaping it, watching it.

Were you working with a coach?
No. I would teach myself. I also do my own choreography. But a lot of what I was doing was learned from my previous choreographer, Barbara Flowers. She passed away a few years ago, and for her to be looking down and have a smile on her face because I got higher artistic marks … you know, it was great.

Was she (*your choreographer*) during your amateur years?
Yes. She was there at '91 Nationals.

Who was your coach who took you through your amateur years?
Diane Rawlinson. And then Dody Teachman was my other coach for a couple of years.

This was before Diane or after?
In the middle – when I came into my 18 year old teenage years, thinking I knew everything …

You went from one coach to the other and then back to the other?
Yes. Dody was Diane's first student.

With all the hard work you had done, were you confident of your skating (*going into the ESPN event*)?
In the amount of time I had to get ready, I was ready skating-wise. My jumps were all there. My programs were there. I worked really hard on them, and I was very confident that my skating wasn't the issue. It was being able to go there and not knowing what to expect and stepping out on the

ice for the first time and then getting a standing ovation. I started crying on the warm-up. I tried to compose myself and kind of halfway got it back, and then I skated last and almost threw up before I went on. I got so emotionally, overwhelmingly upset. It was like, oh my God, I didn't know that it was going to be this great of a moment for me. Going into the second one *(performance)*, I was relaxed and knew what to expect, and it was just go out and have fun.

And the little things like Liz Manley …
High-fiving me. *(Elizabeth was leaving the ice after her performance when she approached Tonya, who was about to begin her own program. In a symbolic gesture of support, Elizabeth clasped Tonya's hands and then 'high-fived' her competitor. A few days later, Tonya would acknowledge her gratitude for Elizabeth's public encouragement on 'Larry King Live' and 'Rivera Live.' Coincidentally, I co-authored a book with Elizabeth Manley that same year called, "As I Am." In it, she stated: "I knew Tonya very well, … had been on a few tours together … she would often break down as she told me about how her husband and mother beat her … I marveled at how she was able to function, let alone skate. In a way, I empathized with Tonya because I could see a little of me in her. She was always struggling for acceptance and approval in the skating community, and I could relate to that. Tonya had incredible talent and an amazing ability to jump but she didn't have the look that the United States Figure Skating Association (USFSA) desired. They wanted the wholesome, girl-next-door image for their champion. Tonya didn't fit that image and she knew she never would … I have no doubt that Tonya Harding was guilty by association, but I believe to this day she doesn't really understand what happened. In some ways, she could even be considered a victim herself.")*

I told Liz afterward, "That's what sport is all about."
It was heartfelt. She did it because she cares. All of the skaters, all of them … I haven't seen Rory in years – it has been years since I've seen her.

I saw her holding your hands.
Yeah. She was like, "Don't worry about it *(when Tonya missed a jump)*, everyone missed the Salchow *(a jump)* tonight." Everybody, I guess, had been backstage watching on the monitor. And, so, I thought that was really cool. And nobody put me down for falling. Everybody said, "Hey, it doesn't matter. You got out there and at least went for it," and I thought that was so cool, too. I guess I am always my worst critic. If I am not perfect,

then it really upsets me. And everyone was like, "It doesn't matter. It doesn't matter. You skated great, and you looked beautiful. Who cares if you fell on your tush a couple of times?"

Do you think this new style of artistic skating you have comes from maturity?
I think so. In another week and a half or in ten days from today, I will be 29, and it definitely came over time, that's for sure.

How did you feel on the plane ride out *(to the event)*? You had your god-parents with you?
I had my godmother with me. *(Linda Lewis, her chosen 'godmother' and unofficial manager. Linda and her husband, Greg, were and are extremely close to Tonya, and she looks upon them and their relatives as the family she wished she had).*

I guess it was comforting to have her there?
Definitely – she goes every place with me. She knows me. She has known me for five and a half years. She knows exactly how I am – what my mood swings are – if I need something. She is always there for me – whatever I need, she is there.

How did you meet her?
Actually, Linda and Greg met my father first, and then I got introduced to them after that. That was in 1994.

They were friends of your father's?
They wrote a song for me. They are songwriters. They went to give it to my father, and they sang for my fan club banquet, and that is when I met them. And we just clicked and have been together ever since.

Before you went to the Olympics?
No, after. This was in July or August – something like that.

So, you have a fan club … you have a lot of dedicated fans, right?
Yes.

And they gave you a banquet?
Yes. And then they had met my father and got to know him first and

everything. And then finally I ended up meeting them. We totally clicked – 100 percent.

So, they are more like your family than your own family?
Yup. Linda and I are closer than a mom and daughter than I could ever ask for ever. I mean, without her, I would probably not be here today because she is the one who has helped me through the worst – the worst times.

Did you live with them for awhile?
A couple of weeks – here and there. *(She laughs. Tonya has made several moves in the past few years, especially after her various breakups with men).*

So you were glad she was there?
Oh, yes. When I look at it now, I don't think I could have traveled all that way by myself and stay in the room by myself and try to keep myself composed and know what I'm doing without her being there.

How did you feel the first time you stepped on the practice ice, being with your contemporaries – some of them you had *(once)* competed *(as an amateur)* against?
The first day was at the practice rink, and it was very cold. I was out there with the men. *(The men competing at the event included U.S. Champion Rudy Galindo; Ukrainian Champion Viacheslav Zagorudniuk; French Champion and World Bronze Medalist Eric Millot; Russian, World, and Olympic Gold Medalist Alexei Urmanov; and Czechoslovakian, World, and Olympic Bronze Medalist Jozef Sabovcik).* There were no women there yet. And, so, I skated with the men and went through my programs and got all the jitters out. What was very, very strange and odd was on that practice session, I was skating okay, and then all of a sudden, I started missing my triple toes *(jumps)*. I fell on three triple toes, and my take-off felt really weird. So, then I thought, I am just going to leave this alone. Obviously, it was just a bad day for it. Then Alexei *(Urmanov)* found a screw on the ice and asked me if it was mine – because he had asked the other guys, and I looked at my blades, and I'll be damned if there wasn't two screws falling out of my blade. That was my screw. We went in the back room, got a screwdriver, and tightened everything back up. And what's very strange was that three days before I had left, I had my blades sharpened and tightened down to make sure everything was okay, brought extra laces with me so that nothing would happen because people always say *(when Tonya performs)*, she had to

stop or she has a lace problem or a dress problem or something. And I was like, I just can't believe this because it was perfect before I left home. They *(her skates)* were not out of my sight once, so I have no idea. I went ahead and fixed it and went back, and, boom, I did my triple toe – no problem whatsoever.

Would you have noticed the loose screw *(before your performance)*?
I would have noticed that my blade was about to fall off when I wiped them down. So, I would have found out. But, jeez, how can this happen? Because for the past four days, they hadn't left my sight, except at my house when I'm not home or when I fall asleep.

That's too much of a weird coincidence, isn't it? *(Tonya was known for having problems during her performances with her skates or costumes. Some believed it was just Tonya's way of getting attention, being dramatic, or stalling for time, especially if she wasn't skating well).*
It is weird. So, anyway, the thing that was really weird – the next night at the competition, I was backstage getting ready, going through the programs and doing what I do on the floor to make sure I am ready to go out there. I had my skates on. It was about eight or ten minutes or so before we were going to go out for warm-up, and Linda, I call her 'Mom,' and she said, "Oh my God, Tonya – your dress." I looked down, and the mesh, the skin colored fabric is mesh, was ripped, and if I had gone out on the ice without fixing it beforehand, my booby probably would have fallen out of my dress. It was right where my boob is, and I'm like, you have got to be kidding me! So, I ran back to the dressing room, and I had some super glue in my bag – pulled my dress down and super glued around it because it is clear and you can't see it – super glued around the little hole that was ripping, so it couldn't tear anymore, adjusted myself, and went out and competed. If I had done my layback *(spin, where the skater's head and shoulders are thrown back and the back is deeply arched)* or my Ina Bauer *(a move that is a variation of the spread eagle that sees the skater moving across the ice in a straight line)*, there is a possibility of the dress actually tearing and me falling out of it. I mean, I could not believe it.

This is so strange.
Very strange – no big deal.

Were you worried when you were on the ice that it was going to rip?
No, because I put it *(the glue)* all around it so it couldn't fray. So, I wasn't concerned about that at all. When I stepped out on the ice for warm-up, and I got a standing ovation, and the people yelling and screaming "We love you Tonya. Go get 'em Tonya"– I started crying. It was overwhelming, just overwhelming. And the second night, everything was great.

It was – the skating, too.
It was.

And every person getting on their feet in the arena …
And the girls giving me hugs on the ice, and Surya and everyone was wonderful. It was fantastic.

Were you surprised by all the media attention?
I knew that it would be *(there)*, but what surprised me is that everybody was so nice.

Did anyone make comments to upset you?
No. Nobody made any rude comments. I don't ever try to hide anything from anybody. I don't have anything to hide, but when anybody asks me questions, they say, "I know you probably don't want to answer this, but could you please tell us this?" And it's okay. They need to understand that those things don't bother me. But they were very gracious about it. And photos – when I was on the ice practicing in 1994 *(before and at the Olympics)*, they didn't care when they took the flash photography. When I was jumping right in front of them, it would make me fall. But here, they didn't do that. They did it when I was spinning or just skating around, and so I was really surprised and happy they were all so nice to me.

They were treating you with respect?
Yeah.

I think it was because you were open and honest, and it shone through.
Also older – more mature, wiser.

You paid your dues?
Yeah.

I believe there were 48 news agencies there.
I don't know for sure. But everybody was so nice, though.

So, that had to make you feel good?
That was great.

When you were there, did you feel like you were trying to prove anything to yourself or to other people?
I guess the only thing I wanted to prove was that I could actually go out and do it for myself. I didn't know, anymore, if I had it in me to go out and perform in front of a lot of people. The first night, I still had doubts, but even though I had the doubts, when I got done and knew how everyone had treated me, it made me feel much more relaxed, so I could go out there the next night and show them what I could do.

Were you nervous between the two programs?
I couldn't go to sleep. I did not go to sleep that night. I fell asleep about 5:15 or 5:30 *(a.m.)*, and I had to get up at 6:30 the next morning for an interview.

Tossing and turning?
I was totally wide awake. I watched TV. I tried playing cards. I tried drinking warm milk. You name it, I was trying it. I just could not go to sleep. After I got done with my interviews at about 10:00, I ate some breakfast then lay down, closed the blinds, and turned off the TV, and slept for about four hours and got up around 1:30. It was about 10:45 when I went to sleep. Then I got up and did a phone interview. Then I got ready to go to practice, and my practice went really great – oh, that was the other thing – I forgot my second body suit that I was going to wear for practice in the dryer at home and my tights. We had a friend who drove all the way down from Pennsylvania. She and her mom had a car, so they took my mom out to a dance shop down the street and got me a body suit and some tights. *(She laughs)*. So, I wore the new outfit that evening for practice, and I skated really good, and I felt really good. I didn't think I had anything to worry about at that point – just to go out and have fun.

And you did, right?
Oh, yeah. I knew that when I landed my double Axel in the beginning, at that point in time, I could just relax. And then when I hit my triple toe, I knew I could do the rest of the program – no problem.

It was so emotional. *(I had never seen an audience so emotionally involved with a skater and her performance. It seemed that everyone in the arena, including the many younger girls who were wearing their hair in Tonya's signature pony-tail style, wanted her to do well. I also noticed that, wherever I went in town, people were talking favorably about Tonya).*
It was. It was great. When I got through and I had a standing ovation, and I knew that I did it for myself, I knew I could actually still do it – because I had no idea.

Were you thanking anybody *(in particular)* in your mind when it was all done?
I was like, Thank God, I made it through this. *(She laughs).*

What happened at the press conference after the competition?
I got off the ice, and ESPN wanted to tape my small comment – a small interview. When I am at home and training – you see, I have athletic-induced asthma, so if I don't cool my body down by walking around or something, I will get into a coughing fit and will end up choking and throwing up. It lasts for hours. Well, anyway, they pulled me into this little tiny room. It was about 110 degrees in there, plus I was so overheated from the excitement and skating, so all of a sudden, boom, I started coughing. I knew I wasn't going to be able to control this. They did the interview really fast. I ran out of the room choking and ran into the bathroom and was choking, coughing, and throwing up, and they were trying to pull me out because I had to get back on the ice with the other girls at the end. They got me some hot tea. My mom had cough drops, and they got me cold, wet towels to put on my head and my back to try and cool me down because I was so overheated my face turned purple.

Doesn't your inhaler work for that?
Normally it does, but once I have lost it, I can't get it back. Once I start coughing, it's gone. I always train myself at the rink to skate around and cool myself down, and I didn't get the opportunity to do that. When I was on the ice, the girls were giving me hugs, and then Surya came out, and I was coughing. And I was like, "Please, stop. I don't want to cough in front of all these people." I went back and was choking, and then I went to the press conference, signed autographs, and coughed all night long. That's when I ended up getting my bronchitis because I had coughed so hard and so much.

What did you do after the press conference? Did you celebrate in any way?
I went to Michael Rosenberg's room and did an interview with another lady. I was there for about 45 minutes, and then Mom and I went back to the room, and my friend Kim and her mom showed up, and we sat in my room and had coffee. I think I had a 'Mountain Dew.'

That's the strongest *(drink)* **you had?**
I didn't have any alcohol whatsoever when I was there – not even on the way home. Not one beer, not one drink – nothing.

Didn't you want to celebrate?
When I am at home, I may go out once a week and have a couple of beers, but I don't drink hard alcohol because it makes me sick. Every once in awhile, maybe once a month, I will try one drink, but I usually end up not liking how I feel after I have it. I don't drink all the time, and when I do, it's maybe two beers.

Did you sleep that night?
Not too much. A little bit. I think I finally fell asleep about 3:30 *(a.m.)*.

Did you call your boyfriend?
Oh, yeah. He was so excited for me.

His name is Darren? *(Tonya was living with him during the period when several of our interviews were conducted).*
Yes.

We don't want to use his last name in the book?
No.

How many interviews did you have?
I have no idea – over 20. I did over 20 there and little ones here and there and some before I left, and with the tiny ones – over 30.

How was the Larry King interview? *(Tonya appeared on 'Larry King Live' shortly after the event).* **Were you nervous?**
Not at all. He was wonderful. He was really nice. When I first met him, he shook my hand and gave me a kiss on the cheek and said it was really nice to meet me.

That was the first time you had met him?
Yes. He was really nice.

I had heard that Tonya was the subject of a Jay Leno joke, which was made in reference to her birthday and was to the effect of: That's one person you don't want to forget on her birthday – a good present would be new wheels for her house. While I didn't tell Tonya what the actual joke was, I did ask her how all the mockery, which was abundant on late night television, made her feel. She responded:
This was after the comeback?

Yes. Does it make you feel bad when you hear things like that?
No. I just think they are being shallow. They are just looking for ways to make people laugh. It doesn't bother me. It kind of ticks me off, but it doesn't bother me. It's like, "Get a life." Learn how to be a comedian instead of playing on other people's emotions and lives.

You probably heard enough of that back then *(after the scandal)*?
Yeah. How would he like it if somebody was doing that to him? Put himself in the other people's shoes.

It has been said that in some skaters' contracts, they have a 'won't skate with Tonya' clause ...
I don't know about that. But I do know that they were told so.

You told me that you had met other skaters *(prior to the ESPN event).* **Some would come to your town** *(or)* **you would see them on tours, and some of them had been nice to you. Is there anybody you want to mention in particular?**
Well, everybody was just fabulous. If I could have written a fairy tale that this would all happen and how the outcome would be and how everybody treated me; I could not have written it any better *(referring to the ESPN competition).*

What about before the ESPN event? Were any skaters nice to you before that?
Oh, yeah ,– Surya Bonaly and Elizabeth Punsalan, Jerod Swallow *(U.S. National Dance Champions)*, Rudy Galindo, Elizabeth Manley. I saw Surya a couple of times and some of the other people on tour when they came into town.

You would go to the show?
No, they'd be practicing at one of the rinks or something, and I'd happen to be there.

And they were always nice to you?
Yeah. Yeah.

When you were banned from skating, did anybody *(from the skating community)* **reach out to you, or did you find that people moved away just so they wouldn't get involved or whatever?**
Locally, people just totally put me to the side. People have talked about it off and on, and there have been people who have stood up for me and have said, "Hey, we know her, and she is a good person. She wouldn't do these types of things." Michelle Kwan *(U.S. National and World Champion)* had done an interview, and she said that she *(I)* had been my *(her)* idol at one time.

That you had been her idol?
That I was her idol – yeah.

You said for the last five and a half years, you had skated on and off and made sure you went through some type of program. Were you referring to making up a program for the ice as if you were going to be judged?
Yeah. The one that I did the first night in Huntington – that program, I had been working on for a really long time. I had it since '91 Skate America.

So, you weren't just going out and practicing your jumps every day; you were also making up programs?
Uh huh.

Was it in the back of your mind to get back into skating?
Well, I always hoped. It was like – just in case. I didn't want to hear the word – to have it all turned around and have them say, Okay, Tonya, here you go: you can skate in two weeks – and have me not been on the ice or been training.

You always wanted to be ready?
I always wanted to make sure that I was at least half way there.

(2)

Little Girl Lost

"I was always called fat and ugly."

Let's start at the beginning – your birthday?
November 12th, 1970.

Where were you born?
Portland, Oregon.

What are your parents' names?
LaVona *(aka Sandy Golden)* Harding, and my father is Albert.

Are they from that area as well?
I couldn't tell you. My mother was married four times before my father. She moved around a lot, I think. California, Pennsylvania, I don't know … East Coast, too. But I am not sure where.

Do you know your grandparents?
I know one of my grandparents. My dad's mom passed away a few years back. And my mom's grandparents, they live down in Taylorsville, California, and I talk to them every once in awhile.

***(You mean)* her parents?**
Uh huh.

Do you know where your family descended from originally?
I have always heard that I'm 'Heinz 57.' I'm Russian, German, French Canadian, and, somewhere along the line, American Eskimo or something. I don't know where that would come from, but it is one of the things that I have heard in my life.

Do you have any half brothers or sisters?
My mother had three boys and a girl, plus me. Her first marriage – she wasn't married very long. Her second marriage – she had twin boys. One of them died shortly after birth from crib death. And then the other one, I think, was in his thirties, and he died. And her daughter, I'm not sure if she's

in her thirties now, but I have no idea where she is – Hawaii, or someplace
– who knows? Her other son – I have no idea where he is, either.

They were all *(born)* before you?
Yes.

Did you meet any of them?
Oh, yeah, I knew them. The oldest, all through my childhood, from five all
the way up to 13-years-old or 11-years-old, or something like that – no, I
was 15, so all the way for ten years of my childhood, this person molested
me.

A man?
Her oldest son.

How much older was he than you?
A lot – if he was alive, he would probably be in his forties today.

So, when you were a little girl, he was in his late teens or early twenties?
Yes.

Do you want to mention their names?
No.

*I told Tonya at this point that if any of my questions made her uncom-
fortable to let me know and not worry about offending me. She stated
that Michael Rosenberg had told her to be honest with me, and he would
later edit anything that may cause problems. She then said:*
We want the book to be honest and tell people how I am and what I had
to go through in my whole life, and maybe people would understand why
I made the choices I did.

Through it, maybe there is going to be another little girl out there …
Who won't make the same mistakes.

**Exactly, because we all make mistakes in life, and if we can have the
opportunity to help someone else through it – that in itself is worth
everything I think.**
Well, I think that a lot of women out there, after they hear what I have to
say in my book, will take *(a look at my)* life differently – I think, in terms

of being abused – and other children and just people in general, on things that I've had to go through – what choices should you or should you not make, and not knowing what to do.

When I mention the book to people, they tell me that it will be a great story – as a story.
Exactly, because it started out as a little fairy tale that ended up bad, and then all of a sudden you end up on the good.

We discussed the interviewing process, and I mentioned that we would get into the issues with her brother later. She responded:
The second brother, or step-brother, whatever you want to call him, I knew him when he was little, and he was always a trouble maker. They ended up putting him in foster homes, and he was shipped to Pennsylvania with his real father. So, I didn't see him – I mean, I was young; I was probably about six, I think, when I last saw him. And my sister was kicked out of the house at 12, or 13, or 14 – early teens. She was a hooker and married to different kinds of people, and I have no idea where she is today. I saw her a couple of times back in '93, and I saw her once in early '94.

Which marriage produced your sister?
I don't know – her third.

When you were born, how old was the next youngest one – the one closest to you in age?
Gosh, I'd say he was probably 12.

Was he one of the twins?
No, that was the youngest, and the next one was probably 18, 19, maybe 20, I don't know. And then the other one was just a couple of years apart.

So there were three?
Yes.

Because one of them had died when he was young, right? He was one of the twins?
Right.

So, you were just this little thing with all these much older ...
Well, they weren't living in the household. The only one who lived in the

household was the youngest brother, and that was off and on because he was in and out of foster homes.

How old was he when he left?
He was 12 or 14. I was five or six.

Did you miss him when he left?
He was really mean.

You were happy rather than sad?
Yeah.

So, it was mainly you *(as a child in the household)*?
It was usually me.

The older one who *(molested you)* ...
The older one lived in town.

And, so, he would come over?
He would come over all the time and ...

Is he still alive?
No. He was killed. He was married and divorced, and he had kids. He was a really bad person – drinking and violations and jail and all kinds of stuff – probation officers, living in probation officers' homes, for as long as I knew him.

How long were your parents together?
They divorced in 1987. They separated in February, and then their divorce was final sometime in the summer.

So, you were about 17?
I was 16. And then my mother ended up getting remarried again in December, and I was 17 then.

It sounds like you had a tough life?
Yeah. From the time I was born to the fifth grade, we moved 13 times – in and out of different schools. I always had my skating, but that is what I always looked for - towards. Nobody ever liked me at school because I came in late, and I had really bad teeth. They were really small and separated. It

was just kind of an ugly duckling thing. I was pretty ugly from all the way up to – jeez, to ... well ... now. *(She laughs)*. I was cute as a little girl, but then when I got into the ages of six, seven, on until up to '91 – my teeth, when I got them fixed, made a big difference. But I didn't see myself as being pretty until about three years ago.

It is interesting you feel that way because, often, when you feel good about yourself on the inside, you feel good about yourself on the out-side.
I think when I met Darren *(Tonya's boyfriend at the time of this interview)*, it made me feel good because he thought I was beautiful. He would always tell me how beautiful I was, and until you hear it from someone very close like that ... Mom and Dad *(Linda and Greg)*, they will always say, "You are beautiful," but I didn't really think of myself that way.

Didn't anyone tell you that you were beautiful when you were a little girl?
No. I was always called fat and ugly.

By whom?
My mother.

Always putting you down?
Oh, always. I am fat. I am ugly. I can eat this. I can't eat that. You're not going to amount to a hill of beans. My mother was an alcoholic. A very bad alcoholic – filling up a thermos three quarters or half full with brandy, and the rest was coffee – at 4:30 in the morning to take me to the rink. She would drink all that, and then once we got home – or after she got home because there were a lot of times I didn't go to school – she would be drink-ing again as soon as she got home, and it made life very hard. You never knew if you were going to get backhanded or whatever. There were so many times when my mother would be upset with me because I didn't skate good and drag me off the ice by my hair, take me to the bathroom, and beat my butt until it was black and blue. And taking a brush to me – hitting me with a brush. She did that in front of people all the time – slapping me. I mean, it was bad. It was bad. And Diane *(Rawlinson, Tonya's first skating coach)* said things to her lots of times, and she *(Tonya's mother)* just told her to mind her own business and teach me how to skate. My dad was always support-ive of me and my skating, and he loved me as best that he could, and he worked hard.

What did your dad do?
When I was little, he worked for a rubber factory, and then after that he hurt his back. But after that, he ended up working for, let's see … a cement company, and he worked for a sporting goods store in the gun department and fishing department. Then he worked for a cop shop where the police officers can go and buy their equipment. Then he worked for a company that manufactured truck beds. When my parents got divorced, I stayed with my father. When my father lost his job, he tried to get other jobs, but nobody wanted to hire him because he was too old, and he didn't have a college education, and he ended up moving and leaving me with my mother when I was 17 and went and moved to Idaho. He lived there until '91, and then in '91, I brought him back over to Portland where I was. He stayed with me, and then I put him up in a place. When I got divorced from Jeff, he ended up staying with him, which was really, really hard on me. Then my father and I didn't talk for awhile, and when he talked to me, it didn't feel right, you know? This was my father talking, but it sure as heck didn't make me feel like he was a dad. But when he moved, I had to stay with my mother again, and her new husband and I did not want to be there. I was not close to my mother at all. There was no respect there whatsoever about anything. It was really hard – really, really hard. I tried to stay away from her house as much as possible except to sleep there.

When was the last time you saw your mother?
I saw her at the rink in 1994 right before I went to Olympics. And she had the gall to walk down into the rink, miked *(microphone)* under her coat. I saw it. They *(the press)* gave her a mike and turned it on and walked down into the rink to try and get me to say stuff. I told her, "You can leave this rink and never come back. I don't want to have anything to do with you anymore. I have put up with this too long." I haven't seen her since.

Have you spoken to her since?
The only time I have spoken to her was on a fake, phony phone call from the *(1994)* Olympic Games. I found out that she had gone on a TV show and said that she had passed out and had to be rushed to the hospital because of her blood pressure. That was bullshit. When I saw it on TV – no – she was trying to act it out, and that is my opinion. Somebody was going to try and fly her over to the Olympics *(in Lillehammer, Norway)* to be with me, and I am glad she didn't show up because that would have really upset me. That is where all my animosity comes from.

I can understand that *(referring to the abuse).* **You were a little girl. How does a little person handle things like that?**
Drive a big truck and have a big dog. *(She laughs).*

I meant when you were little, but maybe that is why you drive a big truck and have the big dog now.
Yeah. Yeah.

How is your dog?
He's fine. He's sleeping on the couch.

What is his name?
Koda.

I shared a story with Tonya about my own dog, which had passed away the year before, and went on to tell her how my father had passed away only a few days later. She responded:
Oh, jeez … Greg's parents both passed away two years ago, and we are right around the anniversary of Grandpa. I knew them, and I was close to them. My grandfather *(Greg's father)* died on the 25th of October, and Grandma *(Greg's mother)* died in either January or February – I think it was on the 6th.

So, this was both of Greg's parents – one right after the other?
Um hm. It was really hard.

I mentioned how much I missed my father, and how I had been an 'ugly duckling' child and had been teased, but how he had always told me I was beautiful and, therefore, instilled a confidence in me. She responded:
I was always teased.

I told Tonya how I believed it was very important for parents to encourage and praise their children – to tell their daughters they are beautiful. I mentioned that I had received this kind of encouragement from my parents and then my husband. She responded:
I didn't get that. My husband told me that I was fat, ugly, had a bubble butt and thunder thighs. I was always put down. He was trying to rule me, run my life. There is that old saying, 'Peter, Peter, pumpkin eater – keep her in

a shell …' and that is definitely what happened. Jeff was very manipulative and jealous, always tearing me down one way or another.

Knowing that we would talk about this in depth during subsequent interviews, I went back to my original line of questioning, attempting to further explore Tonya's early childhood.

What kind of homes did you live in when you were young?

We had our own house, I think, when I was little. I remember first or second grade; we lived in a house in Westland in Oregon. I don't remember where we moved to from there, but most of the houses we moved to were small homes, rentals – we always rented. For a few years, we lived out of a trailer – a 17 foot, fifth wheel. We lived in my Grandma's driveway. We lived with some friends of ours. They took care of me for awhile, and I lived with them for awhile – Scott, Dee, and Terry, or you could just say the Emstrom's. I remember, until fifth grade, we moved to 13 different places, and I went to 13 different schools. That's a lot. No wonder I'm screwed up. *(She laughs)*. And so, I never had any friends. I was always wearing clothes that were totally outdated, not the style. I was never allowed to wear jeans. I had to wear polyester pants and frilly blouses.

Was it due to a lack of money?

My mother was raised in a very strict household – had to wear a uniform to school kind of thing. But she just never came into the times. She never stayed up with fashion. She was never allowed to wear jeans when she was young, and I guess she thought I shouldn't, either. I had clothes that were made – she made them. She sewed a lot of my costumes. She sewed a lot of my clothes, and I would always have to wear them, and they were always so ugly … so ugly.

You were embarrassed?

Oh, totally. I remember she bought this material that was bright yellow with pink, blue, and white checks all over it. She made a blouse for herself, a shirt for my father, and she made me a pantsuit out of this thing – and it was polyester, and my dad and I – when I was little, my dad and I were real close – we were on the same wavelength – he was like, "This is crap. I don't want to wear it." But we had to do it because – don't get me wrong – I love my dad very much, but he was not a strong man when it came to her. She walked all over him. She basically wore the pants in the family.

Did she have a temper with him, too?
Oh, yeah. She had a big temper with him. He was a man. He never raised a hand to her. He never hit her, nothing like that, and so I can respect him for that. But not standing up to her about me or anything was kind of hard, too.

Did they argue a lot?
Yeah. Yeah. They argued all the time. Then they would give me the – "Who do you want to live with? Where do you want to go?" She says, "I don't want her. You take her. She doesn't want to be with me, anyway," which was true. I didn't want to be with her. He says, "I will definitely take her." He was there in that way. He always tried to work, so I give him credit for that, too.

Did he have any other children after *(they split up)*?
No.

You are his only child?
Yeah, but it was very hard. I didn't have any friends because of all the clothes that I had to wear. They were ugly – so ugly. It was no wonder.

Kids can be cruel to each other.
They are. They are.

Anyone who is different in any way may be picked on.
Exactly, and because I came in late *(to school)*, or I got to leave *(early)*, they would always be jealous.

What is your earliest childhood memory?
I was almost three. We were at Lloyd Center – where I teach and skate now. This is before they remodeled the whole mall. They had this archway with bars in it, and there was an ice rink down below. We were walking across it – my mom and me and her son, and I said I wanted to do that *(skate)*, and she said no. And he said, "Whatever she says goes." So, I sat down and started screaming because I wanted to do it. I had a fit. And I guess they said, "Okay, fine." Went down, put some skates on me, and I sat down on the ice, and I kicked at it and picked it up and was eating it. They told me not to do that because it was bad for me and that I had to get up and do what everybody else was doing. And so I did. I got up and skated around. After

that, I told them I liked it and wanted to do it more, so they brought me back a few more times. I told them this was what I wanted to do. I watched skating on TV and watched the bigger kids skating and watched them do well, and I was like, "I want to be an Olympic champion someday. I want to be an ice skater," and they were like, "Yeah, right. You are three, you know this?" So, they got me hooked up with Diane. She took me on as a student. I remember the first time was at this place called Jansen Beach Ice Arena. The rinks were down inside, and you would sit upstairs and watch, and Diane was down teaching, and my mother would give me hand signals, telling me what she wanted me to do out on the ice. At first, when Diane said, "No, I don't take young girls – young students – beginners," I went out and skated circles around her so that way she would have to pay attention to me, and every time she looked over, I would do something so she could see it. Do little spins and little tiny jumps and stuff. You see, I learned how to skate by watching other people. And so I could do some of these things that other people were doing. So, I was showing off in front of her. I was within 15 or 20 feet of her, and I kept twirling around, and I just drove her nuts. Finally, she came up to my mother and said, "She is driving me nuts. I will watch her." So, she stopped *(and watched me)* and said, "Yeah. I think so." I remember she took me on as a student, and here I am 26 years later because I started *(skating)* on my birthday when I was three.

So, you were going to the Lloyd Center just to pleasure skate and learn how to skate, and you went there for a few months before you met up with Diane?
Yes.

When she took you on, you were the youngest?
Yes. As far as I know, or what I heard through the grapevine; I think she said that she would take me on a six month trial basis.

So, being on the ice was your first memory?
Um hm. I don't really remember too much before that. I remember when I was three or four, we used to go hunting.

Who went hunting – your dad and your mom?
Yeah, and they would take me with them. And I remember my dad taking me on my first walk with him. He said, "We will go for a short walk through the woods," and he said, "We don't want to step on anything like

leaves or branches because it will make noise." I said, "Okay," and I was following him, and I remember he would turn around a lot to see if I was still there. I also remember, we were still walking, and he had turned around to see if I was there, and he stepped on a twig and broke it, and I looked up at him and said, "Daddy, shhh!" You know, like, "Be quiet!" And he kind of chuckled and turned around and kept walking. But he couldn't hear me behind him.

You were that quiet?
I was that quiet. He said, "Don't step on any branches or twigs or leaves that will make any noise," and I didn't.

In describing your father, he sounds like he was a good-natured man?
He was. Definitely.

Easy-going, but not strong when it came to your mother?
Yes.

It sounds like maybe alcohol was influencing your mother's decisions?
I'm sure. The earliest time I remember her drinking, I was seven.

Was she ever drunk – out of it?
That I don't know. When I was older, she would be to the point where I would look at it like, yeah, there is no way in hell she could not be snookered *(drunk)*. I mean, drinking that much coffee with that much brandy every single morning. I do remember … the first time I went overseas – to France, I brought back this big Eiffel Tower crystal glass thing *(decanter)* full of brandy. It was really cool looking. I thought, someday, we'll open this up when I am an Olympic champion. Well, she opened it because she was out of brandy. And when she opened it, she broke the top off of it. When she was done with it, she threw it away. This was something that I got for me as a memento of being over there. I couldn't believe it.

Do you pity your mother now, or do you still have resentment towards her or have you moved beyond it?
I forgive her for everything she has ever done to me, but I have no respect, and she is not a person that I want in my life, and I think that is the best for all of us. Yes, I will be sad when she dies because she is my mother, but there is no love. There is no respect. There is nothing there.

But you have forgiven her?
Well, you have to forgive.

You have to, don't you, in order to move on?
You do. You will never forget. You can forgive, but you will never forget. There are so many things in my life – because of what I've had to go through, trying to remember things – well, about 90 percent of the things that come into my head are always the bad things that stick out in my mind because there were so many of them.

How would you describe yourself as a child?
I was a little tiger. I loved skating. You couldn't get me out of my skates. As many times as I could go to the rink, I was there. I don't know – maybe a little hyper. But I wasn't mouthy. I was never bad – you know, like getting into trouble and lying. I didn't do that. I don't know.

Kind of average then?
A normal kid.

What were some of your favorite toys?
I had a four-wheel drive truck. It looked like a Tonka truck.

So you were a tomboy?
I was definitely a tomboy. I hated dolls. I didn't like them … didn't want them. I remember I got one for Christmas, and I didn't like it – just didn't like it at all. I had cowboy and Indian things. I had a set of 87 little toy cars – 'Matchbox' cars and 'Hot Wheels.' I had an entire collection going. When we lived in the last house before my parents got divorced and we moved, I was 15 years old and, in between, when I was in fifth grade - I don't know how old I was in fifth grade – we got robbed probably about 12 times. Stuff was stolen all the time and broken into all the time. One of the cases that my trophies were in was broken into, and some of my medals and trophies were stolen. A couple *(of them)* were broken. I had a collection of silver dollars. I had 15 or 16. My 'Hot Wheels' – they were *(all)* taken.

The neighborhood wasn't good?
It was not a good neighborhood.

Out of the 13 places you lived, were any of them good neighborhoods?
When I lived with Scott and his mom and dad – when we lived in our trailer in their driveway *(that neighborhood was good)*. They were friends of the family. I was skating and he was skating, and his dad and my dad became friends. And then our mothers kind of became friends. They didn't like my mother. Nobody liked my mother because she was so out of it all the time, but we all went hunting and fishing and camping together.

So, living with them was good?
Uh huh.

But living with your parents, it wasn't great – the neighborhoods?
No. I think when we lived in the trailer at my Grandma's – in the driveway – that was a nice neighborhood. In third grade, I think, we lived in two different houses, and I think both of them were okay neighborhoods. And the very first house I remember was a nice neighborhood.

Were you moving so much because of your dad taking different jobs?
Yeah. I guess so.

Did your mother work?
She was a waitress for different outfits.

Did she ever stay home with you? Who looked after you?
No. There would be one working and one not *(working)*. Being a waitress, she would work nights, or if my dad was working nights, she would work days, and I was usually in school.

Do you remember having any friends when you were four or five years old?
No. The only friend that has been there since I was little until now, and is still in my life, is Scott.

What was it about him that you liked?
He was kind of like a brother to me. To this day, we still talk, and we see each other every once in awhile. He was in the Army for quite awhile, and he got back, and I've seen him a few times since he got out of the Army. But he is like a brother to me. We basically grew up together. We skated a little

bit of pairs together. We thought about trying it out. I was always better myself rather than pairs. And then he quit skating and went into football and things like that, and I lived with him and his family for awhile. I don't know. He was like my buddy, my brother, you know? We fought like brother and sister. We went to school together. When I lived with him, I went to school.

Did he stick up for you?
Oh, yeah. We beat up each other – playing football, cowboys and Indians, Tonka trucks.

So he is the kind of person you would have really liked to have had for a brother?
Yeah. I consider him my brother.

How long did you live with Scott and his parents?
We lived there for about a year and a half, and then I lived there for another half a year, I think.

You stayed on when your parents left?
Yes.

Where did your parents go? Why would they leave you?
They went off to find jobs and get another place to live and do their own thing.

Was it a relief when they would go?
Oh, yeah. I missed my dad tremendously. But I didn't care. At least my mother was gone, and nobody had to listen to her, and it was a lot more fun.

How old were you when your parents left you to stay with Scott's family?
Third grade. I think that was when it was – third grade.

How long did you stay with him?
Oh gosh, I don't even know – three quarters of a year for school. We were in that year long school where you go so many months and then you get

three weeks off – year round – is that what it is called – year round school? I went through, I think, two terms there and two vacations, and then we ended up moving away from there and going someplace else.

How did it feel when you first skated?

I don't even remember. I have a couple of pictures of when I was little. One year, I was four or five, and my mother made me into a peacock for Halloween on skates *(most likely a skating carnival put on by the local club)*. And she put real peacock feathers out of my butt. I am serious – totally serious. And I have school pictures – my mom didn't want to take me to a studio and have pictures done – so what does she do? She sends me to school *(when class pictures were being taken)* in my skating outfit with my hair up in French braids with a tiara, so I could have *(skating)* pictures. Believe me. I have proof of that one, too. *(She laughs)*.

That must have been embarrassing – to go to school in your skating outfit?

Believe me! My very first year of freshman high school, my dad had got me a pair of 'Lawman' jeans with the pegged legs instead of the wide legs. It was the first time they were coming out. He got me a really cool pair of jeans and a really cool tee-shirt to go with them and a cool pair of tennis shoes. That was what I was going to wear for my first day of high school. I am standing outside about five minutes before the bus comes, and my mother comes out and sees what I am wearing and drags me into the house by my hair and makes me change my clothes. She takes the scissors and rips them up and tears them up right in front of me.

Your jeans?

Yes. My father had just spent this money that we really didn't have for me on my first day of high school. She put me into a pair of forest green pants with white polka dots with an elastic waistband, with a built-in buckle, with a white blouse, buttoned up the front with a big bow tie at the top that you tie, with big wide sleeves with the long, frilly cuffs on the end, with clogs. That was my first day of high school. She puts me in that *(outfit)*, put me outside. The bus pulls up, and I had to get inside wearing polyester pants, a frilly blouse, and clogs. I sat in the front seat of the bus and that is where I stayed the rest of my high school time.

Even if people wanted to be friendly, you must have withdrawn yourself because ...
Oh God! As soon as I got on the bus, people were laughing at me.

How old were you?
I was 14, almost 15. I was working *(by that time)*. The girl next door – Jeanie – her parents didn't have a lot of money either, and her and I were friends. And then I had met another girl at school who was in three of my classes, and we became locker partners, and her and I were friends until I left high school.

Do you want to mention their names?
Well, Gena was my high school friend. My next door neighbor was Jeanie.

From the ages of four to six, were you participating in any other sports or activities other than skating?
No – just skating. When I was in fifth grade, I tried to play in the school band, and played bells and the tambourine. I tried to play the violin, but I wasn't musically inclined. Good thing my parents spent their money on ice skating. *(She laughs)*.

It is an expensive sport, right?
Very.

How did your parents afford skating?
My dad paid the bills and my mother paid for the skating. Someone else paid for my skating – a lot of it – going to competitions and things like that. And Diane ...

Who was the someone else?
Well, I don't know if I should say.

Was it a family friend?
No. I would have to get her permission first because if I say something then other people may get really mad.

I told Tonya that we didn't have to note the person's name, especially if it was something done out of kindness. Tonya laughed in a very hesitant manner and was clearly uncomfortable talking about it. She responded:
That's all right. I'll let you know after I find out if it's okay. But when I was

14 – at one of the rinks – they had two ice rinks, and then it was an ice rink and a roller ink in the same building, and I would work weekends on the ice side to get myself free ice time instead of being paid.

You mean you worked at the roller rink?
Both rinks.

What did you do?
Floor guard or a skate guard, where you make sure people aren't playing 'chase,' and if anybody gets hurt *(falls down)*, you help them up.

You are on the ice while the kids are skating – during the pleasure skating?
Yes. So, I did that on both ice and roller, and that's how I paid for my ice time.

Diane was your coach then?
Yes.

From the time you were three until you left her at 17?
It was 1989.

And you only left her for two years and then went back to her?
I went back to her in '92.

Then was it after '94 that she wasn't your coach anymore?
Right – it was after the Olympics. It would have put her in a very difficult position with the USFSA *(United States Figure Skating Association, which is the governing body for American amateur figure skating competition)*, and I totally respect that.

Do you still talk to her? Do you still see her?
Oh, yeah. I see her every day that I go to the rink.

Where you teach now?
Yeah, we teach there. We both do.

Do you teach with Diane, or do you each have your own students?
Yes. *(We each have our own students).*

How many students do you have? *(I had veered away from my original questions about her childhood, using the opportunity to gain more information that I thought could be used in the book in a later chapter).*
I have about 17 students, and they range anywhere from four-years-old up to 70.

Do any have potential?
I have quite a few skaters that are really good. I mean, all my skaters are great. I have one – her name is Christine, and she skates in shows. I am getting ready to work on a new program for her for a show she is going to be doing.

Do you do their choreography, too?
Oh, yes. I have another student in her 30's who is doing triples *(jumps)*. Then I have some young kids who, when I got them, weren't doing anything, and now they are doing singles. I got some who were doing singles, and now they are doing doubles.

Is the ice where you train now where you trained all those years?
No. I started there when I was three. I went around to lots of different rinks. Clackamas Town Center is where I skated most of the time before '94 Olympics. That is where I trained before '94 Olympics.

With Diane?
Right. Now, Lloyd Center has been remodeled. It is a new rink compared to what it used to be. But it is really small compared to Clackamas, which is an Olympic size rink. Lloyd Center *(rink)* is about 25 feet shorter and probably 20 feet thinner *(narrower)*.

So, when you started at Lloyd Center with Diane, then you would move with her to ...
Whatever rink she went to.

She is back at the Lloyd Center now?
Yes. She teaches there or Clackamas because they are both owned by the same company.

When did you first get asthma? Have you had it all your life?
I was about seven.

Were you skating when you first noticed you *(would be out of breath)*
...
Yeah– not being able to get through full programs or when I did I was really out of breath or having a hard time breathing. But that was the only time – when I was doing athletics.

Did they take you to the doctor?
Yeah, we went to the doctor, and he said I had athletic-induced asthma.

Do you get it at other times?
No, hardly at all – maybe if I have bad allergies or if I am coughing a lot if I have the flu or a cold.

But it is not something you have every day or have to worry about if you are not skating?
Not really. I keep my inhaler with me at all times, just in case.

Have you ever wound up in the hospital with your asthma?
Yeah.

Tell me about that.
I've gone into a coughing fit before and ended up taking my inhaler, and it just kept going, kept going, kept going, and I took my inhaler one more time, but it didn't work, so I had to go into the hospital because I couldn't breathe. One of the reasons I had asthma – we found out – was because of the mold inside the cold rinks. It attracted mold on the ceilings and boards and everywhere inside the rinks – the moisture. It would cause mold, and that was what I was allergic to – and dust. We live in the country, and our graveled driveway in the summertime is a dust mat. And the yard is muddy now – grass and hay and trees and spiders. I am allergic to them – deadly allergic to spiders. I can't be around them. There is always dust in my house. I can dust one day, and the next it will be covered again, so I will do the dusting once a week.

It has been said that you smoked throughout your amateur career. Do you think the smoking intensified your asthma attacks?
I didn't smoke throughout my amateur career. I only smoked off and on, here and there when we were on tour or something like that. But I didn't smoke until after I was done competing. I only smoked a little here and

there. I have had asthma since I was seven-years-old, and I don't think I picked up a cigarette at seven.

So you don't think smoking affected your skating then?
No.

It didn't intensify your asthma attacks?
No, because I wasn't smoking like I had been after I was done. I started smoking because I was so stressed out from all the bad people out there. Well, not bad people, but things that people were saying – the way people were being mean and rude.

You mean after 1994 *(the scandal)*?
Yeah.

That's when you picked up smoking?
Yeah. I mean, I smoked a little bit in '91 and a little bit in '92, but it was around tour time. It wasn't when I was competing. Oh God – everybody smoked. I'm serious. There were so many people *(skaters)* that smoked, it was not even funny – at the competitions and at some of the parties we went to afterwards. It wasn't just drinking.

Did you have a pet when you were growing up?
I had a dog. His name was Fencey because when I saw him for the first time, he kept trying to poke his head out through the fence and get through the fence.

How old would you have been, and how long did you have him?
I was four, maybe five. Actually, I was probably five. We got the puppy, and I named him, and I had him – Well, let's see, when my mother and father separated in February, she took the dog with her because the place we – my father got couldn't have animals. She took the dog, and three or four years later, it died.

He was old then?
Yeah, real old. But it wasn't my dog anymore. For some reason, it was just a weird dog.

He was weird when you were growing up?

Not when I was little, no. But when I was older, it *(the dog)* was. It was more like my mother's dog.

So you didn't really miss him after?

Well, I lived with it *(the dog)* for a while, and I was sad when it died, but it was so old that I was glad because I didn't want to see it suffer.

Was he a friend to you when you were little?

Yeah. I used to talk to him. *(She laughs)*.

What did he look like?

He looked like a little, tiny German Shepherd. Like half the size of a German Shepherd with a curly tail.

What color was he?

Black, brown, tan, white: like a German Shepherd. As a puppy, he had little, tiny floppy ears, and when he got older, they stood up straight.

You used to talk to him?

When I was little, I remember I used to sit out in the yard and talk to him and play with him and take him all over the place.

It was kind of rough those first few years – emotionally? But I guess, as a kid, you don't know that do you?

I have no idea.

It's probably more when you were a teenager that you would remember …

Well, I remember some bad things. When my parents went hunting and they had her older son come over and watch me, and that was the first time that he molested me.

How old were you?

I was five. I remember because it was at my first house.

Was it touching?

Yeah, Yeah.

What did you do?

Well, I was supposed to mind my older brother. He was the adult in the family. Do what he says. I had no idea. My mother never told me about the birds and the bees. At the grand opening of the ice rink, Clackamas Town Center, Dorothy Hamill *(World and Olympic Champion)* opened it, and I was her guest skater. I was wearing a white dress, and I fell once in the program, and all of a sudden, my dress had blood all over it. I got off the rink to see where I was cut, but I wasn't cut. I was starting my period. My friend's mom came in and told me what was going on because I thought I was dying. I was 11 then. So, I was always told, "This person is older than you. This is the grown up, you do what they say, no questions asked." That was the way I was raised.

So, this guy is coming in and doing stuff …

He did it then. He did it again when I was about nine. Then he tried to do it again when I was 15.

Did you ever tell your dad?

Oh, yeah. I told my dad the time when I was nine-years-old, and he told me to quit lying, and my mother told me to quit lying and to drop it.

You don't talk about things like that, right?

Right – that was not right to say. Then, when he tried it when I was 15-years-old, I was getting ready to go out on my first date with Jeff. I was doing my hair and makeup in a lighted up mirror that you can stand up while I was watching TV in the front room, and he showed up at our house, and my mom had gone to work, and my dad was at work. He shows up drunk as a skunk, comes in, asks where mom and dad are. I said, "They are both at work, and you need to leave because nobody is supposed to be here, even you, when mom and dad aren't here." He was like, "They wouldn't care if I sit and wait for them," and I said, "Well, they will because I am leaving." And I remember he said, "Doesn't your brother get a hug?" I am like, "Okay, fine, give me a hug, but I am getting ready." So, he gave me a hug, and then he tried to kiss me on my cheek. I was like, "Whatever, go away, go away," because I knew he was just drunk – totally drunk, staggering. I told him to go and sit down, and that he could stay until I have to leave, but then he would have to go. He stole money from my parents a lot and all kinds of things. I was sitting doing my hair, and he comes over and sits down on the arm of the chair next to me and pushes me back in the chair and tries to kiss me. I said, "Get the hell away from me. Leave me alone. You are drunk. Go home. Get out of here." And he came back and tried to do it again. So, I burned him with my curling iron and ran upstairs, and he followed me upstairs. I locked myself in the bathroom, and he breaks the door to get in to me. I grab my stuff again and go downstairs to the other bathroom. He breaks that door handle and comes in. So, finally, I go back and say, "Just leave me alone." I ran over and grabbed the telephone and called 911. He came over to me, put his finger in my face and said, "If you say anything to them, you will die." I was standing there in total shock, scared, not knowing what to do. The operator says, "Hello. What is your emergency?" and I said, "Nothing." She said, "Are you sure?" And I said, "Yes," and I went to hang up the phone, but as I was hanging up the phone, I said, "Why don't you just get the hell out of here and leave me alone?" and the lady heard it as I was putting the phone down. She called back, and he tells me the same thing again. "You tell her nothing is wrong." I said, "Okay." She said, "This is the police. Is everything there okay? If it is not okay, say yes." I said, "Yes." She said, "Okay, we are sending out an officer right now." I said, "Thank you. Everything is fine now." She said, "Okay, they will be there real soon." I was hanging up the phone, and he grabs it from me and rips it out of the wall. I started to run out the door, and he tried grabbing me, ripped my shirt. I ran next door and called the police back because they still weren't there – this took about two minutes – and in the time I was waiting for the police to show up, he gets in his car and takes off and leaves. So, I am going to go back to the house and lock all the doors and wait for the police to show up. I went back – went through the entire house locking everything. Then a couple of minutes later there was a knock at the door, and I went and asked, "Who is it?" And they said, "This is the police. Let us in." I said, "No it is not. You're not the police." It was him. He said, "Yeah, you're right, you little bitch. You open this damn door right now" … just going off. Finally after I said, "No," a hundred times, he got back in his car to pull away, and I looked out the window, and he saw me looking out the window, and he pulls back in the driveway again. I am sitting there, and I called the police again, and they told me they should be there any time and to just hold on. I say, "Okay, fine." And then there is another knock on the door, and I was like, "Leave me alone. Just go away and leave me alone." They said, "Ma'am, this is the police." I said, "I heard that before," but they said again, "This is the police." They said, "We have your brother in custody here in cuffs." I said, "Sure." They said, "Look out your window," and sure enough they had him on the ground in handcuffs – three policemen there with him. So, I opened the door, and five minutes later, I was talking to the police, and Jeff shows up – my date. They said, "Who is this?" and I said, "This is my date." And here, I had just gone through this whole thing. My father comes home. They call my mother. She comes home. And they ended up arresting him for child molestation, for driving under the influence, a stolen vehicle, and resisting arrest, and something else. I'm not really sure what it was. And my mother and father came home and said I was full of shit, basically. My mother told me they were going to put him away for life if I testified against him and all this stuff, making me feel horrible and guilty and all this shit. I had no rights. I was a kid. They *(her parents)* said, "She is not going to testify against him."

He walked away?
He walks away.

Did they get him on the stolen vehicle or anything else?
Oh, yeah. They got him on all the other *(charges)* except the child molestation.

Did it ever happen again?
No, it didn't happen again. But he showed up at my dad's and my house and threatened me. He said if he ever caught me by myself anywhere, he would end up killing me. I said, "Get a life. Just leave me alone. Get out of my house. Don't ever come back." He was like, "Well, it is your father's house. He invited me. We are going fishing." I said, "Yeah, right. You have got to be kidding me." I guess it was true. My father got close with him again and started going fishing and hunting. I was like, whatever. So, when my dad left and went to Idaho – yes I was missing him, but on the other hand, that is when it all started.

When you and Jeff broke up, he *(her father)* did the same. (*Tonya told me this during the proposal interview*). He was siding with these abusive guys?
Totally, and he wouldn't believe me at all.

He didn't believe you? You really think he didn't believe it?
No. Nothing.

Did he just think you had a big imagination?
I have no idea, no idea whatsoever.

Or maybe it was because …
He just didn't want to believe the truth.

Didn't want to believe the truth because it would be a scandal or didn't want to believe this could go on in the family, right?
Yeah.

When it happened when you were five – I guess at that age you wouldn't say anything?
I didn't even know that it was wrong. I remember I was laying with him on the couch and watching TV, and he was touching me, but I didn't know that was wrong.

What about when you were nine?
Well, when he did that, it was like, this isn't right. "It is fine. Don't tell Mom and Dad. You are supposed to listen to me." Then when I told one of my friends – I remember telling one of my friends at school – *(she said)* that was wrong and shouldn't be happening, and I told my mom and dad, and they said, "You shouldn't be saying those kinds of things. That can get people into really big trouble. He is your brother and would never do that."

So, at five you didn't say anything, but at nine you did, and no one would believe you?
Exactly. And it had just happened.

What happened to your brother after the incident?
He ended up going to jail for a very short time. My mother made me not press charges. He died in 1988 in a hit and run accident.

How did you feel when he died?
I was really glad that he was out of my life, and I didn't have to watch my back anymore. There were lots of times where he threatened me, and show up at the rink and come right up behind me, and I wouldn't know he was there. This went on from the time I was 16 through to 1988. He would tell me I was lucky I was alive. I better watch my back – things like that. He would show up at the house.

Did he scare you?
Oh, yeah.

So, when he died you felt no grief?
No.

Shouldn't we be mentioning these people by their first names?
No.

Did you ever wish you had brothers and sisters of your own – someone to grow up with and share things with?
Yeah. And then maybe also I wouldn't have got in trouble so much. *(She laughs).* But then on the other hand, I am glad I didn't because that would have been someone else to have go through the shit that I had to go through with our mother. It's a catch-22.

Your current step-father - the one your mother married after she divorced your father – do you know him?
I knew him.

What was he like? Was he a nice man?
He was okay.

Is she still with him?
No she's not. She divorced him. I think she got married again and then divorced. I don't know. I have no clue. It doesn't matter to me what she does. She ruined her life a long time ago and just never got it back.

Do you ever think, though, you should give her another chance?
I gave her plenty.

Do you see any reconciliation with your mother in the future?
No. Absolutely not. That is kind of like the same thing when I kept going back to Jeff. We would separate, and he would sweet-talk me, and I would go back. I would wake up; smell the coffee, leave, and he would sweet-talk me back. You make mistakes and learn from them, and that is one mistake that I learned and I will never do again. You give them a couple of chances. Yeah, she is my mom, but I gave her lots of chances, and she screwed it up every time. And not just little screw ups; I'm talking major screw ups.

Give me some examples of major screw ups.
Selling pictures of me to make money off of me.

This was after '94?
Yes – baby pictures.

To the press?
Yes. Getting wired and getting paid for it – walking down into the rink before I went to the Olympics Games and trying to get me to talk – having it under her coat *(the mike)* so I couldn't see it, but I did. Let's see … never standing up for me. Going on national TV and faking having a problem to get attention. I knew that was a fake. Yes, she has high blood pressure. She went on national TV and sang a song. That was so embarrassing.

Tell me about that.
Supposedly, her blood pressure went up, and she collapsed on the show.

She was on a talk show?
Yes, and I saw it and said, "Oh, please."

I recently saw part of a clip on a show *('Inside Edition' – Famous 911 Calls)* where your mother called you and you said, "It's okay, Mom. Just relax. I am sure it is not a heart attack." What was that all about?
Yeah. She called me at the Olympics to tell me.

To say that she was having a heart attack?
To let me know that she was on the show, and she collapsed, and these other TV people were going to pay to have her come over to be with me at the Olympic Games, and she collapsed. I was glad she wasn't coming because if she had shown up there, it would have really pissed me off.

I told her about the clip I had seen, and she said she didn't know the phone call was taped. So, that was the last straw – the microphone incident?
Oh, yeah, the mike and me telling her to get out and never come back. I don't ever want to see her again, and then she comes on national TV a week later.

Do you remember what show was it?
I think it was Montel Williams, but I'm not positive.

You are away at Olympics during all this?
Yes.

So, she collapses, apparently, on his show and then makes a phone call to you?
Yes.

Did she make the phone call while she was on air?
I don't think so, but I wouldn't know.

As a child, what was your favorite thing to do?
Skating. That was it.

What was your least favorite thing?
Eating liver. My mother fixed liver once or twice a week because she said it was good for me. I also hate oysters because they were always slimy ... gross.

What was your best memory of this period? Would it be the skating?
It would have to be. I didn't like school because everyone teased me all the time. Skating was my life. That was it.

What was your first day of school like?
I don't even know.

You don't remember?
No.

What was your worst memory?
Being molested, I guess.

That's a pretty bad memory for a five-year-old, and you obviously remember it.
Oh, yeah. I remember – I can pinpoint every bad thing that has happened to me, and it sticks out in my mind like it happened yesterday.

Were you brought up religiously?
No.

You didn't go to church?
Supposedly we went to go to church a couple of times, and they told us we had to pay, and my parents said, "Well, we are not going to pay to go to church." Something like that, but I don't know if it was true or not.

Do you know what your religion was?
No. I have no clue. I have a very strong belief, and I think I am basically – *(Tonya didn't want me to say what religion she is).* Just say I have a strong belief and that I know that somebody from up above watches over me.

Have you always felt this way?
No. I found this out in 1995. *(Tonya was introduced to religion by her adopted godparents).*

What kind of student were you? Were you a good student, or would you rather be outside playing or on the ice skating?
I'd rather be on the ice skating when I was little. My grades weren't bad, but because I was always gone so much and changing schools so many times … I did the school work and everything, but a lot of times, I wouldn't get a lot of grades. They would be incomplete.

How long did you stay in school?
All the way to middle of sophomore year, and then I quit and took two years off and then went and got my GED *(General Education Diploma)* at Mount Hood Community College.

So, you would have been how old when you left school?
Fifteen, and I graduated when I was 18. I took two years off school – took my GED when I was almost 18 – in 1988 – the same time, basically, I would have graduated high school. I knew that my education was really important. I wanted to know business and how to communicate and talk to people for my skating, so I really wanted my education, so I decided to go back and do it at that time – when I didn't make the Olympic Games in '88.

When you were little, did you ever have birthday parties or things like that?
I only remember one, and the only reason I remember it was that it was at a – what do you call it – a sundae place – an ice cream parlor, and there was pictures of it. I had seen them, and I remember that one briefly – that's where we were, and I had friends there. I was probably only like five or six.

You never had the annual party with friends over?
Mm nm – usually my birthday was at Northwest Competition.

So, you would be at the competition on your birthday?
Yep, and so sometimes I'd have – people would come up and say, "Happy Birthday," and I remember at one competition it was Halloween and my birthday was going to be right after that, and so they had – it was after Halloween, it was the beginning of November, and so the party would be costumes to make the festivities. I remember that, and I always tried to hang out with everybody, but I never really got to.

Did your parents give you good birthday presents?
Mostly it was clothes made by my mother.

Do you have scrapbooks of when you were little? Did your mother keep things – like when you won a competition and …
I have a few.

So, it would have been her who kept them?
I have no idea who kept it, but it *(the memorabilia)* ended up in scrapbooks in a big box, and I took them. They were left at the house. My father and I moved out when I was 15 to another place, and that box with the scrapbooks and stuff was left, and so I took it with me, and then my father took one of them that had all his stuff in it, and he took a few *(scrapbooks)* with me in it, and the rest of them I have.

Tonya's love of the outdoors began at an early age.

*Tonya with her Dad proudly
displaying their catch-of-the-day.*

Tonya on ice at age 3½.

Tonya around 10 years old.

Tonya on horseback in happier times.

Tonya at competition.

1991 World Silver Medalist after being first American woman to complete triple Axel.

Tonya & Jeff on their wedding day.

Tonya at Lloyd Center.

Tonya with her father.

Tonya with her mother in one of last photos taken together just before their 'split'.

Tonya inside and outside courtroom during 1994 Scandal.

(3)

A "God-Given" Talent

"It was my way of proving to everybody that I was going to amount to something."

What was it about skating that you loved so much?
I liked jumping and spinning.

Was it the feeling of it?
I couldn't tell you.

Did you find that you could forget about other things when skating?
Well, when I was young, I really didn't have any problems.

I explained the Canadian skating system where a young skater goes through various levels of testing and asked: **Is the system in the U.S. the same as in Canada?**
Yeah. They have to go through everything. They have to go through all the testing. *(When Tonya was competing, there were eight levels that a skater was required to pass in the United States while moving up from Juvenile, Novice, and Junior before competing at the Senior level).* When I was skating, there was figures *(School Figures, or the variations of the figure eight patterns that were traced on the ice and then marked, were eliminated from competition in 1990),* and figures was not my strong point until probably the last four, five, maybe six years.

You didn't enjoy figures as much as the jumping and free-skating?
No. No. It was boring.

Like taking a math class?
Yes. Yes.

Did you go through all the normal testing from when you first started skating?
Well, when you first start skating – when I started skating, there was fig-ures, and then you did your freestyle *(or free-skate, including jumps and spins).* Then you got to a certain age when they did the short program and

the long program with the figures. The figures was one event and the freestyle event was in two parts, and that was when I became a Junior. Because it starts out Preliminary or non-test and then Preliminary – I don't remember being in non-test, but sub-Juvenile, Intermediate, Novice, Junior, and Senior.

You went through all those phases?
Yes, but when I was skating, the figures were still there. They didn't get rid of the figures until two or three years after I was done. Damn. I think I started doing the international competitions when I was 11. I think. I was either 11 or 12, one of the two.

How old were you when you began taking lessons more frequently?
I would imagine that I probably took two to three lessons a week when I was little. I believe, as far as I know, that I was skating Monday to Friday.

From what age?
From four up – I'm sure. When I got older, it was probably one lesson a day.

Five days a week?
Um hm, or two lessons a day, because one *(lesson)* was on figures and the other one was on freestyle. When I was little, I had one figure and one freestyle, and when I got older and had two different programs in freestyle, I would skate either one or two figures and then two freestyles.

Do you think you have a natural ability?
Yes I do. I believe I do. I believe I have God-given talent because there are so many skaters out there that have to train years and years and years, and train six – eight hours a day to do what I do in two hours a day.

Right from the start you found it easier – to pick up the jumps and ...
Yes. I actually landed a triple Axel *(considered difficult at the time for men, and near impossible for women, this jump is the only one launched while the skater is moving forward and where three and a half revolutions are completed in the air)* when I was 12. I was a jumper – totally, 100 percent. I loved to jump.

There were only two women in the world *(who had completed the triple Axel in competition when Tonya was competing)* you and ...
Midori Ito *(Japanese World Champion and the first woman to perform the*

triple Axel in competition). I have it on tape where I landed it in a show in 1987.

Did you know Midori Ito well?
I knew her pretty well. I mean, the only time I saw her was at competitions, and she didn't speak very good English, but I could understand her, and we always talked, and she always wished me good luck, and it was that mutual respect of being one of the great athletes.

So you thought she was a great jumper too?
Oh, yeah. Hey she is my equal. There is no other woman out there that is equal to me, you know – in the jump status-wise – at least at that point. *(Since this interview, a few other women have been able to perform the triple Axel).* I've heard that people have done it in practice, but I've also heard that it is cheated. *(She laughs).* I'm sorry *(for laughing),* but that is the one thing that makes me feel good. That is one thing that nobody has ever been able to take away from me, and nobody has been able to duplicate it to this day. Maybe someday another woman might do it and, hey, great for them. But at least this is something that nobody can take away from me. I did it on my own, and nobody can say I didn't do it. So, when I chuckle, I don't mean to be the kind of person that is a bitch about it. I just chuckle because it's one thing I get to hold onto.

By learning quickly, you would get a lot of praise from your coach that would make you really like the sport, don't you think?
Yes. I loved it.

Did you like your coach? Did you get along well with her?
Oh, yeah. I loved my coach. She was almost like a second mom to me, growing up, because I saw her every day, and I stayed with her a lot.

Did you start taking private lessons with her at some age?
She is the one I started with.

Right, but was it one-on-one or would you have been in a class with other kids?
No, one-on-one when I was three.

From the time you were three, you had a one-on-one?
Yup.

Normally, there would be a group *(to begin with)* and the ones who show more talent or interest would start *(private lessons)* ...
Right, but when I first started skating I remember my mother put me in class lessons because I started at two and a half – actually skating. On my *(third)* birthday is when I had my first skating lesson with Diane. I started skating in July or August *(before she turned three in November)*.

Would it be a 15 minute lesson?
15 minutes – half an hour.

And then gradually working up to?
Usually most of my lessons – I mean, every once in awhile I would have a 45 minute lesson, but mostly it was usually 15 minutes or a half hour lesson, like once every day. So, I would have a lesson every day, or we would spread it out to three days a week. So that way I could have my lesson time.

As you got older and you were going to Nationals, I guess things got more intense?
When I was doing figures, I would have a figure lesson, then a free-style lesson, and you know there was usually one lesson one day, another lesson the next day and variant them, and then it got to the point where I was having both each day.

So, you might have been taught for half an hour and then skating on your own?
Right, for the other 15 minutes or half an hour – and practicing.

Describe your coach to me.
She was the person I looked up to and wanted to be like. When I grew up, I wanted to be like her.

Other than coaching, what had she done *(in skating)*?
She was the star *(soloist)* of Ice Capades for several years.

That must have been impressive to you as a little kid?
Oh, yeah.

From a young age, did you want to be an Olympic Champion?
Well, that was what I liked. That was what I wanted to be. I loved skating so much – that was what I wanted to be. I wanted to be like Dorothy

Hamill. I wanted to be an Olympic champion – Peggy Fleming *(U.S. World and Olympic Champion).*

Did you look up to Hamill and Fleming?
They were my favorites when I was growing up – and Scott Hamilton *(U.S., World and Olympic Champion).* Gosh, there are so many people – Brian Boitano *(U.S., World and Olympic Champion).* I looked up to all those people.

What age were you when your parents were told that this child is really talented and she could make a career of this?
I'm sure it was before the age of 10.

Did skating make you feel special? Did it make you feel different from the kids at school?
Yeah. I was always treated differently because I skated.

In a good way?
No. I didn't have many friends because I was always gone to competitions and coming into school late and moving so much. You know I said, I moved 13 times before fifth grade. So …

That has to set you apart, but did you feel good that you were skating?
Yeah. It wasn't like work to me. I loved to do it.

What age would you have been when you did your first competition?
It was in August before I was four. I was almost four, and I won.

Was this a club competition?
It was in Sun Valley, Idaho. I remember that it was the first time that it snowed there in a whole bunch of years – at that time *(in August)* – and I remember I had these panty hose on – the little thin ones. I didn't wear tights back then, and I remember my mom had me in those with a backless dress. I went out to skate, and I went one or two times around the ice and got off because it was so cold out. I said, "I'm not skating." Diane told my mother to do something. She said, "You've got to go out and skate," and I said, "No. I'm not going to skate. It is too cold," and she started to take off my skates. And this girl, who had got off one minute before, was standing there, and she said, "At least now I don't have to worry about competing against you." I wiped my eyes off and told my mom to put my skates back

on – she had only just started (*to take them off*). I went out, did a couple of little jumps and a spin, and I then had to get off. I landed my first Axel at that competition.

At four-years-old? Your first single Axel?
Uh huh. And I remember I was frozen, and my dad had got me this walking, barking dog, and I named him Axel.

You mean a stuffed dog?
It was a robotic dog with batteries, and you turn the switch on. The dog would walk and bark, and I just thought it was the greatest thing since peanut butter.

He bought it after this competition?
Yeah. He bought it right there at the competition.

At four-years-old you were feeling competitive?
Yes. I liked it. All my life I was told, "You can't do this. You never are going to do this. You'll never be anything at all." Anytime anybody challenged me, it was like, "Really? You don't think so? Well, then fine – watch me." I remember at this one competition, I didn't have a triple loop (*a jump*) in my program yet, but I was practicing some on the ice with another student that was also Diane's. We competed against each other. She said, "You will never be able to do that, and I said, "Well, I have already done it before." And she said, "Well, I don't think you can." I said, "Okay, fine. Watch this," and went out and skated around and did one, just to prove her wrong. And I am like, "Nah!"

Do you think the competitive drive is inborn or acquired – to be a champion?
I don't know about that. I think I got mine from what I had to go through my entire life. I think it just happens that I have it, but I don't think that it is something you have to have to compete. You have to just love what you are doing.

What was a typical day like for you in skating and school?
I would get up in the morning. My mother would fill her thermos with half booze and half coffee at 4:30 in the morning and take me to the rink, and I would skate my sessions, and when I was done, she was done drinking.

How long would you be on the ice?
A couple of hours.

Before school?
Um hm. And she would drive me to school. She wouldn't let me change at the rink because of the floors.

Because of the what?
The floors – you know, because they are rubber mats and because I may get sick or dirty or something.

She was paranoid about dirt?
Yeah. So, I would have to change in the car all the time, and that was really embarrassing, but at least I would have a blanket over me.

Would you have a full day of school?
Basically, yes. If I had to be back in the afternoon, if she had to go to work early and my father wouldn't get off until after that time, she would pick me up from school and take me to the rink. If they both were at work, I would take the bus home and watch cartoons.

Did you do any off-ice training at that age?
I remember I took jazz. I tried ballet once and couldn't do it and said, "Forget this," and didn't go back. My hips don't turn out the way the lady *(teacher)* wanted. I did gymnastics for a few years in school.

How involved were your parents in your skating?
All the time.

Both of them?
Uh huh.

In what aspect? Was your mother the typical *(figure skating mother that coaches from the sidelines)* ... I shouldn't say 'typical' because not all of them are.
The mother that tells me what to do, and how to do it, even though she has never done it.

Like the coach sitting in the stands?
Yes. Diane had to always tell her to butt out because she thought she knew it all. And I would end up getting bad habits.

Give me some examples. You would be practicing a jump, and she would tell you how to do it?
She would be sitting inside watching me through the windows, telling me that I was dropping my shoulder or keep my chin up.

Would you listen to her or would you just listen to what your coach was saying?
Oh, I had to or else I would get beat.

So, Diane would confront her, but since your mother was the parent, there is only so much that she could do?
Exactly.

In what way was your dad involved in your skating?
Well, my dad was always supportive. He would take me to the rink a lot of times, went to competitions with me if he didn't have to work. I remember this one competition in Great Falls, Montana. I was at the competition, and I wasn't skating that great. I was missing some of my triple jumps that were in my program. I was pretty young then and was doing triples.

How old is young?
Eleven or 12, and I remember I had a problem. They had a stand where people were selling mementos from the competition. There were these candies in pill bottles, and there was one that was made up that said, 'Terrific Triple Toe – Take one for one triple missed, take two for two triples missed – up to three – no more than four a day.' After my practice session, I got off, and my dad told me he had just got these, and it was so funny. It was candy, and I was old enough to know this, but I thought it was so cute and sweet.

I guess you preferred your dad there _(at competitions)_ rather than your mom?
Oh, Yeah – definitely.

Did your mom push you to become a champion?
No. She never really pushed me to skate. She tried to get me to quit a few

times because it was so expensive. But if I didn't do it, or it wasn't good enough for her, then I would get in trouble. I guess she ice danced before me, and it didn't pan out for her, so maybe she was trying to fulfill her dream through me. Who knows?

I guess unless you got into her head, you would never know.
Exactly.

Was your mother ever embarrassing to you?
Oh, totally, totally. She wore polyester pants that were tight in the thighs and loose at the bottom with fluffy, ugly colored blouses. She never matched anything. She smelled because she didn't take a shower every day. *(I was speaking to a former skater who used to compete against Tonya as a child. She stated that she remembers very well, that Tonya's mother was an unusual woman who was very brash. The one thing that stood out in her mind was the odd odor that emanated from Mrs. Harding).* You don't have to mention those things. She was very embarrassing – on her appearance – that's a good word.

What about verbally?
She talked like a truck driver. Embarrassing – yeah.

That would make you cringe, I guess, when you were a kid?
Oh, yeah. Nobody went around her. Nobody liked her.

Probably the alcohol had some influence?
Yes.

If she was drinking that amount in the morning ...
That was not all she drank. As soon as we got back home, she would pour herself another cup. I mean, it would go on all day, until she left to go to work.

Tonya had been on 'Rivera Live' the previous day, and I told her that when the host mentioned her mother, her facial expression and tone changed, and it was clear that she didn't have good feelings about her mother as opposed to her face lighting up when he spoke about her god-parents. I told her it was a good interview. She responded:
Oh, cool – really cool.

Did your mother and coach ever disagree, and did you feel like you were between the two of them?
Oh, Yeah – they had fights all the time. Of course, I listened to Diane about my skating, but I had to listen to my mother, too.

So you were in the middle?
Yeah. It wasn't Diane's fault by any means because my mother was the one who was wrong.

Was the Axel your first jump? *(Asked because she said she had completed it at four years of age).*
My first major jump – I had already done the half jumps and other singles before I got to the single Axel because the Axel is the last thing you learn.

If you were 11 when you were doing triples, how old were you when you were doing doubles?
I think I was nine when I was doing triples.

You were doing triples before most men are doing them?
(She laughs).

How were you taught? Would Diane explain something to you, and then you would go and practise it yourself?
She would work on everything with me, and then, after my lesson, I would go and work on everything I learned in the lesson.

Who made all your costumes when you were little?
My mother.

So she would dress you for the club shows?
Oh, yeah. I remember she dressed me up as Shirley Temple for a show one year – 'The Good Ship Lollipop.' I remember my mother found this material that she thought was fabulous. It was cocoa brown – dark chocolate brown with red and orange and yellow flowers on it – not spread out – I am talking full *(of flowers)*. She beaded the flowers – red, orange, and yellow – this whole dress. And I had to wear it for practice one day, and Diane told me to take it off. *(She laughs).* And I said, "I can't."

You couldn't because your mother would be sitting there and …
I had told my mother I hated it and I didn't want to wear it, but she made me wear it. It was horrible.

So, you would just go and skate and try and forget you were wearing this thing?
Yeah. It was pretty embarrassing.

When you say your mother beat you, how did she do it?
Grab me by my hair, slap me, kick me, beat me with a brush on my butt.

Would that ever be in front of anybody?
Oh, Yeah – she did it at the rink all the time.

Did Diane try and stop her?
She'd tell her not to do it, but she *(her mother)* would tell Diane to mind her own business.

If someone did that these days, they would be charged with child abuse.
Oh, yeah.

You mentioned that you were always told you were fat and ugly.
Oh, yeah. I was never allowed to eat chips or candy or cookies or peanut butter and jelly. Every once in awhile, I was allowed to eat peanut butter and jelly. I had to eat bran muffins, liver and onions, stews – things like that.

Things that weren't supposedly fattening?
Right. When I was little, I remember she *(her mother)* would always make me take vitamins – 12 of them a day, plus a quarter's *(size)* worth of bee pollen, and I am allergic to bees.

How did you find out you were allergic to bees?
I found out about 10 years ago. I got stung by a bee and had an allergic reaction to it.

What happened?
I had to go to the hospital. My throat swelled up and my eyes puffed out, and I couldn't breath. And one time I've been – well, two times actually –

in '91, I got stung by a bee, and my friend took me to the hospital, and by the time I got to the hospital, I don't remember getting there.

How did it happen?
I was on my way to the rink, and I was at the gas station – this was when I was living with my girlfriend – we had a place together. I went down to get gasoline on my way to the rink, and a bee flew into the window and stung me on my left shoulder – my left shoulder blade behind me. I all of a sudden started feeling real crappy – went right back to the apartment and told my girlfriend, "I'm not going to make it to the hospital. You have to take me. You have to drive me." It was probably a 15 minute drive there, and when we got there, the doctors had to carry me in.

So you had been taking bee pollen all those years?
Yeah. No wonder I had a hard time. *(She laughs)*.

You weren't an overweight child though?
No, absolutely not.

She *(her mother)* was just worried that you were going to gain weight and it was going to affect your skating?
Yup.

Why did she call you ugly? Why would she say that?
Because if I was over the weight that she thought I should be, she would say I was fat and couldn't eat things. There were some times, if I didn't skate good, then I would have to go without dinner. She'd send me to my room without dinner.

It was never like, "Let's just go home. We won't worry about it, and you'll do better tomorrow?"
No. I would get a butt whipping and sent to my room without dinner. No TV, no music, no nothing.

Would she say it was because you were being lazy or because she thought you didn't skate well?
I don't know. I mean, it didn't matter because she was in such a weird mood all the time – being drunk all the time – that it didn't matter. If I came in and looked at her wrong or said something wrong, I would either get slapped or sent to my room. I mean, I went without dinner so many times.

My mother's older son would come over to their house – my trophies would be up on the mantle, and they had the cups on the top, you know. My mother put her quarters from tips in a couple of them, and most of the time I could use it for bus money, or we would take it and cash it in for ice skating lessons or something. Well, he would come in, and he'd steal half of it, and I would be the one getting blamed for it because I took money to go to the bus stop for the bus. And then I would get blamed for it, and I am like, "I didn't take it. I didn't touch it." And she didn't believe me, so I always got sent to my room. And I would say that would happen at least once a week.

Was this the brother who had been giving you problems?
Yes. He was always a trouble maker. I mean, all my mother's kids were bad trouble makers. Because, I mean, they were never raised properly. Her daughter was a prostitute. Her first son was a druggy, stealing, in and out of prison – you name it. *(Tonya interrupted our interview by saying to her dog, "Koda – wake up!)* He is dreaming. *(She said with a laugh).* Her other son was in and out of foster homes and in trouble all the time – running away – you name it. So, … just bad parenting.

What would you do – just sit in your room and wait it out for the night?
Yup. I'd have to go up and figure something to do for the night or just go to bed.

There was no TV up there?
Nope – no TV. My very first radio I got, I was a seventh grader.

Were you ever disciplined by Diane for misbehaving on the ice or missing jumps?
I am sure I was a handful. Aren't most kids?

Were you ever physically disciplined by Diane?
No, never.

So she was always the gentle one then?
Oh, yeah, totally. She treated me with respect. If I was being lazy or mouthy, she would say, "Hey, straighten up, or I am going to quit your lesson."

She sounds like she is a very good coach.
She is a wonderful woman.

While you are coaching now, do you ever use any of her principles that she may have passed on to you?
I'm sure. Because I have been doing it for so long, and because I have achieved much more, I have about six different ways of being able to teach things – feelings on jumps, spins, but for the most part, I use what I learned. And then what I have learned myself over the years – I will also teach that.

Do you attribute the way you teach to the way she taught you?
Yes.

How old were you when you started attending sectionals? *(Regional and sectional competitions are mandatory for figure skaters before competing at the national level).*
I don't even remember. I was young.

Before 10?
I think so.

Did you rise quickly through your tests? Yes. I moved up one *(level)* every year. A lot of people stayed back.

How old were you when you turned Senior?
Twelve.

And you were competing with the senior ladies?
Um hm.

Do you remember anything significant before the age of 10 that stands out in your mind either with skating or school?
When I was young, I remember going fishing and hunting with my parents.

Do you still like fishing and hunting?
Yeah, yeah. Not so much hunting now that I am older. I mean, I like the outdoors – but not shooting Bambi. But I love the outdoors.

Did you love it as a child?
Uh huh.

What was it that you liked about it?
I don't know. Just getting away from town, being out in the woods and going for walks with my dad, and fishing was fun. It was challenging. When I was younger, I used to pick up bottles and cans from the side of the road or rest areas – places like that. That was how I made my money besides cleaning my room or mowing the lawn. I saved up a whole bunch of money, for me. I was pretty young – nine, ten – third grade. I saved my money up because I wanted a 10-speed bicycle. I found one in a store I wanted that was $110.00 or something like that. We went up to a competition in Seattle. I remember we were sitting there before I was going to go out and compete, and my dad told me that if I won, I could take my money and go ahead and buy my 10-speed bicycle up here because we were going to stay an extra two days, and I could get it up there because I had seen it in a store there, too. I had gone out and won the competition and went for the medal ceremony. We were just getting ready to leave and the head judge or referee of the event, and somebody else, came up and asked to speak with my father, my coach, my mom, and me. They took us into a room and said that it had come up to them that my father bribed me with a bike to win the competition. We explained what was going on, but they still said it was bribery. They ended up taking my first place medal away from me and gave me second.

How did you feel?
I felt horrible. I was like, "No way." But it didn't matter because I got my 10-speed anyway.

Did the officials believe the bike was considered to be payment *(which would not have been allowed since amateur skaters at that time could not accept payment)*?
I have no idea. Well, it was against one of my competitors that I competed at every competition. She was very competitive. It was usually me in first and her in second or her in first and me in second. I mean, we went back and forth.

So, it may have been her parents or coach complaining?
It was her parents that complained to the referee. I remember, too – this was

also up in Seattle because there were a lot of competitions we went to up there, and I remember being out in warm-up, and my zipper broke on my dress. It was hooked at the top, but it broke all the way down. I went off to the back *(stage)*. I had pretty much warmed up. There were only a couple of things I hadn't done. We were backstage, and my mom was sewing me up, and they were calling my name, and she was still sewing. They said, "Last call for Tonya Harding. You have 20 seconds or you will be disqualified." I just got on the ice, and they had just started to say *(that she would be disqualified),* and I came out *(she laughs),* and so I went ahead and skated, and they had to cut it off of me.

They had to cut the dress off of you?
Uh, huh– up the zipper where she had sewed it because she had to loop it around the zipper.

Do you remember if you won the competition?
No. I don't remember. *(She laughs).*

Do you remember your youth as a good time or a bad time?
I think it was a good time for me when I was young. From the age of eight or nine, then it started not being so good.

In what way?
Because my mom was drinking so much.

And probably because you were noticing it more?
Oh, yeah.

When you were little, you probably didn't notice that she had the thermos full of ...
Right.

Do you remember how old you were when the USFSA became involved in your career?
Oh, jeez, little. I was always in USFSA. I was always a USFSA skater.

By the time you were ten, they would be looking at you?
No. I was in USFSA events since I was four-years-old. When I competed, I competed through USFSA since I was four-years-old.

So, everything was gearing to get onto the National team at some point?
Yeah, and the Olympic team. I'm trying to think what age I would have been when they really started to notice me. I would say 10 or 11. That's when they started noticing that I had potential.

When the USFSA began to get involved in your skating, would they tell your coach how you should look and act?
Oh, yeah.

I told Tonya that certain skaters in Canada had told me of the pressure they felt from the sport's governing body with respect to weight, costumes, and how they wanted the skater to look. Tonya responded:
If they didn't like my costumes or if I was overweight, or they didn't like my ribbon or something, they would tell her *(Diane)*. They would come in and have judges look at me before I was tested to see if it *(the program)* was okay.

Were you nervous as a kid – competing?
No. I don't think so. I don't really remember. I loved competing when I was young. It was a competition against myself. I was going out there to prove what I could do. Everyone was always telling me, "Oh, you won't be able to do it. You can't do it. You won't amount to anything." Okay … I am a good skater, and I knew it. I knew I had talent. It was my way of proving to everybody that I was going to amount to something.

Did you make friends on the skating circuit when you were young?
Uh huh.

Anyone we would know now, who made it into the top ranks?
Rosalynn Sumners *(U.S. and World Champion).*

You skated with Rosalynn?
I was a few years younger than her. I remember skating with her. Let me think.

What about Debi Thomas *(U.S. and World Champion)*?
Yeah, I skated with Debi. I skated against Debi. Jill Trenary *(U.S. and World Champion)*, Rory Flack. I got to skate with Scott Hamilton a couple of times, and Richard Dwyer *(U.S. competitor and 25 year soloist with Ice Follies)*, and with Peggy *(Fleming)*, Kitty and Peter Carruthers *(U.S., Pair Champions, World, and Olympic medalists)*.

This was when you were little *(referring to the older skaters)*?
When I was little, yeah.

How did you feel when you would meet these people?
Most of the time, I would be getting their autographs. *(She laughs).*

Do you remember meeting Scott *(Hamilton)* **for the first time?**
I don't.

What about any of the women?
Dorothy Hamill opened the Clackamas Town Center, which is in Clackamas, which is a suburb of Portland, and I got to be her guest appearance skater in the show, and I got her autograph then. And Richard Dywer was when I was real little, and I remember watching him skate at Lloyd Center before they remodeled the mall and the rink, and I got his autograph there. Let's see … I don't remember when I got the other ones.

Did you watch a lot of skating on TV when you were young?
Uh huh.

Did you dream that someday you would be on TV?
Yeah, I did.

So you wanted to do this from an early age?
Uh huh.

You knew what you wanted to do and stuck to it?
Well, I found something I was good at and that I liked to do.

It was easy for you to be disciplined in it – have the willpower to stick at it?
Yeah. Yeah. It was hard sometimes because of the pressures from my mom. But for the most part, I tried to do the best that I could.

(4)

Rising Through the Ranks

"Unless I am on my deathbed, I am going to skate."

Much of what I have read about you indicates that people thought you could be an Olympic gold medalist.
Um hm.

So, you were really a protégé in skating? The talent came out young and was apparent to everyone?
Yeah. Yeah.

Before you turned Senior, had you won any noteworthy championships in Junior? What was your record before you turned Senior?
I think I got first, second, or third a couple of times at Northwest Regionals. At all the other competitions, I was usually in the top four.

Was this in Junior?
All the way up – all the time. I don't think I really ever got any lower than seventh.

Before you turned Senior, was there anything *(noteworthy that happened)* from those competitions that stands out in your mind?
I remember when I competed up in Tacoma one year; my blade fell off in the middle of my program. It was pretty funny.

Tell me what happened?
I was skating and did a jump and came down. When I landed, my blade came off. I grabbed my blade and took it off the ice. *(She laughs)*. I remember one time I had a ribbon that matched my dress, and one of the judges came up and told Diane that if I didn't take the ribbon out of my hair, he wasn't going to give me the marks I would deserve, if I deserved them.

Why?
Because he didn't like the ribbon. So, we took the ribbon out.

Some skaters that I have talked to have told me their nerves get to them all the time. It doesn't seem like you were that type of competitor. It sounds like you were the type who says, "I know I am good. I know I can do a good job, and I can't wait to get out onto the ice and show my stuff."
Exactly. Exactly. I always liked to be able to go out and show them what I could do.

Did it also have to do with the applause and the audience?
I have always said that it has to do with not having a loving relationship as much as I should have had as a child. Maybe I liked that *(the audience approval)* – being able to please people. Who knows? I am not a psychologist.

Do you remember anything else from this time?
I don't remember what year it was, but at one of my first Northwest competitions, I had just got brand new boots, and Diane didn't know it. I had only worn the boots three times, and I went out and competed with those boots *(she laughs)*, and she didn't know it. And oh my God, she was so mad.

How did you do at that competition?
Oh, I won. And then I remember at a Northwest competition – it was at Silver Skate, which is in Portland, my hometown. I threw in my triple Axel and landed it, stepped forward, and fell. So, I didn't get credit for it.

Was that the first time you tried the triple Axel?
Yeah.

When were you first credited with doing the triple Axel?
'91 Nationals.

That was the first time you did it in competition? That was the first time that any North American woman had done it in competition?
Right, but I did do it at one of the Northwest competitions, and I landed it, but then I stepped forward and fell, and they didn't give me credit. They said I had to land it and hold it for so many counts.

How long *(was it)* between the Northwest competition and the '91 Nationals?
I was 12. Maybe I was 13 *(at the Northwest competition, which would make*

Tonya 21 years of age at the 1991 Nationals). But I was really young, and I remember the competition was in Portland.

What year was your first Nationals? The first I can find recorded is in '87. You were fifth *(according to my information).*
I was at Nationals when I was a Novice.

How old were you? *(We spent a few moments figuring out what her age would have been).*
I was 11 when I was a Novice. I was 12 when I was a Junior, and 13 when I was a Senior.

At the Novice level, did you ever win *(Nationals)?*
I won lots of competitions, but not Nationals. My first Novice Nationals, I was sixth. I remember watching Jill Trenary skate for the first time at that Nationals.

Was she Novice? Wasn't she older?
She was either Junior or Senior, I don't remember.

So, you went Novice one year and Junior the next *(year)?*
I went up one every year.

You went from Novice to Junior right to Senior?
Yes.

How did you do at Junior?
I was sixth at Junior Nationals. Well, it was at Nationals, but I was there as a Junior. I went up to Senior, and I was a Senior – gosh – I think it was '84. I would have been 14 – well, I was 13 until November …

I know it is hard *(to remember).*
It is. It is really hard. I remember skating against Tiffany Chin *(U.S. Champion)* at a Skate America competition in '85, and I came second.

This would have been as a Junior?
I think I was Senior. And then I went to Nationals, and I was sixth. That *(Nationals)* runs in January, so '86 Nationals I was sixth. At '87 Nationals, I was sixth. I was sixth two years in a row, then I was fifth. I was fourth in '88. I was an alternate.

Who were your competitors in this time period?
Jill Trenary, Debi Thomas, Tiffany Chin, Caryn Kadavy *(U.S. competitor)*.

Who, in your mind, was your biggest competitor?
There wasn't a biggest competitor because I liked them all. I always looked up to them.

They were all older than you, right?
Yeah. So, it was always just exciting for me to skate against them and try to beat them. These people were the best, and I was right there with them getting to compete against them – seeing if I could beat them or not.

How old were you at '87 Nationals?
I was 16.

So, Jill Trenary would have been …
She was 19 or 20 – and Caryn Kadavy. They were both older than me.

All of them would have been older? Debi Thomas?
Right.

So they weren't really your friends?
Oh, yeah, they were my friends. I really liked being able to talk to them. I had to grow up quickly. *(She laughs)*.

How did you feel the first time you stepped on the ice as a Senior?
Well, nervous, a little bit, but excited.

Was that where you saw Jill Trenary skate or was that when you were still Novice?
Novice.

She would have probably been skating Senior at that time?
Either Junior or Senior.

Did you want to compete at that level?
I always wanted to skate with the bigger kids. I was doing the same jumps as they were.

Tell me about your first Senior Nationals.
I don't even remember.

Where did you finish in your first Senior *(Nationals)*? Sixth, you said?
Sixth. Second year – sixth, third year – fifth, fourth year – fourth. I just worked my way up the ladder. *(Later research showed that Tonya placed fifth at her first two Senior National competitions, which were held in 1987 and 1988).*

Do you remember anything else from this period?
I just remember working hard. Going to school – up to a point, of course. Going to school, going to skating – all that.

Did your mother go to Nationals with you?
No. Usually I just went with Diane.

Did you room with any of the other girls?
No. Usually I had my own room. I think I either stayed with Diane or had my own room. I don't remember.

If you were fourth at '88 Nationals, who was ahead of you?
It was Debi Thomas, Jill Trenary, Caryn Kadavy.

In that order?
I think it was Debi Thomas, Caryn Kadavy and Jill Trenary, but I'm not quite sure ... and then me.

Did you feel that you should have been at the 1988 Olympics?
I felt that because I was the alternate that I should have been able to have that opportunity because with the other gal being sick and not being able to finish.

Who was that?
Caryn Kadavy. But of course, I always believed that because Jill Trenary was Carlo Fassi's *(Italian medalist and elite coach)* other student along with Caryn Kadavy ... They were both at the Olympics, and he made her skate the event so I couldn't come and have that opportunity because I could have beaten his good student, his other skater. And so I always felt that was pretty unfair, but she did deserve the opportunity to go ahead and try, so I understood that part.

So, really that was the first Olympics you should have been at?
Mm hm. I missed it by one.

Did you watch it on TV?
Yeah. And I thought Elizabeth Manley *(Elizabeth took silver behind Katarina Witt, the German World and Olympic Gold Medalist)* should have won. Hands down, she should have won, hands down. I mean, that's just the way I feel. I just love her. I just love her. I always thought that her and I – our skating was always very similar. And she is a little power house, and that's how I always thought of myself, too.

She always said that as well, – that your skating was similar – the energy.
Yeah. Yeah.

The following year in 1989, you were third, but you didn't go to Worlds?
Because they were only allowed to take two *(skaters)*.

And who were the two that went?
Oh gosh …

You must have been upset that you didn't go to Worlds?
Well, I was happy with my performance.

My information has it that in '88 you won Skate America and Nations Cup. Is that correct?
Yes.

Then you went to Nationals …
That was '89 Nationals.

And you came in third. Wouldn't you have been a little ticked off that you didn't go to Worlds?
I was disappointed because I had worked really, really hard – really, really hard. And it was just disappointing. I do remember that was when I thought about quitting once. It lasted for a couple of days. *(She laughs).* And then I decided, No, I just want to skate.

You don't remember who the two women were who did go? *(Later research showed that Jill Trenary and U.S., World and Olympic Champion, Kristi Yamaguchi went to the 1989 World Competition).*
No. *(She laughs).* Whoops.

How did you feel when you won Skate America?
Great.

That was huge?
Yeah. It was really cool.

Can you remember who you were up against?
I know Nancy *(Kerrigan, U.S., World and Olympic Medalist)* was there.

Is she around the same age as you?
Yeah. I don't remember who else. I don't know if Jill was in that one or not.

When was the first time you met Nancy Kerrigan?
I don't even remember. I'm thinking it was '88 or '89.

It would probably have been at Nationals?
Most likely – yeah.

Or at one of the top competitions?
At one of the international competitions or possibly even an Olympic festival that happens in the summer.

Nothing sticks out in your mind about meeting her?
Un uh. I do remember that we roomed together a few times at competitions and training seminars.

According to the research I have done, from '90 to '92, it was you, Kristi Yamaguchi, and Nancy Kerrigan *(who were the top three U.S. women and competing against each other).* **Right?**
Yup.

After that, from '92 to '94, it was you, Nancy, Lisa Ervin *(U.S. competitor),* **and Tonia Kwiatkowski** *(U.S. competitor)?*
Right.

And in '94 ...
Michelle Kwan.

And Nicole Bobek *(U.S. competitor)*?
Uh huh.

Was the 1988 Skate America the first major competition that you won?
I don't think that was probably my best accomplishment to then. I think the Skate America in '85, when I came in second to Tiffany Chin, was one of my best.

Why?
It was a major event. I skated great at it, and I was up with the top skaters from all over the world.

But in '88, there would have been the top skaters *(at the competition).*
Yeah, but I was younger back then *(at the 1985 Skate America).*

So it was more of an accomplishment?
Right.

Where was Nations Cup held *(which she won)* **that year?**
I couldn't tell you. You have to realize that I have competed over 500 times. Let me add it up. For 26 years – when I was little, I probably did ten competitions a year all the way up until '91 or '92, and then I was doing six competitions a year – for 20 years. For 20 years at ten a year, and then six a year from '90 to '94; and that's not even including shows, exhibitions.

So it has to be over 500 times performing?
Yeah. I would say 'performing.'

So you didn't go to Worlds, but the following year ...
'90 Nationals.

Do you remember that?
Yup, I remember. I don't remember what placement I was.

Seventh, according to my research.
Going into the free program?

No. That was the total *(placement)*.
I think going into the free program, I was eighth or ninth. I don't remember. That was the first year my triple Axel was in my program, and I had been landing it consistently – skating great. We had a day in between short and long programs. After the short program, I ended up catching pneumonia. By the time I got to compete my long program, I was running a 103 degree temperature. The doctors told me not to skate. They wanted me to disqualify myself. I said, "No. I am going out. I'm skating. Unless I'm on my deathbed, I am going to skate. I am not going to drop out of a competition." And so, I went out and skated. I was barely moving – left stuff out of my program, popped *(when the skater begins to jump, but only completes a half or single rotation)* my triple Axel, and I ended up seventh overall. Two days before that I was landing the triple Axel almost every time. I would have been the first American woman to have ever done it. But then I ended up doing it the next year.

Did you go into that competition with a cold or not feeling good to begin with?
No. There was snow on the ground there. So, going from a warm rink to a cold rink, to a warm rink to outside cold, to the hotel – in and out of cold and hot all day long – I got a cold.

Do you remember where this Nationals was?
Salt Lake City.

So you got a cold. When did you find out you had pneumonia? Or was it just a bad cold?
I knew I had pneumonia. When I got home was when I found out for a fact that I had pneumonia. I mean, I couldn't breathe at all. My chest was hurting. I had fluids. It was horrible.

Do you think this had to do with your asthma?
It could have had something to do with it, but I don't know. I'm not a doctor. It went – boom – into my lungs.

Why were you eighth in the short program? Were you sick then?
Well, see, we had figures then, so we started out with figures, then we went to the short program and then the long program.

But you didn't do well, on the short program either.
No, I did. I think I was something like twelfth in figures, and I pulled up to eighth *(in the short program)*.

You were okay *(health-wise)* in the short program?
I did a clean short *(program)*.

How did you feel about figures? *(We had touched on this during a previous interview, but I wanted Tonya to elaborate because there had been much controversy over dropping figures from competition and how the quality of skating had subsequently lessened).*
It was really hard. It wasn't 'hard' *(per se)*. I was young, and it was boring – really boring. Draw two circles on a piece of paper. Draw two circles on the ice and follow them around, over and over and over, and try to do the same identical thing every time. It was boring. When I was young, it was always at cold ice rinks that I skated. I didn't skate at malls. So you froze to death during figures. You are not moving.

Is it lonely as well, – being out there by yourself, doing the same thing over and over again?
Well, there are other skaters out there doing the same thing, but there is no talking allowed. You have to be quiet. It was always cold. It was always boring, and I didn't really care for it very much. But, at the end of competing for my figures – the last few years of competing in figures – I was getting good at it, really good at it. I was in first or second place after the first two figures. And then when I finally get good at it, they take them away! *(Her voice rises in irritation).* It was like – here I had to do them for all those years. Now people don't have to do them at all. All they do is get to do the fun stuff.

When figures were eliminated from competition, do you think the quality of skating went downhill?
Well, all it is now is freestyle. There is really no determination now – my opinion – if you weren't good at both, you weren't at the top, and it made it a lot harder for people like me. I was a good free stylist – always. If I hadn't had the figures, I may have been an Olympic champion – and a lot younger, too. But, the school figures – you have to be good at both of them *(freestyle and figures)* to be able to do it *(make it to the top)*. The school figures teach you control.

And discipline. Right?

Discipline, control. You have to learn how to move your feet at the same time as your arms to exact precision. Looking back on it now, if I had my choice, I'd have my kids *(students)* doing figures because it would teach them hand, eye, foot coordination. It *(school figures)* was a good thing.

Kids go out now and can jump, but there is ...

No control. Figures taught you complete balance. That's why when I competed it was always *(against)* older people – I think, because the older ones knew what it took to do it – the figures – to have the control to do all these things.

Many of the great skaters I have spoken to hated doing figures, but they all say that there is such a difference in *(the quality of)* skating now *(since figures were eliminated)*.

Yeah, I think so too. I do. I do think so.

(5)

Boyfriends, Husbands, & Horror

"My mom hit me, and she loved me – he hits me, he loves me. It's just the way life goes"

How many people did you date before Jeff Gillooly?
He was my first.

How old were you?
I was 15.

You had no serious boyfriends before him?
Nope.

No dates?
Just little things with boyfriends in high school, you know, where you hold hands in the hallway. I wasn't ever allowed to go and do anything with him by myself.

With Jeff?
Right. My dad went to the movies with us.

How did you meet Jeff?
I met him while I was skating. He was standing there watching me skate.

At the mall?
At Clackamas Town Center.

Why was he watching you skate? Did he just happen to be at the mall?
It was in the evening time, and I was skating on a public session. My dad was picking me up. I had already skated freestyle before that. Jeff and his friends were at the mall to go to one of the stores. One of his friends had to go to the bathroom, and the bathroom was beside the rink. So, he was standing by the side of the rink watching me skate while his friend was in the restroom. His friend came back out, and they were talking. He *(Jeff)* had been staring at me. My friend was skating with me, and I remember

him calling my friend over and asking her what my name was. And I told her to tell him and to tell him how old I was because I was 15.

How old was he?
He was 17.

What was he doing ... going to school?
He had graduated from high school and was working for a company that picked up donations.

Did he ask you out then and there?
We exchanged phone numbers, and I had talked to him a couple of times on the phone, and then I asked my dad if we could go to the movies. We went to the movies, and my dad would sit in the background. Then later, he would drop us off *(wherever they were going)* and pick me back up. Eventually, after a few weeks, I was able to go out *(alone with Jeff)* for a few hours in the late afternoon. But I would have to be home by 7:00.

Your parents were strict?
Oh very, very.

You told me in an earlier interview that you were getting ready to go out with Jeff when your half-brother was at your house going after you. Was that your first date with Jeff?
That was the first date when I actually got to go out by myself with him.

What attracted you to him?
I guess I thought he was cute.

What kind of personality did he have? Was he funny? Did he make you feel good?
I don't even know. I can look back now and think, jeez, how could I even be with a person like that? Obviously, I thought he was a great guy because he was interested in me, and he was my first boyfriend. Other than that, I really don't know. I guess he liked me, and he liked my skating, and so I liked him. *(She laughs)*.

Did you meet his family right away, and did you get along with them?
I met his family a few weeks after we started dating.

Did he live with his parents?
He had lost his dad when he was young, so he lived with his mom and his brother. He had three brothers and two sisters.

So, he was living at home with them when you two met?
Yes, but not all his sisters and *(brothers)*, just his mom and brother.

A younger brother?
Older. Jeff was the youngest.

Did you like his family?
Yes. They all treated me really nice, and everybody seemed okay. Normal family that would have problems – there is always usually one bad seed in the family.

Did they live in a nice place?
A contemporary home – a little house, maybe 1,800 square feet, 1,500 square feet – not big. They lived in a small neighborhood in southeast Portland.

Did you prefer being over at his place rather than at your place where you were having some problems?
Yes – all the time. After my father left me for the first time and went to Idaho, and I had to move in with my mother and her new husband, the only time I was at that house was when I slept. That was it.

Whose house?
At my mother's house.

This is when your dad and mom split up and they divorced and she remarried?
Right, and I had lived with my father. You see, my parents separated in February of '87, and I went with my father, and then my father left in September or October of '87. I don't remember, but he ending up leaving and went to Idaho, and I had to move in with my mother because I wasn't actually working at the time. I mean, I was *(only)* doing part-time work, so I lived there for awhile. But the only time I was at my mother's house with her new husband was when it was bedtime. I would stay out until 9:00 at night – when my curfew was, when I was 17-years-old. I would be home at 9:00 o'clock, go to bed, and leave. Most of the time, during the days that I

wasn't doing anything, I would be at his mom's, sitting having coffee and b.s.'ing with her.

Did you like his mom?
Yeah. She was really nice. I used to take her to the grocery store because she didn't drive.

Do you ever see any of his family now?
No. Nope. *(She laughs).*

Did you and he become serious quickly?
No. I was 15 when we started dating in late August or beginning of September. I was going on 16.

This would have been in 1986 then? *(We spent time figuring out her age during this period).*
Yes. We dated until March of '90 when we married. We didn't get married until I was 19.

When did you get engaged?
We got engaged three years into our relationship.

Were you living together before you got married?
Yes, we did, because when I turned 18, I got the heck out of there *(her mother's house).*

You got your own place?
Yes.

Was it an apartment or a house?
It was a little, tiny house about five minutes from his mom's house and about ten minutes from my mother's house. It was a little, tiny, one bed-room house – just kind of crappy – a starter or renter home. It was not a great area, but it was an okay area. For young kids, it was fine.

When you got engaged, did he make a big deal of it? Was it romantic?
I had gone to a competition, and when I called him after I was done with my competition, he asked me over the phone, and when I got home, he asked me again. It was just at the house – just us two.

Did he give you a ring?
Yes.

Did he surprise you with the ring or was it something you had bought together?
No. He had bought it.

Were you excited and happy that you were going to be marrying him?
Oh, yeah. I thought it was great.

So you really loved him? You were head over heels?
Well, I thought so then, but when I look back now, I was stupid. He used to beat me all the time. He would get pissed off, and he'd beat me. He would go out with the guys, and I would stay home. He wouldn't take me out. Because when he turned 21, I was only 19 – almost 20, and he would go out, and I would end up staying home.

This was after you were married?
Yes, but even before. What was I thinking then? Being stupid and young and naïve – my mom hit me, and she loved me – he hits, he loves me. It is just the way life goes. He's a man, that's how it goes.

Often when you are abused as a kid, you are abused as an adult.
Yes. Now I am an adult. But I wasn't an adult until about two and a half or three years ago. I'd say it was three years ago when it hit me and I started to grow up, and realize, hey, I've been through all this counseling, and my counselors told me I shouldn't be treated like this. And finally, when I got divorced the second time, it was the biggest step for me because as soon as he *(her second husband)* laid a hand on me the first time, I told him – I gave him the ultimatum. I said, "Either you stop doing this – don't ever hit me again, or your ass is out. This is my house. I own it. I paid for it, and you will be gone. Don't ever raise your hand to me again." Two weeks later, he pushed me down the stairs, and I told him to get the blankety-blank out.

What was his name?
His name was Michael. And he did it right in front of my dad the first time.

What did your dad do?
Nothing. He has never really stood up for me either. While I am on that subject, I love my dad to death, but I have no respect for him. In March of

'93, when I finally decided to straighten my shit up and said, okay, I'm leaving – my father stayed with him.

Jeff, you mean?
Yeah. He stayed with him! *(This was said in an incredulous tone)*. He moved in with him and lived there with him, and I was going through a divorce. Yeah. Nice, huh? He *(her father)* was sitting in my kitchen when Michael *(her second husband)* turned around and punched me in the face, and he didn't do anything.

Did you ever confront your dad about these things?
Yes. He said, he didn't want to get involved and I am a big girl and can take care of myself.

You mean a man has punched you in the face, and he said that?
Yeah. Darren *(her boyfriend at the time of this interview and the one who was involved later when Tonya was charged in the 'hubcap' incident)* has no respect for my father. Darren is usually at school when my father is in town, so he doesn't have to be around him very much. I mean, he doesn't mind my father. He is my father. He respects that. He understands that, and he knows I love him, but for him to be around him for any length of time, knowing what my father has done to me – it just really irritates him.

Darren sounds like a good man.
He is a very good man. A couple of weeks ago, we went out for a couple of drinks with some friends. We went out to this place down the street, and this guy said something, and he *(Darren)* was like, "I am tired. I just can't hold it back anymore."

What did this guy say? What do you mean?
Well, this guy had this little red light thingy, pointing this red light thingy on my boobs.

A laser?
Um hm. Yeah. The kid had already been warned by the security person – the bouncer, to put it away and not bring it out. Finally, I said, "Honey, this guy keeps shining that thing on my tits. Can you please take care of it?" And Darren stands up and says, "Hey, man, could you please stop?" He *(the trouble-maker)* was like, "Fuck you." Darren was like, "Excuse me?" And the guy said it again. Anyway, the bouncer came up and said, "Okay. You can

leave. I told you to put it away, and now you are causing a problem." After the kid got kicked out, our truck was keyed again. They were college kids. There were like 14 of them in their group. We had only five people in our group, and three of them were girls. We are like, these guys are becoming assholes, and we don't want to get into a fight, so Darren and I left because they were starting to mouth off because their friend got booted out of the place. And then they started saying shit because it was me.

It sounds like Darren is man enough to walk away from it. Right?
Yes.

Not to get involved?
Yeah. It is hard for him, though. He wants to say something because if he doesn't then he is not standing up for me. I am like, "Honey, we've heard it all. These people are just little people who don't even matter to us."

Are they doing this because …
They are male.

Because it is you *(knowing who she is)***?**
Well, I think it is because they know who I am and because nobody really knows about him *(Darren)*. I mean, I get marriage proposals on the internet. I have probably had a hundred of them.

Are you kidding?
I am not kidding. I get so many e-mails and letters from people who say they love me and all this crap, and they want to marry me, and I am like, "Get a life." But I think that now Darren has been put into that light as my other half, now people think they can try and challenge him. He is with her. Let's see if we can tick him off.

Is he older or younger than you?
He's younger – 11 months younger.

Does he go to school?
He is a union electrician.

About your dad – he sounds like he is a nice man, but a weak man?
Yes. He has been that way all my life. He is a big teddy bear. He just doesn't growl. I mean, I have heard about him growling a couple of times when

I wasn't there. But, not ever standing up for me – not ever standing up to my biological mother – I mean, nothing.

Did he ever remarry?
No. I wish he would.

At this point, I checked the tape, concerned that it wasn't working properly, and told Tonya that I wouldn't want to have to ask her all the questions again. At the beginning of our interview, she had joked that she wasn't looking forward to talking about Jeff. I said: **That would really make your day? Having to ask you all the questions again?** *She responded:*
Oh, no. Just being able to talk to you is fun. That's what I like about you. I tried to work with a lady before in '94, when I was going to write a book, and I just could not talk to her. I just couldn't open up and be able to just talk to her like a normal person. She would ask me these real horrible questions, and I just couldn't handle it then. I mean, right in the middle of everything *(the Olympic scandal)*. I just couldn't deal with it. And she was just very pushy, and I couldn't talk to her. And that is what I like about you because you are just … I think it has to do with *(the fact)* that I'm a lot more grown up, too. But you are very easy to talk to, and I enjoy just being able to talk.

I thanked Tonya and told her that most women, including myself, have been through difficulties, and sometimes they are not easy to talk about, and that we obviously 'clicked.' **Okay, back to Jeff. You were saying he was abusive to you. Did that ever show up before you were living together?**
No. He was fine. He worked, and I saw him for a couple of hours in the evening time before we moved in together, but that was only for a couple of times a week and maybe once on the weekend, and I would be able to see him for an afternoon. But once we moved in together, he became very abusive. When he turned 21, he started going out and wouldn't come home until the wee hours of the morning, and *(he would be)* just really, really abusive to me. He would be mad or would punch me, hit me or kick me – whatever. And I would take it because I thought I deserved it for being bad. "Oh, sorry, I didn't clean the house good enough" or "I didn't clean the house because I didn't get to it."

You ended up apologizing all the time or wondering what you did to deserve this. Right?
Right.

Do you think he was he fooling around?
I don't know for a fact. When we separated and started going for the divorce in '91 when I got back from tour – I found this out in '93, so it was way after – that he had got an apartment for this girl when we were separated, and they were seeing each other. We ended up getting back together and resolving things because we went for counseling and got all better. So, I thought I would give it another shot. This was marriage, and I wanted to make sure I was giving it 150 percent. We got back together in September of '91 and were together until March of '93. Then in July of '93, I went through with the divorce and was going through our storage unit and was putting my stuff in a different unit when I found papers that showed he still had the apartment going. I mean, receipts in his name plus a box of toys, lingerie, magazines ,and all this stuff – completely taped up with no markings on it, in the very back corner.

What do you mean by 'toys' – kid's toys?
No.

Sex toys?
Yeah. Who knew? Anyway, I found out it was the girl who did my nails. He had been having an affair with her from '91 to '93 when we were still married. And that is who he is married to now!

Nice guy ...
Yeah, and she was my nail girl! *(Said in a comical fashion)*.

It is laughable now, isn't it?
And her name is Nancy! Can you believe that? *(We both laughed)*. And if I thought I was a bitch sometimes – let me tell you this gal is so rude. After that, she didn't do my nails anymore. I mean, she was such a bitch.

We want to put humor in the book because if you can laugh at yourself ...
That's what I think. It really helps you to grow. But to find out two years later and then – oh God.

Tell me about your wedding.

We got married in a house. *(She laughs)*. This little, tiny chapel house.

Did you have a lot of people there?

There were about 30 people. We had the reception at one of his parent's friend's house.

Did you wear a wedding dress?

Yeah, a friend of mine made my dress for me because I didn't have a lot of money. We paid for our own wedding. But I had my dress made, and he bought me a little ring – little, real little – a $299.00 little ring. But the money was not the important thing. It was the thought that counts. It was a little ring, but it was cute.

Who was your maid of honor? Did you have someone stand up for you?

Yes, my friend Stephanie. She is no longer my friend. Her parents became really good friends with my father, and when Stephanie and I lived together once in '91 – that's who I lived with – we got an apartment together when I was going through my divorce with Jeff the first time, and we lived together, and she ended up meeting a guy and moving out. And when Jeff and I got back together, I let the apartment lapse, and we moved into another place.

Why isn't she your friend now?

When Stephanie lived with me the second time – her and her husband and kid – because I needed a place to stay too, and it was a nice house, and it was less expensive with them *(living there)* and me, they ended up trashing the house completely. The lease was in my name, and I had to pay the bills for the house to be fixed when they decided to move out. I ended up not living there after all. I stayed with some other people. Her parents had some of my stuff in their storage unit that I wanted to get, and I have no idea what happened to it. But I had told my father, "Listen. If you are going to be in my life – a part of my life – then you need to do what is right. And if these people want to take advantage of me and do this shit to me, then I would appreciate it if you wouldn't hang around with them. Well, he didn't listen. To this day, he still has contact with these people, and he has done that to me so many times. People take advantage of me with either money or whatever, and I put those people out of my life, and he stays in contact with them – comes into town and stays with them.

Was Stephanie a skater?
No. I met her at Clackamas Town Center. I worked for 'Spud City,' which was a potato place. Her dad was the manager.

Was it a store?
No, a restaurant.

In the mall? A fast food place?
That's exactly it. He *(Stephanie's father)* would do the coffee in the morning, and he would sit there and talk to all the people, and they would all watch me skate – the mall walkers. For a couple of years, I had been talking to him. Well, he gave me a job. I would open the place up, get the coffee, get everything running – for two hours, and then he or somebody else would come in and take over, and then I would be able to go down and skate, and then after I was done skating, I could come back and work for three or four more hours.

You worked hard then?
Yeah. I enjoyed doing it, and that was how I met Stephanie – through him because she worked for him in the afternoons. We became friends.

How many years have you known her?
I probably met her when I was 18 or so.

For her to be your maid of honor when you were 19, you must have really liked her?
Oh, Yeah, and I didn't have a lot of friends either. Diane came to my first wedding, and she stood up as sort of one of the …

Bridesmaids?
Kind of, yeah.

Were your mom and dad at the wedding?
My dad was at the wedding.

Why wasn't your mother there?
I didn't invite her.

You weren't talking to her in '91?
Yes, but we had a falling out then because of her husband. At least, I think she wasn't there. No, no, no, no. I'm sorry. She was there for that one, but wasn't there for my second one.

We can talk about that later.
It is all so confusing.

Tonya and I then discussed about changing last names after getting married and how confusing it can be. She said:
I know. I am Harding, and then Gillooly, and then Smith, and then back to Harding.

Were you a Smith too? I was a Smith.
(Tonya laughed hard). My second marriage was to a Smith.

My marriage to the 'Smith' lasted nine months.
Mine lasted 99 days. 99 *(days)* – 9 *(months)* – isn't that funny?

I thought mine was the shortest *(marriage)*.
(She laughs). You know what? Anymore *(marriages)*... I mean, nowadays, it is great. Everybody knows who I am anyway. But it will be so nice to say, "Tonya *(she gives me Darren's last name)*. Of course, the *(she says his last name)* part will not be in the book because we don't want his last name in the book.

But what if you get married before the book comes out?
Well, if I did get married, then people will know.

Wouldn't it be 'Tonya Harding *(Darren's last name)*'?
No. I am going to drop my last name. Yes, I am. Except for skating events – like Peggy Fleming does, because I think she goes by 'Peggy Fleming' for everything but her marriage, and that's the way I would be, too. But it will be so nice to say 'Mrs. *(she says Darren's last name)*, instead of saying, "This is Tonya Harding calling." *(And having people say)*, "Are you the skater?" "Yeah." *(They say,)* "I've missed you." I mean, that part is great, but it would just be great to be part of him.

I told Tonya that I had reverted back to my maiden name after my divorce in honor of my father. She responded:

I don't really have anything – I mean, my skating – the Harding name is the only thing I had, but I look at it that 'Harding' has not been a pretty page in my life. It hasn't been. So, why not start fresh?

You are who you are now because of everything you went through in your past. You wouldn't have met Darren or your god-mother or have all the good things that are happening now if you had not gone through what you did in the past.

I know. It's just great to have everything turned around.

It's all a journey, right? One step at a time and hope to do your best?

It is. Going from one planet to another, and *(I've been to)* Mars a couple of times. *(She laughs).*

So, your wedding day was nice?

It was.

Did you go anywhere for your honeymoon?

Our friends pitched in and got us a hotel room down the street, and we all sat and watched movies, and then we left. I didn't have a honeymoon. Didn't have anything, and it was that night that he filmed me. *(Her voice rises in anger).*

Tell me what happened?

Well, we got this video camcorder for our wedding present. We used it at the wedding, and when we came home, we were walking through the door, and I was shit-faced. I mean, I was totally trashed – barely walking. I wasn't old enough to drink, but we were in somebody else's house. So, when we came in the door, I remember I was being flirty and funny. I lifted my dress to show him my garter on camera. I was trying to be sexy, and, of course, I can never do that, and I turned around and showed him my butt. I lifted my dress and showed him my butt, and I was laughing and that was it. Well, then, later that night, we – you know – he filmed it.

But you knew he was filming it, right?

No. I knew he was filming when we walked in the door.

What was he filming?
You know – the video, the magazine that is out now.

I have not seen anything and have only heard snippets about this.
It was horrible. Horrible!

Did he have the camera set up in the room?
Someplace. He set it up someplace in the room when I was putting on my lingerie, and I have no idea where it was. I didn't see him set it up – nothing.

So he was in the video too?
Oh, yes. It is in 'Penthouse' magazine. I didn't even know it. I found out in '94 when I showed up in a lawyer's office because 'Penthouse' had pictures of me.

They had taken the pictures from the video?
Yes. They were going to do it *(print them)* no matter what.

When did he sell them?
In '94, right after he got out of prison – or right before. I don't even know the dates now.

Did he make a ton of money on this?
Yup. I made money, too. But the point was, I settled out of court. They were going to do it anyway, no matter what. So, I figured, if they were going to do it no matter what, I better get paid something out of this. So, finally, instead of taking them to court and suing them for all this money, and it being publicized big and everything again *(as was the '94 scandal)* in the court system, I decided to settle it out of court, and they had to pay me so much money.

Had the pictures already been published?
They had them all ready to go.

So it was ready to go – it was going through anyway?
Yup.

You couldn't stop it?
No.

Were you and Jeff still together then?
Oh no, no, no, no, no.

So when did this happen?
In January '94 is when I came home from Nationals. Then I went to Olympics in February. I went through all the court shit in March. That *(the 'Penthouse' issue)* happened in May, June – I couldn't even tell you anymore. So, it probably was right before he went to prison. *(More on the video in Chapter '11.')* And, oh, I can tell you something else. When I came home from the Olympic Games – I had my bag of stuff that I had got from the Olympic Association. I had a medal and a really nice camera. He took both of them – took both of them. Talk about being pissed off. I ended up leaving half of my stuff. I had crystal. I had beautiful dishes. I had stuff that I had collected from other countries. My friends came over to move me out the one day he wasn't going to be there. He had to be at his lawyer's office, and they were trying to get all my stuff out of there when he showed up. I had to leave half my stuff – stuff that was really important to me.

Does he have it now?
Oh, no. I am sure he either gave it away or sold it. But he has done lots of shit like that before. In '91, after I had won Nationals and had gone to Worlds – let's see, in '92, excuse me, right before I went to Olympics *(in Albertville, France, where Tonya placed fourth)*, I had received a really cool camera for the Olympics – they give it to you at Nationals in your bag of goodies. One of the photographers that I knew really well, – his name was Tom, out of Portland – he used to take pictures of me all the time for 'The Oregonian' *(a newspaper)*. I did a photo shoot at the Coliseum *(a rink)* around the boards. They had a 'Budweiser' sign on the boards, and they had some other signs up there, and I thought it would be really cool because I'm in my skates, and so I got up on the rail, and I laid across the rail above the 'Budweiser' sign, and he took a picture of me – just for me – so I could have it. He blew it up, and I put it in a really cool frame. I mean, it was really cool looking. It had been hanging up on my wall. When I left him *(Jeff)* in '93 and my dad ended up staying there – when I was carrying some of the stuff out of my house, I had the picture. I had my camera and a whole bunch of other stuff, and he *(Jeff)* came out and knocked me on the

ground. Everything went flying out of my hands. He took the camera and threw it on the ground – broke into smithereens. Took my picture, jumped up and down on it, broke it, took it out *(of the frame)*, and ripped it in half.

Was this because you were leaving him again?
Yes.

And he didn't want you to go?
Oh, no. He just didn't want me to have anything that was important to me. Just thinking of this stuff – it is all coming back to me – ahh! I need to take a pillow and punch it or *(slap)* a wash rag on the sink – wham, wham, wham! *(She laughs)*.

This is good that you are remembering.
You are getting so much more than you thought. I remember in '93, before I left, I ended up staying with another *(friend)* – her name was Angela, and she was one of my other skating friends. Kind of like a team thing. She pushed me, and I pushed her. We'd jump and skate together. I had stayed with them *(Angela's family)* for a couple of weeks because we *(Jeff and her)* were going to try and work things out, until I said, "No, I just can't do this anymore." Well, one night, I had gone out with my friend Wendy. We went shopping at the mall. I told him *(Jeff)* I was going to be back at a certain time, and I was running late, and I called him. I was about half an hour late – that was it – because we wanted to get something to eat. I knew he had already eaten with his friends. So, I called him up and told him I was on my way home in just a few minutes and that we were just finishing up our dinner. He told me to get my ass home. I was like, "I will be there when I get there," which was not even half an hour late. Got there *(home)*, and Wendy left, and had said, "If you have a problem, just jump in the car and come out and stay with me." I said, "That's great. Thank you," because she didn't like him. My other friend, Stephanie, didn't like him. Nobody liked him. Well, now I know why. Like they say, 'Love is blind.' Anyway, I got in the house, and he just started going off on me – literally, going off on me. I said, "I am not going to do this. I am staying at Wendy's house, and we will deal with this tomorrow after you calm down." He didn't calm down. He got ten times worse. I went to get a bag and my clothes – skating clothes and jeans and a shirt for the next day, and my jammies – then went to get my curling iron and makeup. He came in, threw my bag down, punched me, and pushed me through the stained glass window into the bathtub,

cutting me all over the place. Then he grabbed me, pulled me out of the
bathtub, and throws me on the floor. I get up and run into the other room,
trying to shut the door. He broke the door in, came in, grabbed me by my
leg, and twisted my leg and ankle so hard, I thought it was going to break.
I am screaming and yelling. He finally threw my leg down, slapped me, and
walks out of the room. I get up, grabbed my bag. I had my skate bag, my
purse and my coat, and I run out the door and go to jump in my truck. He
runs out after me, throws the hood up on the truck, grabbed the coil wire,
and ripped it off – completely rips it off. I mean, it wasn't good anymore. I
go to get out of the truck and go to get in the car. We had a Lincoln
Continental with the suicide doors – a big car, you know, a '67. It was
parked in the driveway, and our driveway was on a good, I'd say, 30 degree
angle.

Were you terrified at this point?
Oh, terrified. I was totally hysterical – terrified.

Were you worried that he was going to kill you?
Oh, easily. I mean, I had cuts and bruises all over my face from his hitting
and punching me. I had thought he was going to break my leg – threatening me all this time. So, anyway, I go to grab my stuff, and I got in the car.
I had opened up the door – he was standing in front of the driver door,
screaming and yelling at me. And I had thrown my stuff in the car, and then
he goes in front of the car and lifts up the hood and rips off the other one
– *(coil)* wire so I couldn't leave. And I am like, "What are you doing?" I
reach in and go to grab my stuff – the stuff I had thrown on the seat – my
skates and everything – grabbed that stuff and I had a hold of the door at
the same time, and it was on an angle, so my hand and my hip were on the
door holding it *(open)*. All of a sudden, as I was getting ready to get out of
the car, he kicks the door and slams my hand in the door. The door actually shut – literally shut on my hand. I dropped everything and opened the
door, grabbed my stuff. He went in the house. He turned around and
walked into the house, and I have no idea what he was doing – no idea.
Grabbed my stuff, picked it up, and started running. There was a drugstore
– at that time – about one mile up the road. I start running, carrying my
skate bag, my purse, my clothes bag, and my coat, in 'Ked's' tennis shoes.
Running down the street, and he comes running after me. I kept running.
I just ran as fast as I could. I had pretty good endurance back then, but I
was carrying all this stuff. My adrenaline was so high that I kept running.

Finally, he stopped. He is yelling and screaming, "I am going to get you, bitch." You name it, he said it to me. Finally, he stopped. I had kept running, and I noticed he had turned around. I just kept running and was finally about eight blocks from the stores where I knew there was a telephone. So I started walking because I was getting so tired. All of a sudden, I could hear the truck coming. He had jumped back in the truck, had put the coil wire back on it and fixed it, and was coming. So I started running again.

Is this a lonely road?
It is black. It is a neighborhood, but it was one long, black street with one house on it. But it was the only way I could go to get there. Finally, I make it out to the main road, and I could hear him coming, so I started running again. And there is a new housing development there, behind the store. I heard him and saw him turn on to the main road, so I ran into the new housing development. I ran in and hid in some trees and saw him drive by and park on the other side. Then I saw him coming running down. So, I am running through these trees in a new housing development – couldn't see a damn thing – tripped a couple of times. Finally, he saw me, ran around the other side, and jumped back in the truck. I made it to the store, which was closed because it was 11:00 at night. I hid behind a huge, huge pillar. He drove through the parking lot looking for me. I made sure he couldn't see me behind this pillar. Whichever way he went, I went the other way around the pillar. Finally, I heard him drive off. I put a quarter in the phone to call my girlfriend, and she said, "I will be right there." When he had grabbed me by my hair – when I ran, I was so sweaty; my hair was completely matted up. When my friend got there and took me back to her house – the police were already on their way because she called them – the police got there, and my girlfriend and the policewoman pulled out a handful – I am not talking just a little, I am talking a handful of matted hair that he had actually pulled out of my head and was stuck in the matted hair in the back (*of my head*). She (*the policewoman*) put it in a baggy.

Did you go to the hospital?
My hand was completely smashed (*hurt badly*). Nothing was broken, but it was totally smashed on the fingers.

Did you go to the hospital? Did the police take you to the hospital?
I don't think I went to the hospital.

So it was cuts and bruises?
Right. The kind of stuff you can treat at home.

Luckily, nothing was broken.
Exactly.

Did the police charge him?
The police went to the house, and he wasn't there. They went to his work the next day to arrest him, and he talked his way out of it. They didn't arrest him.

He was pretty smooth, wasn't he?
Oh, he could be a *(Dr)*. Jekyll and *(Mr)*. Hyde. He schmoozed the people from the USFSA on tour. He got them to thinking that he was this great thing. That is why they wanted me back with him, and as soon as we would be in the *(hotel)* room, he would beat the crap out of me.

They wanted you to go back with him?
Remember, I told you that a USFSA person called me in '93, right after I divorced him, after my counselor had died, right before '94 Nationals ...

I don't remember you telling me this.
In '93, after we were already divorced ...

This is after everything you just told me took place?
Oh, yeah. This is right before '94 Nationals when all this shit happened – he had found out ... okay, let me start at the beginning. I got a call from a USFSA person, stating that they thought I had a stable life when I was with him. And if I was not with him, I would not get the marks that I deserved.

They thought you were more stable with him?
Yes, because that is how much they had been tricked. No one knew what happened behind the scenes. Even Diane didn't know. He had told her I was a crybaby.

Did he tell people that you were lying about him hitting you?
Oh, yeah! She *(Diane)* wouldn't even believe me. She would say, "Oh, you hit your head on a corner of something again." She did not believe me until the day he turned me in and said that I was the one who planned this whole

thing on Nancy. Until that day, Diane never believed me. He had her fooled.

You mean you would come to the rink with bruises on your face ...
Oh, yeah, all over the place.

Black eyes, whatever ...
And wearing so much damn makeup, you would not believe.

And did you tell her you had hit your head or did you tell her Jeff had hit you?
Oh, yes. I told her lots of times. "Jeff has hit me. He is beating me up." She would say, "Tonya, now let's not exaggerate."

Why wouldn't people believe you?
I don't know. Excuse my language, but I think a lot of people had their head up their ass. I'm sorry.

We had come to the end of the tape, and I asked her if she wanted to continue. She responded:
Sure. Sure. I'm on a roll. *(She laughs)*. When you get me going on bad shit like this, I could talk and let you know it all.

This is very interesting to me. How your coach and people around you thought that you were bullshitting.
Yeah. All the time.

Why would she and people think that? Were you dramatic?
No. He got to her, too.

Did they really think he was a nice guy?
Oh, Diane thought he was great for me because he was older and mature – because he fooled them, totally fooled everybody. He did not fool Angela, her mom and dad, my friend Stephanie – all these people saw him do bad things to me, but do you think anybody would ever come forward and stand up for me? No! *(Her voice was steadily rising)*. Because they don't want to ruin their reputations because of what had happened to me. So, let me finish that one part. I had gone to the competition and came third – should have won. I really believe I should have won.

What competition was this?

I don't even remember, but it was in '93. When I got the call – it was before this competition – *(where they told me)* that I had to be back with him. And I said, "No, I am not going back. I am going to prove to you guys *(the USFSA)* that I can do this on my own. I have done it on my own all along. You guys just didn't understand that."

They believed your mental state would be better if you were with him, and therefore better able to compete?

Because I am a married woman rather than a single woman – so anyway, somebody at the rink had overhead Angela and I talking and told Jeff that the only reason I was with him was so that I could make it to the Olympics and that I was going to leave him after I was done *(at the Olympics)*. Because after the Olympic Games, I wanted to retire *(from amateur competition)*, and if that was what it was going to take – that I was going to have to spend two or three months with him, then that was what I was going to do. After he put me through so much shit and used me. He took me for everything I had in my divorce – everything I paid for. He hardly worked. He worked off and on. He probably worked two and a half years, three years out of the seven we were together.

You were only divorced from him once?

Right – we never got through the full divorce the other *(first)* time that I went through it. I had divorced him the second time *(after the second separation)*.

Give me the chronological order *(regarding the divorces)*.

In '91, after I got back from tour ...

The 'Tom Collins Tour'? *(Then owned by Tom Collins, and called 'Champions on Ice,' this production tours the United States in the spring and invites those amateur skaters who have performed well, on the world scene during the previous season).*

Yes, in June. He had threatened me on the phone with a shot gun that he was going to kill me when I was still on tour. So I went directly home to Dody's *(Teachman)* house, who was my coach *(at the time)* – stayed with her. She and her husband took me over *(to my house)* to get my stuff.

Why was he going to kill you?

Who knows?

What was his reason?
I don't even remember.

Was he jealous of you?
Major league – I am sure of it.

So if you are out on tour, he may have thought you were doing stuff?
Yeah, but I was in my room every single night. I didn't go out and party with everybody.

So you get into a fight, he is threatening to kill you over the phone, you go to Dody's?
Yes. I went straight to Dody's. She picked me up from the airport, and I filed for divorce, and then we ended up reconciling – I think it was in October.

Of the same year?
Yeah, because I didn't think I could do it without him.

Do what?
Make it on my own and stuff. I never lived out on my own ever before, and I was basically dependent on him.

For what?
Well, because he was the one who carried the job and paid the bills and did all that stuff. All I had to do was skate – and being told all along that I'll never amount to a hill of beans, I'm stupid, I'm ugly … there will never be anybody else out there who will take me. I tried dating a couple of other people and just couldn't find anybody that really would treat me good or anything like that, and I got to the point where I was really lonely and couldn't figure out how to make things work. Do you know what I mean?

I do understand. A guy can be beating you, but you can also be dependent on him.
Yes, and I guess that is what I was. I didn't think I could make it without him anymore. So, I thought, Okay, I am going to try this one more time. We had been through counseling, and I thought I would try one more time. He was good calling me and saying, "Hey let's work it out" and "I love you" – always saying the right things to get me back, and I'd be stupid enough to go back and get beat up again.

You didn't go through with the divorce?
No, we cancelled it. We reconciled and went all the way through a whole, entire year without him hitting me, and so I thought everything was fine. Well, that's because he was having an affair! So, then in '93, when I left him in March ...

That was after the *(violent)* incidents *(she had just related)*?
Yes.

You didn't go back with him after that period *(of incidents)*?
No. We went through the divorce, and then in September of '93, after we had already been divorced, I ended up having to go back to him in October because I was told to by a USFSA representative *(to do it)* unless I didn't want the marks. If I wanted to make the Olympic team, I needed to make myself have a stable life.

You mean *(the USFSA believed)* the judges would favor you more if you were married and stable?
I guess so.

Or was it because *(the USFSA thought)* your performance *(from consistent training, without other pressures)* would be better if you were married? The judges *(certainly)* wouldn't be marking you on whether you were married or not. They are *(supposed to be)* marking you on your performance. Right?
I really can't tell you. All I know is that they said I had a stable life when I was with him – married, settled down. *(They said, when I was with him,)* I was always training. I was always coming to competitions *(prepared)*, and they wanted to make sure that I was still going to be that way to go to the Olympic Games.

Was he trying to get you back during this time?
No. He was with the person who is his wife now. He was with her.

Did you tell him why you were coming back – that it was for your career ... that it was for the USFSA?
No. No.

So, how did you get back with him?
I contacted him and said, "Come on. Let's try it again," and I was just like, you know, dreading every minute of this. But we stayed in separate rooms.

How did you explain the separate rooms to him if he thought you were going back *(as a married couple)*?
Because we were working it out. We were going to try and work it out. We weren't just going to jump back into things. I said, "I'd really like to try and work this out to see if we can, you know, be friends and live under the same roof and then go back to having a married life, basically."

Would you have stayed with him if things had have worked out?
No. As soon as I was done with Nationals, I was going to move out and back in with Angela – my training partner. It was already set with her parents.

You were sure?
Oh, yeah. I hated him. And I do not use that word. I mean, I don't hate people.

You knew you hated him then?
I hate this man.

I know you hate him now, but did you hate him then?
I hate him for what he did to me.

What about before *(1994)* Nationals?
I didn't hate him. I disliked him. I didn't like how he treated me, and I didn't like him as a person.

So you told people you were going back together, but you were staying in separate rooms?
Ah, yup – we sure did.

Did you tell him to leave the girlfriend if you were going to go back together?
Yup.

And did he?
He agreed to, but he never did.

So, at this point, it is more of an image thing?
Yup. I told him I had money coming in. I said, "I will pay for half of the bills if we can just work on this – work on getting things back to the way they were. We stayed in separate rooms. Then when he found out from somebody at the rink that I was only there to further my career and that I was going to leave – I think it was about two and a half or three weeks before Nationals, and when he found out, he came unglued. I got the shit kicked out of me so bad. I had back and blue eyes. I had bruises all over me, and that's when I had to go in and start training at night. He is thinking *(she surmised)*, Now I am going to have to come up with all the money to pay for all the bills because she is not going to be here – she is my money making machine. So, then he decided to ruin me. He told me he'd ruin me. He told me that if you are not going to be with me, you're not going to be with anybody.

Did he just come home one night and say that – when he found out from someone at the rink?
Oh, no. He had showed up at the rink, and he was standing there talking to somebody, and as soon as I had done skating and we left and went home, he confronted me. Totally, when we got back home. I mean, it was bad.

You never directly told him?
Oh, no. He had used me so much over the past seven years that for three months of me using him, I didn't think was that bad – especially when it meant the rest of my life. You know, I figured if I can make it on the Olympic team, they can't kick me off the Olympic team if I'm not with him. But to at least make it there – make it that far, I thought, well, I can deal with it. And if he hits me a few times, I've dealt with it before; I'll just deal with it again.

Did you move into his house when you came back *(to him)*?
Yes, I did.

Did you sleep with him at all?
Nope, not until he took me.

Really?

Yup. It was sad, and I don't know if Michael *(her manager)* is going to want this in it *(the book)* or not, but, ah – you're sitting down right?

Yes.

Okay, because this is going to shock you really bad. When I got back from the Olympics – excuse me, it was from Nationals *(January '94, where Tonya won the competition and where Nancy Kerrigan was attacked and was forced to withdraw),* before the Olympics, and we ended up seeing the lawyers, and right before I went in to see the FBI people to tell them the truth of what I knew *(about the attack on Nancy),* at that point, him *(Jeff)* and two other guys – don't know who they were because I couldn't see who they were … they were in a different car – decided to drive me up into the mountains, put a gun to my head, and take themselves upon me.

All three of them?

Yeah. He stood there and watched the other two men do it. And he decided to do it, too. They said, if I didn't cooperate and say exactly what he *(Jeff)* told me to say, they were going to take me out. I had a gun at the back of my head and *(was raped)* on the back of a truck of a car, and they told me this is what you are going to say. This is what you are going to do, and if you don't, you're not going to be here anymore.

***I was obviously horrified and expressed same. I asked:* What were you thinking *(during this)*?**

That I wished they had pulled the trigger. It would have been better than to go through that a second time. I mean, I had already been raped before.

By who?

By a friend of mine, who I knew for eight years.

When you were how old?

When I was separated from Jeff the first time in '91. I used to hang out with all his friends, and this one guy, who I knew who used to work at the rink, had a steady girlfriend and was going to ask her to marry him, and he was having problems with her, and I went over to his house – we all hung out there a lot. He was talking to me about her, and he was in tears, wondering what to do. He had a portrait of me on the wall. I had given it to him. It was just paper, and he asked me if I could sign it. I said, "Well, sure. No problem." Well, I bent down and began to sign it on the bottom of the painting, and he grabbed me and threw me to the floor. I fought him and fought him and fought him, but it didn't work.

Did you go to the police?
No. I didn't go to the police.

Why?
Because at that point in time, I was National Champion. I was Skate America Champion. I mean, I wasn't going to ruin my career.

In those days, there was that sort of fairy tale image of the women ice skaters?
Yeah. I mean, I wouldn't be popular. People would take me to task just like they do now. I have never brought it out that I have been raped twice. Why people don't understand why I didn't come forward *(regarding Nancy Kerrigan)* – that's the reason I didn't come forward! *(She was obviously upset).* And I told his *(Jeff's)* story *(to the FBI officials)* – tried to tell his story, and they knew I was lying. They said, "Do you know what hindering the prosecution is?" I said, "No." They said, "It is when you don't tell someone the truth when you find out about it and you hold back. Are you lying to us now?" "Yes. I am." "Okay, so would you like to start over?" "Yes, I would." Then my lawyer took me into another room and said, "Listen, if you don't want to go to jail, you need to come out and tell them exactly what is going on and what you know." And I told my lawyer what had happened to me, and he said, "Don't worry. We will get protection for you." I went back in there. I told them the truth – everything. Left, I went back to my dad's house, and there were FBI sitting out in the parking lot, and Jeff walked right past them, broke into my dad's apartment, and came in and saw me. Was that protection?

So, the assault with him and the two other guys took place after Nationals and before Olympics?
Yes. I wish he would have pulled the gun *(trigger).* I wish he would have shot me in the back of the head because then I wouldn't have had to go through it. No woman should have to go through that.

What were you doing while this *(the assault)* was going on?
Screaming, yelling, bleeding ... I was totally bloody by the time I got home.
When I got home, my clothes were bloody.

Was it any of those guys *(who were later implicated in the scandal)* who were involved?
Well, one of them sounded like one of them. The other person, I don't
know who it was.

You didn't see them?
He wouldn't let me turn around to see them. He pulled up and we parked
and we started talking. He said somebody was meeting us, and we needed
to talk. They took me out of the car – when they pulled up, they were
behind us, and they had their headlights on, and then when we got out of
the car, Jeff turns me around and says, "Face the other way," and so that is
when I turned around, and that is when he put a gun to my ... he did! He
put a gun to my head and *(Due to the graphic nature of this incident and
Tonya's ongoing embarrassment and shame, she requested that I not include the
exact details of the assault for this book. Her recount to me, however, explained
why she did not know who the other two attackers were)*. When they were
done, they got in their car and left. I crawled in the car and rode home with
him. The next day was when he had his lawyer's appointment, and I got my
shit *(possessions from the house)* out. *(Further details about the events that led
up to the rape are revealed in Chapter '9')*.

Here is another one *(story about her troublesome relationship with Jeff)*.
In September, right before we were deciding to get back together supposedly, I had *(originally)* decided I am not going to do this *(reconcile with him
for the sake of her career)*. I am going to take my chances before the competition. I had gone out with my girlfriend – came back to my apartment. I
was riding my motorcycle. I didn't have a car. I had a little 250 Ninja bike.
And, I left my girlfriend at a bar. I told her I had to get up and go to the
rink in the morning because it was 9:30 at night. Got home and walked
into the apartment. My door was open, and my purse was gone – nothing
else was gone, just my purse, and I was like, Oh my God. Then all of a sudden my cell phone rings, which I had with me, and it was him. He said,
"Where are you?" I said, "I'm at my apartment." And he said, "I am right
here, now." And I am like, Okay. Hung up the phone, grabbed my helmet,
and ran from the apartment. I was just getting on my bike, and he pulled

up. He was yelling and screaming at me. I told him I wanted my purse back, and he said it was in the truck. So, I went to the truck to get it, and he came out and grabbed me and threw my purse back into his truck again. I ran to my apartment. He followed me into the apartment, pulls a gun up to my face, and pretends he is going to shoot me. Then he says, "Maybe I should just shoot myself," and he puts it up to his head. I'm like, "Don't do that. Don't be stupid. Don't shoot the gun. Just put the gun down." I mean, I didn't want to see him kill himself. I didn't want to see him kill me, either. So, anyway, I said, "Just forget this. Just leave me alone. I'm leaving." Left, walked out of my apartment, started to walk to my bike, got off the curb, and walked into the parking lot itself, which is only about a hundred yards from my apartment door, and he pulls the gun out again and says something to me, and I started to turn around, and the gun went off. Something hit me in the head, and I went flying backwards onto the ground. I was sitting there bleeding. People came running. He pulls the gun on to all these other people, telling them to get away from me. I am screaming and yelling because I was hurt. Drags me into the truck. People were trying to stop him. He was pointing the gun at all these people, who were in their jammies. The police station was right across the street from me. He drags me into the truck and pulls out of there, hitting a man on the way out, running into him – bumping him. Chases down the road – the police are chasing him. He has a shotgun and a handgun in the rig. He runs through a few different red lights, and they finally catch up to us and pull him over. One went around him, and the other went behind him. Pulls him over, tells him to put his arms up. I was bleeding – couldn't figure out what the hell was going on. They told me to put my hands up. I had one hand up. They couldn't see the other one, and so they started yelling at me, but I was holding my head. They take him out. They take me out. They put us in the same goddamn police car – after the people just told them, he had shot me! And tells me, while they are sitting in their cop car talking – "You better tell them it was just an accident, or I will have you taken out." What am I supposed to do? "Yeah *(she told the authorities)*, it was an accident. The gun just accidentally went off. Didn't know it was loaded."

Did they charge him?
No. He wasn't charged with anything at all. Nothing – not even assaulting the other man – putting the gun into other people's faces and telling them to back the fuck off.

Did they charge him with carrying a gun?
They took his weapons from him. They let him go *(she was almost yelling in obvious anger)*, and they wouldn't take me home. The police sent me home with him! After he shot me. Well, he shot the ground – that is what happened. It was asphalt cement – the asphalt had a two and a half thing *(hole)* from where he shot it. It was the asphalt that hit me in the head. I had to pay $300.00 to fix the little hole because my apartment was going to sue me for it. I mean, I have had restraining orders on this person before, and he violated the restraining orders, and the police won't do a goddamn thing about it. I mean, the police don't want to do anything. He was violating my restraining order *(in a previous incident – see below)*, and the policeman told me to be quiet and stand over on the side while he talks to him.

You had a restraining order on him?
Yeah. That was in '91.

When you left him the first time?
Yup – chased me down – him and his brothers and sister chased me down to a boat place, threatened to break my legs in front of people, and took my boat. The cop said, "You know, your restraining order isn't any good here." And the policeman said, "I'm sorry. I can't do anything for you" and let him go, and he took my boat.

Did you ever get it back?
Well, yes, I did, actually, for about two and a half weeks because I got a friend of mine that had a truck because I didn't have a truck to pull up – because it was sitting in his front yard – and got a friend of mine to pull up in front and hook it on, and we drove off with it. So, I stole my *(own)* boat back off his mom's property.

Are you a bit nervous that when the book comes out of him reading this stuff? Because he probably will, right?
I have no idea. I cannot let myself have to worry about him. I mean, what am I going to do? Walk around with my eyes on the back of my head for the rest of my life wondering if he is going to show up and hurt me? I mean, like they say, it is hearsay. It is my word against his. Of course, I have a whole bunch of witnesses.

And after that *(all the violent incidences)*, **the United States Figure Skating Association is telling you to go back with him?**
Yeah. But, like, how I am supposed to be able to tell anybody that this shit is going on?

Because they wouldn't believe you?
Exactly, because they never believed me before!

But weren't you so afraid of him by that point that …
Yes. I was terrified.

Well, then, how could you move back with him?
Because I had *(received)* an ultimatum. I had to take my chances *(on moving back in with Jeff)*. And maybe not even make it on the Olympic team … *(if she didn't resume her marriage)*. *(I had)* done this *(trained for the Olympics)* for the last four years for absolutely nothing *(if the USFSA followed up on their supposed ultimatum)* or go back with him *(and please the USFSA)* and *(her plans were to)* stay in a different room – stay away from him as much as possible – do my thing, make it on the Olympic team and go on and have a happy life.

Do you have the names of the people *(from the USFSA)* **who asked you to go back?**
I can't do that. That's something I can't do.

So, we will just say 'officials' from the United States Figure Skating Association?
Yup. One in particular. He had this person wrapped around his finger. This person was calling him all the time! I couldn't believe it.

What you went through after Nationals *(referring to the rape)* **… I can't believe you went through that.** *(I was still reeling from she had told me about the assault).*
Why do you think I wanted to kill myself a couple of times?

I didn't know about this *(the rape)*.
Right – nobody … the only people who know this about me is Mom – Linda and Greg, they both know, and Darren.

What about Michael *(Rosenberg)*?
No. He knows I was raped, but I sure as hell didn't tell him the details. What was I ... I mean, Michael hated this person.

This *(details of the assault)* **is important to put in** *(the book)*.
Michael hated him. That's the reason I had to leave him *(Michael Rosenberg – meaning that Jeff was the reason Michael had severed their professional relationship)* the first time.

I told her Michael had told me that he had stopped representing her because of Jeff. I also asked her if I could tell Michael what she had told me regarding the assault. She responded:
Yes. He *(Michael)* said, "Tell her everything, and then when I read it, we will decide whether we are going to have it in there *(the book)* or not."

I told Tonya that when I watched the 1994 events unravel on television, I thought I saw Jeff with her at the airport upon her arrival home from the Olympics, and asked: **When you came home after the Olympics, he** *(Jeff)* **was with you at the airport, wasn't he?**
At Olympics? No, it was from Nationals.

So after the Olympics, you two were apart?
Oh, yes. I think. I don't even remember. I am sure we were not together. I am sure we were not together at that point in time.

When you were with the FBI and went into another room with your lawyer, did you tell him what had happened *(about the rape)*?
No. I didn't tell him that. Like I said, nobody but Linda and Greg and Darren know this.

Was that because you were ashamed of it?
I mean, I told them that I had a gun put to my head, but I didn't tell him the rest. I told him I am being threatened. I had a gun put to my head. I was told to say this or I would be taken out. I want protection before I say anything.

And why didn't you tell them the whole truth about that? Were you ashamed?
Yeah. I mean, it was the second time I had been raped, and to be raped by three men.

Even though it is totally not your fault – you are a total victim – you are still ashamed of it?
The first time I was raped, I never told anybody because I knew the person. It was a friend of mine.

But it's true, isn't it? Women are ashamed.
You don't really want people to know that you had to go through that. It's embarrassing.

Say you weren't a celebrity and you were a normal person and that happened to you, you would still feel that kind of shame?
Well, I probably would have told somebody then.

Because it's not going to be all over the newspapers and the world?
Exactly.

So you didn't tell the FBI or anyone?
Nobody to this day – until I started talking to you – nobody except my mom, well, Linda, Greg, and Darren know what has happened to me.

And now Michael *(Rosenberg)* knows?
And now Michael knows.

So, when you went back into the room, you told the FBI that you were being threatened …
Yes.

And you had a gun to your head …
Yes. I told the FBI I was being threatened, and I was going to be taken out if I didn't tell this story. *(More on the FBI questioning in Chapter '9.')*

When you told your lawyer what happened – say with the gun to your head – did he not want you to charge Jeff? Couldn't they have got you to charge him with threats or something like that?
There was nothing I could do about it. That's why I asked for protection, and then they gave me protection, and he walked right through all my …

I guess there would have had to have been a witness. Otherwise it is …
Hearsay. It is my word against his, and that's how it always was. And

because he was older than me, nobody ever believed me. Not even my own God-damn father believed me. My own coach didn't even believe me.

But your dad saw him hit you that one time.
My dad saw him hit me lots of times. He never stood up for me – nothing.

So when he didn't believe you …
He didn't believe it. He didn't believe that he could do anything like that to me. I mean, my father lived with the guy after we were divorced.

So he didn't believe that he would hold a gun to your head and say, "I am going to kill you," or whatever?
No. No.

And the hitting part … What? Your father would think that maybe you deserved it or something?
Who knows? I have no idea.

And why should you have to get into their heads (now) to try to figure it all out.
(She laughs).

So you only told your lawyer, at the time, that he had been threatening you?
Yes.

After the lawyers offered protection – how did Jeff break into your father's house? What happened?
He showed up at my father's house in the evening time. It was dark out. And there were police cars – not police cars, but FBI cars or whatever – government cars.

This was where you were staying now – you went to your dad's place?
At my father's – yes – at his apartment. And there was a couple of cars parked out there, along the edges (of the parking lot), you know, and (he) just pulled in, parked, got out, walked up, and walked right in my dad's front door. And I'm like – ahh.

What did he say to you?
He was like, "So, how did it go? Tell me what you said. Tell me how it went." Of course, I lied through my teeth. "Oh, I told them exactly what you wanted me to and stuff." Yeah.

Is that the last time you spoke to him?
No. The last time I spoke to him was when the 'Penthouse' thing went through.

So nobody knows? That is why these people were never charged with this?
Right, but I don't know for a fact who the other two people were. I mean, I have a feeling who one of them was, but I have no idea, and I can't make an accusation and not know for a fact.

But you know he *(Jeff)* was involved?
Oh, yeah. He had a gun to my head.

When you went home with him that night *(after the rape)*, what did you do?
Well, let me see. I cleaned myself up in the bathroom. I soaked in the bathtub for about an hour, trying to clean myself internally. I don't even remember what I did after that. I think I just went to my room, and I just stayed in there. I remember I was sitting in the corner next to the window for awhile.

You were numb? Your mind has gone blank?
I didn't want to be here anymore.

What happened the next day?
The next day, I called my friend when he *(Jeff)* left the house, and I told her, "You need to get over here and get me out of here now."

Angela?
No. Stephanie. So, Stephanie, one of her brothers, her two uncles, and her dad brought over a truck and another car to help me get out.

That was it, as far as you living with him?
Yes, and he showed up as I was getting ready to leave. I was still packing up stuff.

Didn't he go to Olympics with you?
No. He showed up at Nationals after the long program day because I was so freaked out *(after the attack on Nancy)*. He came home with me from Nationals.

Right, but this was before all that garbage *(the rape)* had happened to you?
Right – that all started that day when we came home.

When did you try and kill yourself?
About two days afterwards.

After the assault with the three of them?
Yes.

How did you try and kill yourself?
I drove as fast as I could in my car on a straightaway and tried to flip it. Didn't work. I spun around in circles and wound up in the opposite direction, facing the other way.

Did you tell your therapist any of this? *(Tonya later received counseling).*
I don't know if I did or not. I could never really open up and tell people anything.

We discussed the book, the proposal, and I commented that perhaps by her telling her story, it may help another battered woman. She responded:
If I had millions of dollars, I would donate so much to helping battered women. You have no idea. I mean, I wanted to put together a skating show to raise the $50,000.00 for the Special Olympics' kids that I had to raise *(as part of her punishment)*. I wanted to put a skating show on for that and also another one where I could do it for battered women – abused women, and donate all the proceeds to them. And nobody would ever give me that opportunity to raise money for helping other people.

Maybe when this book is out ...
Maybe people will understand me a little better. You know, not judge me so wrongly.

This is your book. Do you want the story about the three of them *(the assault)* in there *(the book)*?
Well, that is why you need to ask Michael.

If it is okay with Michael?
I don't want you to tell *(the exact details of how it was done to her)*, but yes – that the rape happened by three people with a gun to my head. I think people will understand.

I think it has to be done as tastefully as possible. We won't dwell, on it.
Right.

We will say it happened and …
Right, and was one of the reasons I didn't come forward.

You said, 'one of the reasons,' were there other reasons you didn't come forward?
Well, I had a gun put to my head, and they said if I didn't go along with what they said, they said, I would be taken care of there – right in the same spot I was in then.

There were no other reasons why you didn't come forward?
No.

You were terrified and, so much so, that two days later you were trying to take yourself out?
Yeah.

This still has to affect you? I mean, how can a woman go through that?
And getting my life threatened by other people through him and some other people. What was it – oh God – might have been '96 – it might have been '95 or '96 – I tried it again.

You tried what again? To kill yourself?
Yes.

How? What happened?
Same way. I had a faster car. I had a Corvette with a glass top. I took the glass off and headed to the beach. I just couldn't put up with it anymore. I

couldn't deal with life anymore. I couldn't deal with how people were so mean and why people would want to take me out. What did I ever do to anybody? You know? It didn't make sense. I lost 28 pounds. I was down to 90 pounds. I was way skinny – couldn't eat, couldn't sleep. People were following me. People were wrecking my stuff. I just said, "Screw it."

And what happened?
Nothing actually happened. I mean, I tried.

You started driving faster?
Driving faster and faster and faster. I thought about driving off of a cliff, driving off the road, trying to flip it, trying to do anything. I ended up at the beach and sat at the beach for a couple of hours. I walked on the beach by myself and turned around and came back. But I really thought about it, but I just couldn't do it. *(She laughs).* You know, I laugh about it now, but the reason I am here today is because I can help somebody else. The Lord kept me here – not letting me flip my car, not letting me drive off a cliff or something because there is a purpose for me being here. Right after that, I was like, Obviously, the Lord must want me here for a purpose. And so I decided to fight. I am going to keep fighting. I am going to keep going and never give up.

(6)

Walking a Tightrope

*"I was always trying to please everybody.
To this day, I try to please everybody."*

Prior to this interview, both Tonya and I had learned that Robert Wagenhoffer had passed away from complications due to AIDS. Robert was an American figure skater who after retiring from competition became a choreographer for many of the elite skaters. Before beginning the planned interview that follows, I asked Tonya: Were you very upset when you learned that Robert had passed away?
Yes. I cried. I had met him *(Robert)* when I was very young – skating. I think the first time was probably at a Nationals competition.

He would have been competing?
I think so, but I really don't remember. The last time I saw him, I think, was up in Sun Valley. It was a few years back. I went up and was skating just for fun. I think I ran into him up there. Gosh, I don't remember the last time I saw him.

You liked him, didn't you?
Oh, yeah. Yeah. He was always very positive towards me and always stood up for me.

After everything that had happened *(to you)*, he was still positive *(toward you)*?
Yeah. I mean, he was the type of person who said, "Hey, people make mistakes."

He was going to prepare your program *(for the ESPN event in Huntington)*. Wasn't Michael *(Rosenberg)* going to arrange that?
Uh huh. Well, Michael was working on it, and he was going to have him choreograph my program for me, but because we had such a short time and I had basically had it done, we decided not to at the last minute.

I would like to go back to your skating and talk about how your personal life was affecting it. Was Jeff involved in your skating?
He wasn't involved in my skating, but he wanted to be involved in it, but I wouldn't allow that. He is not a skater, and he did not know anything about it.

Would he make suggestions?
Yeah. Yeah. If Diane suggested something, or if she didn't like how I was training, then she would bring Jeff into it because he was my husband and maybe he could make me do it. I was like, Hey, wait a minute. This is my skating – period. I don't want all these other people involved in my skating. Diane is my coach, and I am her student, and that is the way it is going to be.

So, he would make suggestions regarding choreography or how you should be training?
Just how I should be training and things like that.

Let's discuss the period from the time you met him at 15 until the time you moved in together at 18. You were living with your parents until they split up ...
Right, then I lived with my father until he left. Then I lived with my mother and her new husband until I was 18.

And then you moved in with Jeff ...
Yes. I had to get out of her hair. *(She laughs).*

So you have never totally lived on your own?
Oh, I have lived on my own. I lived on my own all of '94 – I mean, I was dating somebody, but I wasn't ...

Living with him?
Yeah. And then when I got married, he moved in and – the second time, to Michael *(her second husband)*, and then he moved into my house, and 99 days later, he was out. And I lived in my house on my own, took care of myself, and then I sold my house in '97. I also lived on my own in '91 and in '93. A girlfriend lived with me.

When you were dating Jeff and living at home with your parents, was your mother still involved in your skating?
Yes. She always took me to the rink.

Even when you were 15 or 16?
Yes. Well, she took me. I mean, she wouldn't let me drive.

When she left *(the family)*, was that a relief?
Yeah. Definitely.

So now, she was not by your side at the skating rink?
She wasn't trying to tell me what to do. She always tried to tell me how to skate, and Diane hated that. She had told her lots of times, "Stay out of it. You are not a coach. You don't know what is wrong." But she always continued to try and tell me how to do it. So, we had a lot of conflicts there. There wasn't anybody around this area – even Diane – Diane had only done one or two triples, and here I am – *(doing)* triples.

You mentioned that your mother would give you hand signals *(while watching her skate)*. What kind of hand signals?
She had hand signals for each jump or spin or whatever.

What do you mean? She wanted you to do the jump a certain way?
Well, she would make a hand signal – like an "A" with your hands, and that would be Axel. I can pretty easily read lips. If they are done slow enough, I can read them. She would say, "Double Salchow" or "Double Loop" or whatever.

This was during competition?
No. During competition, she pretty much sat, and my coach was taking care of me.

So this was during practices?
Uh huh.

Are these things she wanted you to work on or she wanted to look at?
Who knows? *(She laughs)*. *(After her mother left)*, I would take the bus, or my father would take me to the rink, or by that time, I could get a ride with some of the other parents. Once I turned 16, my dad let me take the car to

the rink. If he had to go to work that day, depending on what time he had to go in – if he didn't have to go in until 11:00 or 12:00, then I could take the car and go to the rink, or else he would take me to the rink. Sometimes, I would take him to work and then drop him off. I would skate in the evening time and then go back and pick him up.

You got your driver's license when you were 16?
Uh huh. I had my permit when I was 15, and then on my birthday or the day after my birthday – it was pretty close, it may have been the 20th, I went and got my driver's license.

You couldn't wait, I guess?
I couldn't wait. I couldn't wait. I was so excited. *(She laughs)*.

By the time your mother had moved out, you were dating Jeff?
Oh, yeah. I had been dating him for awhile.

At this time – in 1987 – you were fifth at Nationals. Was he impressed by that?
Yes. He thought my skating was great.

Was he encouraging and supportive?
Well, basically, yes. On the days I didn't go in, he would bitch at me and say, "Hey, you are supposed to be training." And I was like, "Wait a second." I am either sick, or I had hurt something, or I just didn't feel like going in that day; I just didn't feel well. I have always had people telling me what to do. *(She laughs)*. Not to put in the book, but even Darren sometimes *(when Tonya was living with Darren, she didn't want this in the original autobiography, but after they broke up, she gave permission to include)* – we've had two instances where he'd say something to me and try to tell me something, and I am like, "Whoa! Back the trolley up. You know nothing about skating. You know nothing about the politics involved in it. Back off. I don't tell you about electrician work. So you don't tell me how to skate."

For so long, you were pulled *(in different directions)* by so many people
...
Yeah. You can't please everybody. If you please yourself, that is all that matters. I was always trying to please everybody. Still, to this day, I try to please

everybody. But I know that is not going to happen, so I try to let it go and deal with it. It's like, Hey, if I am happy with myself, my agent is happy with me, Darren is happy, my family – that is all that matters. You know?

Well, that is a good lesson to learn. Some people take all their lives before they realize that.
Exactly. That is just what I was going to say. Sometimes it takes forever to get there. But I feel fortunate enough that all the bad things that have happened to me made me what I am today. And nobody is going to pull the wool over my eyes ever again. I just won't put up with it.

How far into your relationship with Jeff did he start getting more involved in your skating?
He wasn't really involved in it. He always tried to tell me what to do.

What about trying to act as your manager?
No. He wanted to try and manage me after Michael *(Rosenberg - her manager)* and I split. I am like, "No." I said, "You don't know anything about the skating world. Don't even try and do that. This is my skating. You ruined it with Michael, and now I am on my own again." And so, he was never involved in my skating itself.

How did he ruin it with Michael?
Well, Michael just couldn't stand him. He *(Jeff)* was such a jerk – threatening me while I was on tour. He was just a real pain in the neck.

Was he phoning Michael and talking to him?
No. He *(Jeff)* didn't like him *(Michael)*. He didn't want to talk to him. He didn't like how he was managing me. He *(Jeff)* was such an idiot, it was pathetic.

So he would say something to you, and you would say something to Michael?
Well, Michael could not stand him. He *(Jeff)* was just an idiot.

Michael would say to you, as long as you are married to him, I can't deal with it?
He was a lot better than that. He would say, "Tonya ..." It was really hard, dealing with Jeff, trying to keep him *(happy)* and wanting to do what

Michael wanted me to do. I was being pulled in both directions. And I just couldn't deal with it. And then Michael couldn't deal with him – not wanting me to do things. We just decided it would be better if we parted ways.

When did you and Michael split?
In '92 *(according to Michael Rosenberg, it was in 1993)* – sad day in skating.

Did you go back with Michael prior to the '94 Olympics?
No. I have always stayed in touch with Michael. I care a lot about Michael and his family. His youngest daughter, Amy – her and I went shopping when I was down there *(in California where Michael lived at the time)*. We hung out together. They were really cool to me, and they always have been. Now Whitney *(Michael's other daughter)* and I – it is like we have known each other for years. We get along so good. At the competition *(ESPN)*, we hung out. She took care of me and made sure everything was all right. She is just a doll.

Did Jeff have big dreams for you?
I don't think back then he thought anything about that. But I think once he saw how much money I was making in '91 and '92, then, I think, he was a little bit more into that.

He thought this could be lucrative?
Yeah. Yeah. That he wouldn't have to work. He was pretty lazy.

What work did he do?
He worked at OLCC – 'Oregon Liquor Control Commission,' in a warehouse, throwing boxes of booze.

So, nothing …
Nothing lucrative, no.

So when he started seeing dollar signs, that's when he became more involved, right?
That's when he started pushing me more.

Did he have big dreams for himself – that he was going to have a lot of money one day?
With him? For himself, no. He always wished, but he never put anything into it – to work hard and make something for himself.

He was ambitious, but lazy?
Yeah. He worked, but then he didn't.

Did you ever support him?
Oh, yeah. Oh, yeah.

After you were married?
Yes, after we were married. There were times he was laid off. There were times when he would quit his job and be laid off for quite a few months. There were times when I was totally supporting us 100 percent. I bought our car. I bought our truck. I bought the boat. And he took it all. I didn't even end up with the furniture!

Did you make money from skating at 16?
No, not until '91.

When you won Nationals?
Yeah.

And the money would be from going on the 'Tom Collins *(Champions on Ice)* Tour'?
Exactly. I did a Texaco commercial in '91 up in Canada in Vancouver. It was really hard work, but it was fun, and I landed lots and lots of jumps for them on the video, plus I landed two quads – two quad loops on the video.

Did you get money for that? Back then amateurs weren't allowed to take money *(directly)*. Did it go into a trust?
Yeah. It had to go into a trust at the Association, and then you would send them your bills for skating or whatever – costuming, makeup, things like that, and they would reimburse you, but you had to send them in receipts and all that stuff.

Did you do many commercials or endorsements back then?
No. I did Texaco. When I was young, I did Alpen-Rose Dairy Milk. *(She laughs)*.

A commercial?
Yes, and I think that was about it.

So, you weren't making a whole lot of money from endorsements?
No, but that was really good money for that. I mean, that did help pay for costumes and all that.

Texaco? They paid you well?
Yes.

From the ages of 15 to 18, how heavy was your training in this period?
I was doing two to four sessions a day.

Did you have a choreographer?
I was working with Barbara Flowers.

At this point, who was funding your skating?
In '87, 'Blue Cross, Blue Shield' of Oregon sponsored me for one year. Then – you can't say the name *(she told me who the donor was and what the person had done for Tonya)*.

Is this the same person you mentioned before *(she had not told me who the donor was in the previous interview)*?
Yeah.

At 16, you were working part-time?
Yes, I was working part-time. I paid for my ice time that way and some of my lesson time, and some of it was just given to me. Once I made it in '91, when I made it on tour and went to Worlds, then I didn't have to pay for my ice time. So, once I made it on the World team, I didn't have to pay for ice time. I only had to pay for lesson time.

Before you moved in with Jeff, what was a typical day for you during this period?
Getting up early in the morning, going to the rink, skating a couple of sessions, then going to school. After school, sometimes I would work my part-time job. I would be working two or three days a week for a couple of hours and then go to the rink afterwards. Most of the time, my mother worked in the afternoons and my dad too, but she didn't leave until 3:30 or 4:30 in the afternoon, so sometimes she would drop me off at the rink, but most of the time I took the bus. The bus stop was one block away, and I went directly to the rink.

Would she go with you in the morning?
Most of the time – either her or my father.

What hours did you skate on a school day?
When I was younger, I skated from 4:45 until 7:30 *(a.m.)* and then went directly to school, and then I'd skate in the afternoon too. As I got older, it would be 6:00 or 6:45 until 9:00 *(a.m.)*. Then when I wasn't in school anymore and I was driving myself – I guess '93 – I was skating from 6:45 until 10:00 in the morning, taking a couple of breaks.

During this period, how often would you see Jeff?
A few times a week.

After skating?
Yeah. If I was in school and he wasn't working, I would see him. If he was working, I would see him for an hour or maybe two in the evening time after he got off work.

It was during this period that you left Diane for awhile?
That was when I was 18.

What happened?
I just got to the point where I was a typical teenager, and thought I knew more than she did. *(She laughs)*.

You would argue?
Yeah. We started arguing a lot, and I didn't like the way she was teaching. I wanted to do it different. I thought I knew more. It wasn't working out. We both decided I would go over to Dody, who was Diane's very first student, and let her work with me. So, I went with Dody for a couple of years and then went back to Diane.

Why did you do that?
Well, at the time, things weren't going as good as they should have been with Dody.

In what way? What do you mean?
Jeff was back in the picture again. This sounds horrible, but she got pregnant and was about to blossom right after Olympics and before Worlds. I started getting into fights with Jeff about it, and he made me quit her.

He didn't think it would look right?
I don't know. I have no idea, but it was either that or get beat up.

He wanted you back with ...
Diane, because he knew he could manipulate her. He could not manipulate Dody. Dody saw right through him and didn't want him around. I even lived with Dody and her husband and kids right after '91 tour when I moved in with her. That's when I left him for the first time. She picked me up at the airport, and I went home with her. That's when he threatened me with a shotgun. I lived with her until I got a place with my girlfriend.

What was it about him that she *(Diane)* liked?
I have no idea. I really don't. When I get upset, I cry, okay? I mean, if I get really mad and really upset, if I'm not screaming, I'm crying because it hurts so bad to have to be screaming. So, he'd always tell her, "Oh, she is faking it. She's just crying so you will feel bad." Things like that. It is like, "Wait a second." You know?

Did you feel like sometimes they were pairing up against you?
Oh, yes. They did. They did. We had a huge meeting at her house, with her, her husband, Jeff, and me, and she was telling him what she wants me to do.

She would tell Jeff with you sitting there?
Yeah, and it was like, "Wait a second." She was like, "This is what Tonya needs to do, and this is what she needs to do, and this is what she needs to do, and I am counting on you to help her achieve these things."

Did you ask her to take you back, telling her you weren't with Dody anymore?
Yes. I went to her and asked her to take me back. And it took a lot, too. I had to have another meeting.

With her and Jeff?
Oh, yeah, promising I will do this, and do this, and do this, and this – twist myself into a pretzel for you. When it came to my skating, she had only done one or two triples in her life, and I had been doing triples since I was 11 or 12. By that time, by the time I was 18, I was doing them all the time, and I was finding different ways of being able to do them easier or better,

or whatever, and she didn't want me to change anything. So, it was total dis-agreement on how it stood to be done.

You said you were rebellious as a teenager. Were you headstrong? Did you want to do things your own way?
Exactly. Yes. I was never in trouble. I never did anything wrong. The first time I have ever been in trouble with the police was in '94 when this *(the scandal)* all happened. I have only had four speeding tickets all my life. And I've never hit anybody on purpose. I've been rear-ended. I did hit somebody once – rear ended – when they were backing up at an intersection, but they found out it wasn't my fault. I mean, I just bumped them at a red light. But I have never been in trouble with the police – ever, ever! I never even stole a piece of candy when I was growing up.

What about the rumor that you have a bad temper?
I only have a bad temper when I am pushed to the max. And then watch out! No. *(She laughs)*. I don't have a bad temper anymore, really. I mean, I won't take shit off of anybody anymore. It used to be that the only way I knew how to protect myself was to be fighting back – you know?

Verbally?
Verbally, exactly. Of course, I have been hit a couple of times, or grabbed a couple of times, where I have turned around and laid somebody out. I mean, I hit Jeff a couple of times. And I was dating this one guy for a year and a couple of months, and we got into this fight, and he grabs me – he pushed me out of the way, and I walked out the door, and he came up and grabbed me to turn me around, and I knocked – I punched him right in the face, and said, "Don't you touch me." And the time I was telling you about when he *(Jeff)* threw – pushed me through the shower door – I remember once during that fight – it was in the bedroom – when Jeff was twisting my leg, I punched him because he was hitting on me, and I punched him, and that just made him mad.

If you are being physically threatened …
If I am being physically threatened by anybody, I am not going to back down. I am not a bully or anything like that. I mean, I can take a lot. But if somebody was to come up and hit me or push me or grab me, I can defend myself. But it's not like – it's so funny, I could not believe it – a cou-ple of weekends ago we went out with some friends, and Darren and I got

into a spat, and he threw his keys at me, so I could leave. These other two people that were with us had two friends with them, and they were girls, and this one was just yuk, you know? I wasn't really talking to them at all because I don't like them. But the other two people we were with – I liked them. Anyway, Darren was a little bit tipsy, and this – excuse me – this bitch tells Darren, "Why don't you just shut the fuck up." And I am like, "Excuse me. Who the hell do you think you are telling him to shut the fuck up?" I said, "You have nothing to do with us, so why don't you keep your mouth shut and mind your own business?" So, the two girls got in my face, and I am trying to get Darren out of the place. "Let's just go home. " Finally, we were leaving, and our friends are holding this girl back. She just wanted to kick my butt. I was just like, "Go away. You aren't even part of my circle. You are nothing to me," and I turned around to walk out. Well, somebody said that I ended up getting into a fist fight with two girls that night at the place.

Was it in the newspapers?
No. No. Somebody had told one of Darren's buddies at school that he had heard it. I was like, "Wait a second. I didn't hit anybody!" *(She laughs).* I just thought it was funny. People make up stuff just to see what they can get out of it, you know? But, I mean, I don't have a bad temper at all. The thing I get mad at the most is people cutting me off and then slamming on their brakes or having to go through a telephone conversation with a computer – push this button, listen to all these messages, and push this button – that stuff irritates me, and then finally when you get to somebody, they don't want to talk to you? Oh – they are just being rude.

Your nerves must have been bad when you were with Jeff?
They were horrible. They were really horrible, and telling me I am fat and ugly all the time, and that I had to diet. I should eat this and I shouldn't eat that.

He was trying to control what you were eating?
Oh, he tried to control everything. Finally, I grew up and realized I didn't need that. I mean, I still went through that *(the abuse and control)* until I got to Michael *(her second husband)*, and when Michael hit me, it was almost like – boom – I am not taking this anymore.

How did it feel to be back with Diane? Dody sounds like she was a good coach.
Dody was wonderful, and Dody is still wonderful. She did so much for me. I landed my first triple Axel in competition with her.

How so?
Because she was at '91 Nationals with me – her and Barbara Flowers.

Do you keep in touch with Dody today?
I see her every once in awhile.

Do you have a good relationship with Diane?
Oh, yes. We have a very cordial, business *(relationship)*, but are still friends.

Do you feel if you really needed something, you could still go to her?
Oh, easily.

Where does Dody teach?
She is at the other rink.

So, you are all still in the same area *(at the time of this interview)*?
Uh huh.

We reviewed her main competitors during 1991, and I asked: **When did you first meet Kristi Yamaguchi?** *(At the 1991 U.S. Nationals, Tonya placed first and Kristi was second. At the 1991 World Championships, Kristi claimed the gold medal while Tonya took silver).*
I couldn't tell you. We all skated at Nationals, but we really didn't know each other really well, until '91. We had been at training seminars together – *(we would)* see each other at Nationals or Pacific Coast Championships.

Did you have any kind of relationship with her?
Well, we all went out together and did things on tour, and we were always friends.

The '91 'Tom Collins *(Champions on Ice)* Tour'?
Um hm. I mean, we were always nice to each other. Everybody was always very nice to each other.

How many tours did you go on?
'91, '92, and part of '93. Tommy always took care of us. We always stayed
in nice hotels. It was hard living out of a suitcase basically for a month and
a half. I came home a couple of times to change clothes. I would get more
clothes. I ended up coming home to Dody in '91. Tommy would take us to
shows. One year, he gave us rollerblades. He always took care of us. He gave
us warm-ups and bags.

That was the year Liz Manley was thrown off the tour. *(Elizabeth had*
been accused of taking drugs, which she denied). **Do you remember that?**
I remember it, but I never heard why. A personal thing, I think. I never
heard what the reasons were. But as far as I know, and I can be honest about
this, I know when she was around me, she wasn't doing that *(drugs)* – if that
was what it was.

I have heard stories that competitive skaters don't let their skates out of
their sight because of what someone else may do to them. Have you ever
had an incident like that happen to you?
Yes. I have had my blades ruined a couple of times. People would take
something to them. I remember when we were on tour, nobody did anything to my blades, but just from walking back and forth or slipping on
mats or whatever, I had my blades sharpened a couple of times on tour. Oh,
gosh – what's his name? He is kind of odd. He skates on his hands ...

Gary Beacom *(Canadian competitor, known for his unique skating style,*
and who also spent time in a U.S. prison for tax related charges)?
Gary Beacom – yeah. He did *(sharpened)* my blades a couple of times on
tour. But there have been instances – a couple of times, where people have
ruined my blades.

This would have been at competitions?
Yes.

Was this in the late '80's or early '90's?
Earlier, I think. One pair, somebody took something to them. I remember
one was at a Northwest competition – you know, you get Northwest, then
Coast, and then Nationals, and one was at another competition when I was
younger.

How would you know *(that your blades were ruined)*? **Did you just get out onto the ice and all of a sudden you can't skate?**
You'd be slipping and sliding everywhere. One time it was like that, and the other time, I came back in, and my boots were on the floor, and my stuff was on the floor, and I picked up my boots and looked at them and noticed there were little chunks out of my blades and scratches all over the sides. We had to hone them out as best as we could.

Did that go on at Nationals?
I don't know if it did or not, but I always kept my skates in my sight.

If your skates are off ...
They are on me *(carrying them)*. *(She laughs)*.

So you know where they are at all times?
Right.

Did you ever hear of such incidents *(at a major competition)*?
No. Not really. I don't think so. I mean, when I was younger, but I didn't really pay attention to that kind of stuff then. I knew there were kids who had their boots stolen at competitions, but I don't think that was done on purpose – I have no idea.

Of course, watching your skates – I mean, without your skates ...
You are nothing. You can't put on a pair of rentals and go. *(She laughs)*.

When was the first time you met Nancy *(Kerrigan)*? *(I had asked this in a previous interview, but she hadn't been able to remember then)*.
I think I met both of them *(Kristi and Nancy)* at a training seminar for the first time.

Did you get along well with Nancy?
Yeah. Everybody got along well with everybody. I mean, her and I roomed together. I'm sure one of them was at the training camps, and we roomed together on tour – different competitions we would go to where you are assigned a roommate. Her and I stayed together.

How did you get along with each other?
Fine.

Was there ever any friction?
No. We were both two young girls who skated good. Competition to me is like, if you are going to do this, you have to work hard, and it is totally up to you. It is a luck, luck situation. You can be skating perfect every single day, and then all of a sudden, you can step out *(on the ice)* and have a bad day. And so, I never thought of her as my competitor – the same with Kristi or any of them. Sure, we were competing against each other, but we were just friends out there trying to do the best that we could do at what we do.

So it is more of a competition against yourself?
Exactly. Exactly.

If you win and everybody else is falling down, I guess that's not the way you want to win?
No. I would rather go out there and see two people do a perfect program and be judged on how they accomplished it.

When you and Nancy were rooming together, were you like girlfriends or would you each just go about your own business?
When we were at competition – we would all go down together and eat. On tour, we would go shopping. I did my thing, she did her thing, but then we sat there and would watch TV or whatever.

But you didn't become close friends?
Well, I never really had a lot of money, and not really the nicest kind of clothes. So, I think people – and I was always youngest. I don't know. Other people clicked easier with other people than with me. And I have no idea – I think it was probably because of Jeff.

Did you feel self-conscious?
All the time.

Why?
Because I was fat and ugly.

You thought that then? Even in '91 when you were the World Silver Medalist?
Um hm. I thought I was a great skater, but I didn't think I was pretty. When you hear it all the time, you tend to believe that kind of stuff.

Did you think Nancy or Kristi were better than you in some ways? I'm not referring to skating.
I don't know. They had great childhoods. They had great lives. I think I was more envious of that. I always wished that I had it as good as they did.

It seemed liked they had perfect lives?
Yeah.

And you had to fight for everything you had?
Um hm. And I think, also, and I don't know if we want to put it in the book or not, but I think there was a little bit of jealousy on some of the girls' parts, and the guys' parts too, where I didn't click with a lot of them because I was doing a lot more than they were doing.

The triple Axel?
Yeah.

When you went on tour, would you perform the triple Axel?
Yeah, but I got a lot of support, too. But, I mean, every once in awhile it was like ... I don't know ...

Tell me how you felt? It is important.
I guess I felt – if people weren't talking to me, or if they were doing their own thing, it was just because they were jealous of my skating, or if they just didn't like how my life was. I didn't have the kind of life that they had.

I may be way off-base here, but it sounds as if you may have given up your triple Axel to have the kind of life some of them had. Am I right?
Yeah. And also, I was more of a tomboy than I was a lady. I didn't like to sit around, do my nails, and gossip. I would rather be out and do something else, you know?

Play pool?
Yeah. I was more in tune with the guys than I was with the girls.

So, if the girls are sitting around yakking, or whatever, and the guys are going out to ...
Play pool downstairs or something – yeah. Or they would all go out to a dance place, and of course, when I was married, I couldn't do those things

or I would get in really big trouble. A lot of times, I would just stay in the room by myself. People would come in and see me. The first tour in '91, I hung out a lot with Liz *(Manley)*. She kind of took me under her wing and showed me the ropes. And I really looked up to her. I still do. From everything she has been through, too. It has been almost like a Christmas miracle. It is amazing how people pull through things.

Who were some of your guy friends on tour?
Paul Duchesnay *(Canadian born, World Ice Dance Champion who, along with his sister, Isabelle, competed for France)*. He and I were always really cool friends. We hung out and had coffee together. Now he drinks his coffee the same way I do. Paul and his sister, Isabelle, Liz, Todd Eldredge *(U.S. and World Champion)*.

What about Rudy *(Galindo)?*
Yes. Rudy was always nice to me. And then there were a lot of people from the Seattle area that I saw at competitions.

Do you ever see Todd now?
Not now. When we were on tours and shows, we would do jump for jump. I always thought that was fun. I always thought they should do a competition between Midori *(Ito)* and I, called 'East versus West.' And do a jump for jump competition. It would be so much fun – doing a jump competition where you get three chances, and if you hit it the first time, you can either keep it or you can go on to see if you can do a better one, and you can get to choose whatever one you get *(you want)*.

Were you doing quads *(a four revolution jump)* as a teenager?
Yes. Quad Salchows and quad Loops *(variations of the difficult jump)*. On the 'Texaco' commercial I did in '91, I landed it. I haven't done one in years, but I am sure I can probably still do it.

Before you moved in with Jeff, did your relationship with him affect your skating?
I think it did.

Were you trying to impress him?
Yeah. I was trying to impress him.

So you were setting the *(wrong)* ground rules for what was to come later on?
Yes. Big mistake. *(She laughs).*

How did he become so chummy with the USFSA authorities later on?
Well, when we were in – well, that will tell who it is – but, he chummed up with a couple of the higher officials when we were on tour after Worlds.

In 1991?
Yes, because we were together *(her and Jeff)*. There was '91 Nationals, and then we went to Worlds, and then there was a tour that I went on for a month over there *(in Europe)*. He *(Jeff)* flew there after Worlds to go on the tour with me. So, he chummed up and schmoozed up with these people so much that they thought I had a stable life with him, even though once we got back to the room, he beat the crap out of me. There were a couple of times he beat me up on tour, and I tried to get him to go home, but he just wouldn't.

How did the other skaters like Jeff being on tour?
Oh, they didn't mind. He schmoozed and schmoozed and schmoozed, until we were in the room. I mean, I wanted him to leave after the first week we were there because he got pissed off for some reason, and he had hit me a few times – kicked me a few times, but I always had to put that smile on after I got out of that room.

You would try and hide it?
Yeah– as much as you possibly can. In '93, before Nationals, I had bruises all over my face. I skated *(practised)* at midnight, so I didn't have to go into the rink early in the morning and see everybody and let them see all the bruises all over me. I remember at one point, I was wearing so much make-up that I looked like a clown. It was so packed on under my eye and on my cheekbone – I tried to cover it because I had to go and skate, but it was so bruised up, you could still see it through the makeup.

And I guess it is the kind of thing you don't want to tell people – my husband is beating me?
Yeah.

Did he ever apologize to you after he beat you up? Would he say, "I'm sorry and that will never happen again"?
Oh, he said that all the time.

What would bring it on? Was it booze? Did he drink a lot?
He would drink, but not a lot, unless he was out partying or something.

So it could be booze or anything?
He had a total *(Dr).* Jekyll and *(Mr).* Hyde personality, and he could schmooze or talk his way out of anything.

So you would never know when a beating was coming on?
No. No.

Anything could bring it on?
Yeah— it didn't matter.

Did you ever provoke him? That is a horrible thing to say because no man should ever hit a woman, but did you ever get mad enough with him, and you would sometimes push his buttons?
Oh, yeah— any woman can push a man's buttons.

But he shouldn't haul off and hit her.
Exactly – I mean, I'm not saying that I am innocent and that I didn't do anything wrong because when I get yelled at, I start yelling back.

You wouldn't cower in a corner?
Well, I did. I did a lot. But there were those times that I would start speaking back, and then I'd get it even more. I remember hitting him one time to get him off me, and that was the wrong thing to do.

That was when he pushed you through the bathroom ...
Yeah.

Other than that, how did you like the European tour? Did you go to cities you had never been to before?
We went to a few different cities – Sweden and Switzerland. Switzerland was beautiful. I had never seen so much snow in my life. I thought Finland

and Sweden were similar to here – lots of trees and green and pretty – and Germany – I expected the Autobahn to be like it is on TV with the banked corners. It's not. It's a straight road that is probably a hundred miles long, and you can go as fast as you want. *(She laughs)*.

Did you go to Italy?
Yeah, we went to Italy, and everybody went out to dinner the last night before everyone was going to leave, and the wine over there – yuck – it tasted like crap, but let me tell you, everyone was toasted, including the bus driver.

How long was the tour – six weeks?
No. It was four. It was a month long – it might have been three.

It must have been exciting for you – you hadn't seen a lot. You had been to different competitions over there, but ...
Right, but even being on the tour, though, you still don't get to see a lot of stuff that you would normally see.

True. You are in hotels and skating rinks.
Yeah, and you are at the rink, and you are out and gone. When we were in Berlin, we stayed at the Hotel Berlin, and it was right across the street from the zoo, and I didn't get a chance to go to the zoo because we were only there for one night, but you could hear the lions roaring, and it was pretty cool.

Did you take lots of pictures?
No.

Did Jeff stay with you the whole time?
Yes, he sure did.

Did he have to pay for his own airfare and trip?
No. He didn't have to. They told him he could go along because he schmoozed them. He talked them into it. They wanted me with him. That's what it is supposed to be.

Taken during the 'apology show' ('Breaking the Ice') with Nancy.

Tonya competing at ESPN Pro Competition during 'Comeback Skate'.

Tonya with Canadian Champion, Elizabeth Manley at ESPN 'Comeback Skate'.

*Tonya led away to jail after
'hubcap' incident.*

*Tonya explains her side of the story
to Larry King.*

*Promotional Shot for TNN
Television Special.*

*Poster from Tonya's movie,
'Breakaway'.*

Tonya & Koda.

Tonya & one of her trucks.

*Tonya after celebrity boxing bout
with Paula Jones.*

Tonya Pro Boxing.

Tonya with Michael Rosenberg &
his daughter Whitney.

Tonya with her godmother,
Linda Lewis.

Tonya teaching skating.

Tonya at home in Washington.

(7)

The Accident That Would Change Everything

*"Right – I'm going to roll my truck on its side to get publicity.
I have tried to stay away from publicity."*

*Tonya and I had been speaking 'off the record' prior to this interview,
and she told me she had suffered a minor mishap with her foot. Her large
dog had stepped on it, causing an injury that forced her to stop skating
for awhile. Shortly thereafter, on January 6, 2000 – exactly six years to
the day after the attack on Nancy Kerrigan – Tonya was involved in a
car accident while driving to the rink, and subsequently she suffered further injury to her foot. As with all incidents that involved the skater, the
accident was quickly picked up by the media. Following is my interview
with Tonya that took place a few days later.*

Tell me about the problem with your foot.
The doctor is wondering if I hit my foot in the truck *(which caused the ini-
tial wound to reopen)* because it started getting better, and then after the
accident is when it really started bothering me, and I went to the doctor for
it. I don't even know for a fact if it was just the dog or if I hit it during the
accident and that's what made it open up again.

It was originally hurt when the dog jumped on it?
Yeah, but that was in the beginning of December, and then it healed, and
it was fine, and then all of a sudden it started hurting again.

What did the doctor say?
I have to go in and see him on Thursday and see how it is healing. If it does-
n't heal up in two weeks – he wants to see me this week and again next
week, and if it doesn't heal up, then there is the possibility that I may have
to have surgery.

What does he think it is?
It is a blood hematoma inside my foot between my pinkie toe and the other
toe. It is round and about half an inch. It has a canal where it is draining
from it out in between both of my toes.

Is that like a blood clot?
It is called a sinus canal that is draining, and it is from the hematoma, and if it doesn't stop draining – which it has – it has stopped so far, but if I take a shower and rub it, it may open up again. So, I really don't know. When I take my shower, I just leave it alone.

So, it could have been aggravated by the accident?
Exactly.

You may have had it *(when the dog stepped on it)* and it healed, and then the accident reopened it?
Exactly. So I have no idea at this point what's up with it.

Are you able to get into a pair of skates?
No. I can wear one pair of tennis shoes, one pair of tie-up shoes, and my boots. That's it.

What about teaching your kids?
I teach them in my tennis shoes on the side *(of the rink),* and I have only taught one day.

Since before Christmas?
Yeah. I missed all that work time because of me not feeling well. Even to this day, I am still get shooting pains down my back, and I haven't gone to the doctor for that. I did mention it to Dr. ... *(she told me the doctor's name),* and he said he would check it out when I came in on Thursday because it has got worse in the last week.

This has been since the accident?
Right.

Did you have the pain before the accident?
No. I think what happened is that I am probably out of whack – not lined up. He also said there is a slight probability that I might have whiplash. Well, I mean, I was whipped around in the truck like a little rag doll.

Tell me about the day of the accident and what happened.
I got up in the morning, left my house, and was heading up First Avenue to a coffee shop to get my first cup of coffee to go to the rink. I stopped at

the first stop sign. When I pulled up to the stop sign, I noticed it was a little bit slick out. So, that right there put me on alert. It is a little bit slippery
out, okay, I'd better be careful. I left the stop sign and am going straight
down the road. The truck is an automatic and hadn't shifted into third gear
yet, so I was going 25 miles an hour. All of a sudden, the rear end of the
truck went left. It slid out from behind me and went into an oncoming traffic lane, and I let go of the gasoline *(pedal)* and turned the wheel to the left,
trying to get it to come back to me. But it didn't come back. It was still
going, and there was a car right there, so I turned the wheel to the right and
gassed it, and it went back over to my lane, onto the side of the road. It hit
the fence on the left hand front and, from the momentum, hit the left rear
and rolled around on the back of the truck. The fence was at the back of
the truck and got wrapped up in my hitch and bumper from the momentum of hitting it, and it *(the truck)* turned onto its side – onto its right side.

What were you thinking *(upon losing control of the truck)*?
I was thinking, Oh my God. When I couldn't get it back in control, the
only thing going through my mind was to get the hell off of this road. Don't
hit anybody. Don't involve anybody else in this. I was more willing to wreck
the truck than to put somebody else's life in danger. It was really close. The
man I almost hit went off the side of the road. It is a back wide area where
it happened.

Was this in the country or the city?
The city – a city road – it is in front of a cement truck factory, and there
was a spot where the cement trucks pull over. Well, when the man saw what
was happening, he went over there, and he tried to stop, but every time he
tried to stop, he slid all the way into the curb. So, he knew how slippery it
was, too. The man came over – I was sitting on the side of my truck – the
truck was sitting on its side, and I was hanging from my seat belt and was
totally hysterical. I saw the fence coming and turned my head and just held
on tight to the steering wheel, trying to hold myself there. I thought it was
going to stop. I was bouncing around – then all of a sudden it was like I was
dizzy. When the truck tipped over, everything was kind of like weird in my
eyes.

Were you in shock? Were you crying?
Oh, yeah. Oh, yeah. At that point, I am hanging there, and I realize that
I'm on the side of my truck, and I reached up and turned my key off, so it

wasn't running. The man I almost hit and two other men opened up the door. Somebody else was on the other side and was telling me everything was okay. This man jumped inside the truck with me, and he was holding me – it was an older gentleman – probably in his 40's – he was holding me to try and calm me down and make sure I was okay. Somebody said they were going to call the police, and I said, "Please, don't call the police. If you are going to call them, don't mention my name."

Did the man who was helping you know who you were?
He didn't know until he was in the truck with me.

Did you tell him who you were or did he recognize you?
Well, I told the people, "Please don't call the police and tell them Tonya Harding has been in a wreck. Just tell them there has been a wreck." He said, "Everything is going to be fine. I saw everything, and you did the right thing." I mean, it was black ice, and it was so icy out.

What was the weather like? Was it snowing?
No. It was a little bit foggy – not bad – kind of clear, but foggy.

Was there snow on the ground?
No, but the grass in the front yard was crunchy. The mud puddles were all ice. The police could see where the truck came out behind me, and he *(the police officer)* could see where the truck's tires went all the way over to the fence. He did not cite me for losing control of my vehicle. In fact, he commended me on my driving and said I did the right thing for avoiding a head-on collision and avoiding bringing somebody else into a car accident.

You could have killed yourself by doing this.
I wasn't concerned about myself. I was more concerned about the person coming at me because there were three or four cars behind him. I remember he was in a sports utility vehicle. I don't remember what kind. I don't remember what color. I just remember that it was a sports utility vehicle. He was the one who jumped in the truck with me. He was trying to help me and calm me down. He asked if I was hurting anywhere, and I said, "No, not right this minute. I don't feel anything. I can move." I said, "Right at this minute, I am more scared than anything." I had just wrecked my truck, and Darren was going to be so upset. I am hanging by my seatbelt, and I said, "Can you please reach down and unfasten my seatbelt. It is

killing me. It is choking me." He said, "Well, I don't want to move you in case something is wrong." I said, "I don't think anything is wrong right now. Please, it is choking me." And so he held onto me, and reached down and undid my seatbelt. He held onto me so I didn't fall down. Then I am standing on the right side of my door with this man, and I was shaking, and he was trying to calm me down. I am standing in the truck, and all of a sudden I feel like – I don't know – I am enclosed in something because I have a little bit of claustrophobia, and I was like – I have to get out of here. I was going to freak out if I stay in this thing anymore.

You got panicky?
Yes. I started panicking. He said, "Okay, let me help you out." I said, "I think I can crawl out of this thing." I grabbed onto some stuff and pulled myself up. There was another gentleman outside holding the door open and another two standing there. Right at that time the fire department showed up, and I got down and was sitting on the tire. The *(people from the)* fire department checked me out and asked me if I was hurting anywhere – if I hit my head. I had hit my head when I hit the fence or when I tipped over – I don't know, but I had hit it on the side of the window. It wasn't bad though. I wasn't cut. They asked me if I wanted to go to the hospital. I said, "No," and I signed a piece of paper saying that I refused to take the ambulance. I told them, "If I feel bad later, I will go."

What did the truck look like?
Totaled – my truck is totaled – all sides of it. I hit the left front, the hood, part of the bumper, left front. I hit the left back. Then I hit the complete back, and when it flipped on its side, it got the right side, so I got all four corner panels, plus the hood, the bumpers, the mirrors, and my windshield was cracked. My windshield cracked when it hit.

What kind of truck is it?
It is a Ford 250 – a '92. We had it for two years. I got it secondhand. I bought this one because – you see, the media doesn't seem to understand, when they take pictures of people's vehicles that are celebrities, then people know what those vehicles are. My last vehicle that they had taken pictures of and then printed in the paper got stolen from the mall. And then they come out here and they try to take pictures of it again, and Darren got really upset, and his face was in the picture – in the 'Columbian' paper. I told him, "Darren, shut up."

When was this?
Right in front of the truck when they got it up onto all fours. The media
showed up.
The fire department had taken off. The policeman was there, and he was
very, very nice, and the other witness who stayed was the manager of a
'Thrifty Auto Supply' up at the corner who has waited on me before. He
was the other witness who saw it all happen. Everyone commended me on
my driving, saying I did the right thing and that there was no way I could
have gotten it *(the truck)* back. It was total black ice. I couldn't even see it.
When I was walking around the truck from one side to the other side, you
could stand there and move your feet around. It was that icy.

How did you get hold of Darren?
The policeman let me use his phone in his car, and I called Darren. I was
hysterical. I said, "Honey, I've been in a car accident. I'm right up the street.
It is really icy out. Be careful." He is like, "Oh my God. How is the truck?"
I said, "The truck is on its side." He says, "Oh my God." He hangs up and
comes up, and he has his glasses on because he wears contacts. He just threw
on anything. I mean, he had *(she laughs)* hat head. He was still in bed
because he didn't have to go to work early, so he was home. He gets there,
parks, and comes over and asks me how I'm doing and gives me hugs. After
he made sure I was okay, he was like, "Oh my God." So, they called a tow
truck that came and pulled it up on its side.

Had the media arrived yet?
No. The media showed up five minutes after we got it up onto all fours. It
was hooked in the fence. The truck driver was trying to cut it off of our
bumper and hitch because it was all wound up in it. Then we got it cut off,
and we moved it to the other side of the street where the policeman was
parked. It was then – when Darren parked the truck across the other side
of the street, that the media showed up. Darren was talking to the policeman and me, and the media started taking pictures of the truck. They did-
n't even come up to me and ask me if I was okay or anything – nothing. I
was still in shock from going through this. I was sitting in the Jeep because
I was cold, and he *(Darren)* was taking care of all the business. I had already
talked to the police.

Is it Darren's Jeep?
It is Darren's Jeep. My name is not on it at all. The truck is in his name, and

I am a co-owner because he has more money in it than I do, and they started taking pictures of the truck, and he is like, "Stop. Stop taking pictures of my truck. I don't want this in the newspaper." Well, then he *(a photographer)* started taking pictures of the Jeep with me in it. He *(Darren)* told them he didn't want it in the newspapers.

Is this one reporter or many reporters?
There is one reporter and one cameraman. The cameraman starts taking pictures of Darren's jeep, and Darren runs after him and says, "Stop taking pictures of my Jeep. If you don't stop taking pictures of my Jeep, I'm going to break that f'ing camera." So, basically, it came out in the newspapers that Darren threatened this man. But then the man went on a TV interview and said, "Hey, if it had been me, I would have probably reacted in the same way." He said, "I can understand why he acted that way," which basically covered Darren's ass.

Was Darren concerned that it was going to get in the paper because of who you are?
Because they are his rigs and because the last time I had two rigs that were in the paper, they were stolen or were keyed or had flat tires. So, he was like, "Wait a minute. You cannot take a picture of this Jeep, legally."

What were you thinking while this was going on?
Darren, shut the hell up. If you don't do anything and you don't say anything, they don't print anything.

You know that *(to be true)*, right?
I know, but this was his first time dealing with them. In two and a half years, he has avoided the media. At least they didn't know his name. They asked him his name, and he said, "John Doe." *(She laughs)*. So, they just put in the newspaper that a friend of Tonya's got upset for taking photographs, and they were going to sue him *(the cameraman)*. *(She laughs)*. It was kind of funny. But I was like, "Darren, you have to shut up. You can't open your mouth."

When did you realize that this was on the anniversary date of the attack on Nancy?
It was 2:30 or 3:00 o'clock in the afternoon when I heard it on the radio. They said I rolled my truck six times and that alcohol was involved. I am

like, Wait a second. So, I ended up talking to Michael *(Rosenberg)* and told him what was going on and that I wanted to call the radio station. Be nice to them and tell them the facts so they would stop spreading the rumors. I called the radio station, and I ended up getting hold of the AM station instead of the FM station, and I started talking to this man who was very, very nice, and I said that I just wanted to clear up a few facts that had been said about me. He said, "Well, hold on. I'll see if I can get hold of the gal *(the disc jockey)*, and I will transfer you over." Well, he didn't transfer. When he called her, I was still on the line, and I could hear everything they were saying. He said, "Guess what? I have Tonya Harding on the line." And she is like, "No way. Is she pissed?" *(She laughs)*. And he said, "No. She is not mad. She just wants to clarify some things about what you've been saying." And she said, "Oh, shit. I am in really big trouble." And I am sitting there listening, and he comes back on the phone, and he says, "If you want to give her a call right now, she will pick up the phone." He gives me the number. So I hung up the phone, and I called her, and she was like, "Oh, I would never say anything I didn't get off of a good source." And so I asked her where she heard it from. She said, "I heard it from the AP wire." I said, "I would just like to clarify the facts with you so you are not broadcasting anything that is not true." So, I told her there was no alcohol involved – that I was not cited – nothing. So, I clarified it, but she was the one who started it. I really think she was the one who started it. But, I let it go and had a nice little conversation with her. She played the conversation 15 minutes later, and she said, "You know? I really thought Tonya was going to be very upset with me for saying these things, but she was very polite to me, and I thought that was really nice." I was like, Wow. I really could have gone off on her, but I didn't. I hate when people start saying shit like that. I mean, that's how the whole thing in '94 got blown out of proportion. Ahh! That's when I heard it – on the radio. She was announcing it, saying all that stuff was involved and, by the way, it is January 6th, the same day as the attack on Nancy Kerrigan. Maybe she is doing this as a publicity stunt.

You are going to roll your truck as a publicity stunt?
Right – I'm going to roll my truck on its side to get publicity. I have tried to stay away from publicity.

You have been with Darren for a long time and have been avoiding it. This was the first time that he was involved *(in an incident with you that caught the media's attention)*?

Oh, yeah, yeah. Darren wished he had the opportunity to tell the photographer he was sorry. You know, *(she thought he may say)* I was really upset about Tonya and the truck, and I just wanted to take care of business without people interfering. *(She says)* And it would have been different – it would totally have been different, if they had come up to me and asked, "Tonya, are you okay?" Just something. "Do you mind if we ask you a couple of questions?" Or, "Do you mind if we take a picture of your truck?" If they had been polite and had come up and said something to me instead of just taking pictures of shit. It was so rude.

Did it make the national papers?

I'm not sure. Supposedly it went on AP wire, but I am not sure. You can't believe anything unless you see it with your own eyes.

I didn't hear about it up here *(in Canada)*.

I have friends in Georgia, and they said they didn't know about it. I was talking to them last night, and they said, "You were in an accident? Oh my God. Are you okay?" I thought it had hit the east coast. *(She laughs)*.

Maybe by you stepping in and making the phone call, it stopped it from snowballing.

Right. Exactly. Exactly. That is what I was hoping – to stop it in its tracks, so it wouldn't go further. You know, after all this shit I have been through, it is like, why lower myself to other people's levels just because I want to get mad or something like that. I don't get mad that often anymore because I know the truth. And other people saw the truth. Other people know the truth. It's just like, Hey, you report something. I know it's your job, but I'm going to clarify it for you, and to me, that's always the best way to do it. It's not their fault that I crashed my truck.

When you were skating in the early '90's, you told me you wanted to please people because you didn't get that love at home, and that can escalate where you want to explain things to people. You don't want anyone to think badly of you. But that can go opposite because they can misinterpret why you are explaining, and then you can get frustrated.

Exactly. Exactly. But there are so many people out there that just want to go off on people, and I have to admit, back in '91 or '92, I probably would have. I would have said, "Hey! Get the hell out of my face. What are you doing?" But now I realize, if I want to be respected, I have to give them respect, too, because they are just doing their job.

And you like yourself now?
I do. I like myself. I have nothing to be ashamed of. I can walk around and hold my head high. I am a good person with a good heart, and I am a great skater. I have nothing to be ashamed of. Hey, everybody makes mistakes in their life, and just because I happened to be hanging out with the wrong people and made some mistakes doesn't mean that I make those mistakes for the rest of my life. I learned from them. But trying to deal with the insurance companies is frustrating because you have so much into it, and you pay full coverage for two years, that you'd think they would replace it. At least replace it. But insurance companies always try and low-ball you.

Is it because people think you have money?
People have thought that I have had money all my life. I only had money for one year.

What year did you have money?
In '94. I had money then, and that's from the lawsuit that I settled out of court, and my name made a whole bunch of money that I never saw a penny of. To this day, I am still paying taxes for money that I never saw. It went into a trust account in my lawyer's name with my name on it.

Which lawsuit was this?
New York – the magazine *('Penthouse' re the sale of the wedding night video)* – but people have always thought that I have had money, but I am just like everybody else. I have my ups. I have my downs. With the money that I made from the lawsuit, I bought a house and I bought a car.

Our interview was abruptly cut off as Tonya had to take another call.

(8)

Self-Esteem & Misinformation

"They always try and make me out to be this trailer park trash. That's what they said I was – trailer park trash."

I had been researching materials to further educate myself about what had been documented regarding Tonya's childhood and other informa-tion that was being circulated on the internet. This interview (which was conducted in early 2000) was originally intended to allow her to refute what had been printed in a particular book. However, from the onset, our discussion veered in another direction. Because I believed what she was telling me may prove interesting, and because I thought it to be important to understand Tonya's self-esteem issues, I continued in this light for awhile before turning my attention to the planned interview.

What is your weight now, compared to what it was at the height of your competitive career? *(There were rumors that she had gained a substan-tial amount of weight since her car accident).*
I was thin until I was 15-years-old and I was in a car accident with my mother.

Tell me about that first.
We were driving down 82nd Avenue, which is a street by the Clackamas Town Center, because we lived out there, and were on our way to a store of some kind – or home – I don't remember where we were going, but any-way, somebody stopped in front of us, and there was a car in front of the, and there was a car behind us. And somebody came up behind us, ran a red light, and hit the person behind us, and supposedly they were going about 60 miles per hour. It ended up that we rear ended the next person, and so on and so on, and it turned out that I crushed some of my discs in my back. But at first, they said I was going to be paralyzed because I was paralyzed for about ten and a half hours.

You mean you couldn't move any part of your body?
I could move my arms, but I couldn't feel the lower half of my body.

Where you in the hospital?
Yeah. We were there all day and into the night time, and then after about
ten and a half hours, I felt tingling in my feet, and so I turned out to be
okay. But I never had surgery or anything because I always said, "As long as
I can walk and talk and skate, I'm going to do it."

Did you get back to skating almost right away, or did it take you awhile?
It was about two months that I took off. And, of course, when I took off
that time, then I couldn't skate very much or do anything. And so I got fat.
I gained about 20 pounds.

How much were you before the car accident?
I was probably 98 pounds.

And you gained how much?
Probably about 20 pounds or 15 pounds or so. Then I went back skating,
and because I was so heavy, and my body not being used to it, I ended up
coming down *(from a jump)* and I twisted my ankle, and I was off for about
a week after that – came back, and then that's when I broke my jaw bone.

How did you do that?
I fell on a jump *(she laughs)*. Because I was heavy and I was trying to throw
myself into the air to try and do all these triples and stuff, and that's when
I broke my jaw bone, and I was off for – I have no idea. It must have been
another month and a half – two months. Couldn't stand it anymore, so I
got back up, started going back to the rink, and just decided, Hey, you
know, I am tired of this, and it is because of my weight. So, I went on this
really extreme diet.

Involving what ... what kind of diet?
Lots of exercise, lots of water – I ate broccoli and cheese every single day
and a bran muffin. No mayonnaise, no butter, no chips, no candies, not lots
of pastas or anything like that. No hamburgers, no chips, no nothing.

Low fat, low cal?
Yeah. Just getting the energy to skate in the morning is basically all I was
after.

Did you lose the weight?
I lost 26 pounds in 31 days. I went up to 126 pounds, and I got back down,

and I was entered into a competition, and by the time I was ready to go to the competition, I was back down to 98 pounds.

Was 126 the highest you have ever been? *(She would gain more weight in the future – see Chapter '13')*
Oh, Yeah, and I never want to go back there again.

What is your weight now?
I've been off *(skating)* for two months now.

Well, what was your weight in Huntington? *(Approximately four months prior to this interview).*
In Huntington, I was 101.

What are you now?
Now I'm about 109.

So, just by not *(skating)* ... because of your car accident and foot?
I haven't been able to do anything. I mean, my exercise is going to the rink and skating myself and teaching. When I am teaching, I am into what my students are doing – showing them – I'm chasing them around the rink.

You don't just stand by the boards?
No, and it's always energetic. My metabolism is always going.

So you don't have to worry about dieting?
No, but when I'm off, I do watch what I eat. I don't eat a lot. I have my coffee in the morning or afternoon or whatever, and when I get hungry, I eat. Usually, I get a little bit snacky *(hungry)* about 2:00 *(p.m.)* or so. So, I might go in and have half a bagel or a raisin cinnamon English muffin. I may have one of those. Then I eat dinner about 7:00 or 7:30.

So you have never had an eating disorder like some women in skating do? *(I used the example of vomiting after eating).*
No. I can understand why women get to that point because if you have people telling you that you are fat, you're ugly, you're fat, you're fat, you're fat, and you try to lose the weight and something doesn't happen – it doesn't go anywhere; I can understand why women throw up to try and get rid of the weight.

Especially in competitive sports where there is the image *(factor)*?
Well, yeah, the image – that is the whole thing. If people tell you that you
are fat, then your self-esteem goes down, and then you feel horrible, and
you don't want to feel that way. You want to make everybody happy, so then
you try to fix the situation.

**When you were heavy after the accident, did you ever consider that –
did it ever cross your mind?**
No. No. Because I knew if I worked hard enough, I could do it.

When did people start telling you that you were too fat?
When I was young, my mother told me that all the time. I was never
allowed any candy or junk food or anything like that.

But you weren't a fat child?
No.

She would tell you that you were fat, and you thought you were?
I didn't think I was. My dad didn't think I was. But my mother thought I
was, so I never got to eat any of the stuff that normal kids get to eat.

Was your self-esteem high when you were a little kid?
No. I don't think I knew what it meant.

So, it was mainly your mother telling you that *(you were fat)* **when you
were a child and Jeff when you were married?**
Yeah, and also in my teenage years, my coach told us that we needed to
make sure that she *(Tonya)* watches her weight. She needs to stay between
this *(weight)* and this *(weight)*. You know. So there was a point when my
coach at the time was weighing everybody in once a week or twice a week.
I really thought that was pretty stupid because right there that turns your
total attitude where you have to be worried all the time. Oh my God, she
is going to weigh me in so I'd better make sure that I don't eat this tonight
or whatever. I mean, I can see how people get that way, you know?

**Did people from the United States Figure Skating Association ever say,
"She needs to lose a couple of pounds?"**
No. No.

You also said that when you were growing up, you didn't like your teeth?
Well, when I was growing up, I had big spaces between my teeth. So, when my big teeth came in, they weren't big, they were still little teeth. So I was always ashamed of my teeth growing up because I had little, teeny, tiny teeth next to my two teeth in the middle, and as I was growing up until seventh grade, I had this big gap in between my teeth, and I was pretty ugly.

Did people make fun of you?
Yeah. I got it all the time, and finally I got braces in seventh grade, and I had those on for about nine months, and my mother didn't want to hear me bitch and complain anymore when we had them tightened, so she had them taken off.

The braces worked?
Yes. The braces brought my two front teeth together, and the other ones straightened out. And then in '91, when I won Nationals, there was a man that won his Nationals in porcelain veneers.

He did what?
He made porcelain veneers, and he went to his Nationals and won with his porcelain veneers.

You mean a skater?
No, a dentist. You know – a person that does teeth.

Yes, but what do you mean – that he went to his Nationals?
Let me finish the story. He was a competitive person – this man does porcelain veneers – that is what he does for a living. Well, there is a big, huge contest that happens every year for dentists out there for these porcelain veneers, and you take your porcelain veneers, and you go to this contest. Well, it was his Nationals. It was like a Nationals competition, and this man won. He worked at – I think it was a State University Hospital or something. Well, he got in touch with my dentist and said that he would donate a set of porcelain veneers for me, and he donated six porcelain veneers.

At the front?
Yes, on the top. Then my dentist donated his time, and all I had to do was pay for the equipment. It only cost me $250.00 to have the whole thing done.

Was this all done after you won the '91 Nationals?
Right after – I mean, right after; before I went to Worlds next month, they offered to do this for me to help me feel better and to feel good about myself going into my first Worlds competition. So, they donated all this for me, and I went and had it all done at my dentist's office, and it made me look good.

That's nice.
Yeah. It was totally cool. I could never have ever imagined because it was like $6,000.00 worth of work.

So, he did it out of the goodness of his heart?
Yeah.

Should we mention his name?
I don't even know his name. It was '91. It was kind of like a congratulations thing and a good luck thing.

This next set of questions is regarding the book … *(I told Tonya the name of the book, which had been released prior to the 1994 Olympics and claimed to have the 'exclusive inside story' about her. According to Tonya, the book was not authorized by her)* to dispute some of the things they are saying and also to refresh your memory. It mentions in the book about your training partner, Angela. You told me about her before – she was your good friend, and you would skate together and test each other jumping?
Yes. I knew more than she did, but she pushed me. We stroked *(skated)* together around the rink, just keeping going – just keeping ourselves going. And to make it through my programs – when she knew I was getting tired – "Come on, come on" – that kind of training partner.

How did it end up with Angela? Do you see her anymore?
I don't see her anymore. She was not allowed to … I, at one point, wanted to offer to help her out, financially, for lesson time and stuff, for boots or whatever. But her parents could not accept that, and it was all because of what had happened.

After '94 *(the scandal)*?
And she had to basically disassociate herself from me, so she wouldn't get into trouble. You know? It wasn't her parents. Her parents liked me. I stayed

with them. They took me into their home. One of the times, they came over to get me when Jeff was threatening to beat me up and everything. They were the ones who came. Her and her mom and dad came over to get me, and Jeff started to try and fight him *(Angela's father)* – pushing him to start something because they were taking me out of that house.

It was her coaches that wanted her to disassociate with you?
Yes.

Had she been planning to compete nationally?
Oh, yeah. She was still competing.

So you met her at the rink?
Uh huh.

You haven't seen her since '94?
I have seen her a couple of times at the rink when I have gone into the rink before.

In the book, someone from the rink where you skated *(I gave a name to Tonya, but she didn't know who the person was)*, said that your mother was 'horrible.' She called you names. She beat you. She wouldn't let you come off the ice to go to the bathroom. Are these things true?
Oh, yeah. She used to beat me in front of everybody. Hit me with a hair-brush. Drag me on the floor by my hair into the bathroom and beat me – in front of everybody.

She *(the person quoted in the book)* said she wouldn't let you come off the ice to go to the bathroom. So, if you had to go to the bathroom ...
I had to hold it until it was time for me to get off. Sometimes, if I really had to go, I would go and ask Diane. Usually, you had to ask permission to get off the ice in figures – not in freestyle, and if I had to go really bad and she wouldn't let me off, I would go and ask Diane, and Diane would tell me to go ahead and go.

So, you are a little kid and you are skating around and you have to go to the bathroom so you look up at your mother and say, "I have to go to the bathroom."
Yes. She sits right there in the windows, the windows on the side – you know the glass across the front, so you can watch?

There is glass between you and her?
Uh huh.

And she would shake her head no – that you can't go?
Yeah, and if it got to the point where I would go back to my patch area *(area that figures were practised on)* and I would start doing it, and then I would go back over and – "I have to go to the bathroom." And if she got to the point where she just got fed up with it, she would come out there and drag my ass to the bathroom and make me go to the bathroom and throw me back out on the ice.

When you say she beat you, did she ever use her hands?
She used her hands; she used whatever was close.

Did she hit you anywhere on your body ... did it matter ...?
Didn't matter.

In the book, it says your cousin *(I told Tonya the name mentioned in the book)* ...
I don't know him.

He says that your mother wanted you to be a skater even before you were born.
Probably. She tried to skate. She was a dancer, but she couldn't do it. And that was probably six years before I was there. And then when I came into the picture and I wanted to skate, it was like her dream was coming true. Who knows?

Was she raised by a wealthy family? That's what it also says in this book.
Yes, as far as I know. She had to wear certain dress codes, going to school and all that stuff.

Does that mean your grandparents were wealthy or was she adopted into that family?
No. She was – I don't know – she was born to her own parents – my grand-ma and grandpa. She wasn't brought in.

According to this book, she says she was raised by a wealthy family.
Well, then I guess it's true *(laughing)*. I know my great, great, great grand-mother was wealthy. And I know my grandma and grandpa had money, but how much, I have no idea.

But I guess after she had been married to your father and had already been through a few husbands, they wouldn't have been giving her their money at that point?
No.

And in this book, your mother has a horse story. *(Apparently)* she got you a pony to keep you out of skating because it was costing too much money, but you wanted both, so she got rid of the pony.
Yeah, right.

Is this true?
Bullshit. We lived within the city limits. If there was ever a pony, it must have been a stuffed one because there wasn't any live one around, let me tell you. We lived within the city limits. Let's see ... supposedly, the first house I lived in was a downtown area. Then the house I remember being my first house when I was in first grade, second grade, kindergarten, was up in Westwinds – city limits, and they got me a puppy when I was six-years-old – five-years-old. I was five.

But no pony?
No pony.

This book says that everybody at the rink said you were fearless, that you didn't cry when your mother beat you.
I would scream and yell at her to stop. That it hurts. Ow, ow, don't do that!

They said there were never any tears. Is that true?
There were sometimes. A lot of times, you know, I would try to hold it back because I was so embarrassed, and then there were some times that hey it hurt like heck, so ...

You couldn't help it?
Yeah.

It also says that falls never bothered you – other kids may be timid if they fell, but you would fall down, get up, and keep going.
Yep. That's true.

Did older kids dare you to do jumps?
All the time.

Give me some examples. What would they do?
Okay, let's see. I was skating in a competition in Montana, and we were on practice, and one of the girls I skated with was quite a few years older than I was – six years older than I was. And I was doing more jumps than she was, and I had been trying a triple loop at home.

How old were you then?
I think I was turning 12 that weekend because Northwest Championships – that was what it was called – was always at my birthday time. My birthday was on the 12th, and the competition was usually the 8th to the 12th. I remember being out on practice, and she was like – I tried and tried and tried to do it, and I couldn't do it. I kept falling out of it. And then finally she says, "I know you can't do it. You haven't been able to do it yet. What makes you think you are able to do it now? I am like, "Are you daring me to land it? I know I can land one of these. I know I can." She says, "Well, prove it then. If you think you can land it, then go do it." *(I said,)* "All right," and I went and I did it.

You sound like you were a determined kid.
Yeah. I have always been determined. If it's one thing, I am determined. It's either going to be done the right way or it's not going to be done at all. And I mean, even to this day, I remember in my lesson time – usually I had my lesson time where mine would go to the end of the session, usually I would warm up the first fifteen minutes, and then I would have my half an hour after that, and I would always be – I mean, the Zamboni would be ready to come out on the ice, and I would be like, "Just one more – one more time. I'm just going to do it *(a jump)* one last time." And usually the very last time, knowing that I had to do it because I had to get off the ice – I would do it.

So, you would stay out until you did it?
Um hm – as long as I possibly could. Most of the time it was the triple Axel.

The book also says that most of the food you ate when you were young was food you *(your family)* had hunted or fished for.
No. I mean, yeah, we went fishing and hunting and everything like that, and we had venison and fish.

So, if your dad caught something, you would eat it? *(It wasn't hunting for sport?)*
Yeah– like half of the American public. But my mother would go to the store and buy beef and hamburger, like everyone else, too.

I think it is trying to make you sound like you come from the back-woods.
No. We ate normal food. But that helped – with the sturgeon that my parents caught and the deer and the elk they caught – I mean, they never took any does – it was always the bucks like it is supposed to be, and that helped out on the cost of meat through the year.

I can relate to that – my dad fished all the time, and we ate the fish, and my brothers fish to this day.
My dad still does it today.

This book sounds as if they are exaggerating …
Oh, I know. They *(the media)* always try and make me out to be this trailer park trash. That's what they said I was – trailer park trash. That's what they always called me – the media, people, just because I lived in trailers. It doesn't mean that I lived in a mobile home park.

And it doesn't matter anyway *(if she did live in a mobile home park, does it?*
Well, hey, people do what they have to do to live, and if they have to live in a trailer to live, then that is fine because they have a roof over their head and a place to sleep, and if they can put food in their mouth, that is all that should matter. They are not taking anything else from anybody else. You know that is one thing that I have – I have a lot of pride, and I don't like to accept things from other people – unless it gets to the point of the most dire needs – to be needing something.

And your parents both had jobs – they were doing what they could?
Yeah. It's like today. I have a job and everything, but I mean, if it got to the point where I was short *(of money)* and I couldn't do anything about it and

someone offered, the only way I would accept it is if I could pay you back with my next paycheck. I mean, as soon as I get the money, it is yours. It's not like I'm going to keep some and here you go – here is a little bit. It would have to be paid back immediately.

You would take another job *(if you were short of money)* if you had to?
Yeah, but you know, it's so hard out there in society for a person like me. I mean, I've tried to get jobs at a grocery store at like – you know, or like *(a store)* that has groceries, apparel and all kinds of things. I have tried to get jobs at the mall, even automotive places for drivers, and a lot of people just don't hire me because of who I am.

Because of the reputation you have beforehand?
Yes. They think I would ruin their business. And then there was a place we go to for dinner up the street. The owners know me really well, Darren and I, and at one point, before I got my teaching job, she had offered me work there, and I was going to start working there, and I had to memorize the whole menu and everything, and I was doing that, and then in about three weeks, I got my job at the rink. On the other hand, Darren was like, "I do not want you working there." I do not want you working in a place …" because I would have been a waitress, but I would have been in the bar area where they serve meals because I was over 21, and I could work there, so hey, no big deal, but he didn't really want me doing that kind of work.

How did you get the job at the rink?
I went in and talked to them. I pushed my way into the rinks as many times as I possibly could until I got my job.

The same rink – you kept going back?
Well, they told me I had a job for the longest time, and then just before they opened, they said, "Well, hey, we decided not to hire you."

You are now working at the Lloyd Center?
I work at the Lloyd Center – right. The other rink was only five minutes from my house, so that is why I wanted the job there. So, when I didn't get the job there, I went over to the Lloyd Center and said, "Please, please – can I have a job?" *(They said,)* "Sure, no problem – we'd love to have you here." Because they knew – because I had been skating there – how many people are there when I come in. If I am there every single day, they probably have

ten more people a day coming in than when I wasn't there. I brought in a lot of revenue.

Were the students assigned you as a coach, or did they select you?
No, they selected me. As soon as they found out I was teaching, I got so many phone calls.

I guess if I was a parent and I wanted my child to learn how to skate, and one of the best skaters in the world was available to teach them ...
Well, that is how my kids and their parents look at it. The parents said, "We don't care. She *(the student)* likes you."

Did they announce that you were going to be teaching there?
No. It just happened. It came overnight. It was really neat.

And now you have 17 students?
Uh huh. That's the total, and during the summer is when I work with all of them.

Do you have any students that may be going to Nationals at some point? Do you have any that are in the competitive circuit?
They are, but they are in ISI and not USFSA.

What is ISI?
It's just another competitive ...

Branch?
Yeah. Yeah. It is younger levels.

So, some of them have potential?
Yes. I have a couple who just love to skate, and they are getting better and better every day. One of them I work with is an older girl, and she does competitions for adults. Her and five other women who do these adult competitions want me to take them to their competition. I felt that was really cool. The only thing that would hold me back – the thing Diane taught me was that if you go to competitions, everything should be paid for you by your students. And so they are going to divide my cost to go, and that was the only thing that was stopping them from before.

If you ever did get a student that was at the competitive level of the USFSA, would you be allowed to go *(as a coach)* with that person?
No. That ban hurts the most.

The ban is for coaching as well as skating?
I could teach a USFSA skater, but I would have to send another coach to competitions.

Unless they allowed the ban to be lifted?
Well, not … I mean, I don't understand that part of it. It's like …

It's an official ban …
I have no idea. That's the only part of the ban that I don't understand. If I am allowed to teach kids, and I have proven myself to be a good coach and a reputable person, then why shouldn't I be allowed to take my kids to competition?

Tonya and I discussed the rules of coaching, and I pointed out that from what I had learned from other elite skaters in the United States anyone, apparently, who wants to coach can go to any rink, pay the insurance, and become an official coach, but in Canada, even the most elite skater must go through years of training before they can accompany a student to the national level. I advised Tonya to be patient. She responded:
Well, you know, I have waited this long to do things. That is one thing that I have learned – to be patient. Eventually, maybe one day, something might happen. If it doesn't, it doesn't. I am not going to worry about it. I have a couple of coaches at the rink that I'm sure wouldn't mind taking my kids to competition, and I would know they would be in good hands, and I know they wouldn't try and steal them away from me or they wouldn't try and take the credit either.

Diane could go …
Well, Diane is one of the people. But I know there are people out there who would take the credit for it.

Well, first you have to get the student who has the potential and who is at that level.
Right.

Back to the hunting and fishing – were you just a little kid when you first started hunting?
Yeah. I was three.

Did you actually shoot something when you were three?
No. No. No. No. No. I just followed my father through the woods and just went along. You know?

Were you shooting animals ...
No. The very first time I ever shot anything I was 13.

What was it?
A deer – it was a five point buck. It was beautiful, absolutely beautiful. You know, I was always led to believe that we were hunting for the meat that we had to live on for the year. You know – yes it's sad that I'm shooting an animal, but at the time, it was helping us put food on the table, and I was like so excited that I was able to do this – for years, I had been learning how to do this – and when I shot it and it went down, I almost dropped the rifle. I just started shaking – I mean, shaking so bad. Oh my God, I have killed this thing. So, it was like, I was led to believe one way and then when I did it, it was like, Ah shit. But now that I am older, too, if I didn't have the money, which the last few years I haven't, and if I had to go out and shoot a deer to put meat on my table for a year, then I would do it. I mean, I am not ashamed of it.

After that first deer, did you shoot other deer?
Nope.

That is the only deer you have ever killed?
Yep. *(At the time of this interview).*

But if you had to do it to put food on the table for yourself or your family, you would?
Yes. I don't go out and kill things for the sport of it or think it is fun. If I go with other people hunting, then I am going along to watch or to be out in the woods because I love the outdoors. But I haven't been able to shoot anything.

Fishing is different, though – you would fish?
I haven't fished since I was little. I went fishing once. I think I was 22 or 23.

So, you're not out there hunting and fishing *(as per what people think)?*
No. No. I like to go out and shoot paper cups and pop cans and stuff. You know? That's fun to do.

You shoot target practice?
Yes.

Do you own a gun?
No.

Does Darren own a gun?
No. Well, he has his hunting rifle and shotgun that his Dad gave him.

Does Darren hunt?
Yes, he does.

And it doesn't bother you that Darren hunts?
He doesn't get anything anyway. *(She laughs).*

I told Tonya how I was against hunting; she responded:
Well, there are so many people out there that are so against it, but there are many people out there that aren't against it. There are so many who do it for the sport, and I don't like that. That is wrong. That is totally wrong. I mean, If I am going to go out – if I am with somebody who is going to shoot a deer, or if I have to go out and put food on my table and I shoot a deer, I am still going to feel just as bad, but I got food on my table. I take every part of it that is good. I strip it. I will take it to the butcher, and he will do it for me. That way, there's no waste. And that's the way to do it. Not like some people who go out there, and they kill them for their hooves or their antlers or just their hindquarters or something, and I hate that because that is so much of a waste.

So, hunting and fishing are not part of your life right now?
Well, I have gone hunting. I have gone along – not this year, but the year before, and I didn't get anything. But also, I wasn't working. We had a one income household.

With Darren?
Yes.

So you were hunting to put food on the table?
Yes, and for a lot of people, they have never tasted it. It is really good.

I told Tonya how my mother was raised on a farm and how her family would eat venison and that she used to clean the deer herself.
There's a lot of vitamins in the meat. In the olden days, or in the older days, people were a lot more healthy back then, too. You know?

Back to the book – is it true that your first pair of skates came from Goodwill?
Yes, and they were blue – baby blue – the ugliest things you have ever seen in your life.

Did your mom do a lot of shopping at Goodwill?
That's where I got 90 percent of my clothes. I never got anything new except underwear and socks until I'd say eighth grade year – seventh grade year – something like that, and I would get a couple of new shirts or a sweater, but most of the time, it came either from Goodwill or she made it, and they were the ugliest things. They were so ugly.

How long did you wear the blue skates for?
I don't think it was for very long – probably just a few months.

Were your next skates used ones?
I couldn't tell you. I don't think I started getting into brand new skates until I was probably seven or eight.

In the book, it was said that you told reporters the main reason you wanted to go to Olympics was that the Olympic rings were like dollar signs to you.
No.

Is that not true?
Not true.

Was that something they just …
I remember people asking me, "Is the only reason why you're going to the Olympics because of money?" And I said, "Money is like the icing on the cake." I said, "I want to go to the Olympics because I deserve it and I

trained hard. I worked hard. I won. I deserve to go." And when they said, "No, I'm sorry, you can't go," then I sued them. I got a full-blown lawsuit for, what was it – like 21 million dollars or something – and told them, "Hey, either you let me skate and do what I am supposed to be able to do because I earned it or I am going to sue you for what I could have made afterwards if I won."

Who would you have been suing – the ISU *(International Skating Union)* **or the IOC – the Olympic Committee?**
No – the United States Figure Skating Association.

They had no legal basis for not sending you?
No.

I think people have to remember that back in '94, before all this happened, an Olympic gold medalist wasn't guaranteed to be making piles and piles of money like they are now. It was lucky if they got in Ice Capades, right?
Yeah.

It was only after all this *(the 1994 scandal)* **that the professional skating world took off and went** *(through-the-roof)* **dollar-wise?**
It has been known that people get big endorsements after winning Olympic Games, but it is never a guarantee. I mean, life is not a guarantee. You could go there and win and people just don't like you.

(9)

1994 Nationals – The Whack Heard Round the World

*"He tried to destroy my career because if I was not with him,
I was not going to be with anybody else. That's what he said."*

Take me through the 1994 Nationals – what you remember – starting with your arrival. What was it like? How were you feeling?
Well, it was like any other competition to me. Got there, and waiting in line to check in – I was actually standing in line with Michelle Kwan's parents and Michelle Kwan, and just b.s.'ing with them and saying hi to everybody. Once we got checked in, I don't remember anything more, per se, except, you know, we did the normal things – getting up, going to practice, and if I had two practices a day, usually one was in the morning and one was in the afternoon or evening. And I had gone to a couple of practices and was doing pretty good.

It wasn't really any different than any other Nationals?
Un uh. It was the same as it always was. You know, seeing all my friends that I don't see except for at competitions. I mean, it was just a normal competition. And the arena was absolutely beautiful and really good ice – real springy, I remember. Hot, though; it was really hot. The day that Nancy got hurt, I remember I had a practice before her because we were in different groups of practice sessions, and my practice was before hers, and then we had a later practice at the – because there was two rinks, and one practice – the night one – was going to be at the main arena. And I remember I went to practise at the practice arena – the first one, came back, and Diane didn't want me stressed. Take a nap and get up and eat something, and then we would go to practice later. And I remember …

Did you fly in with Diane?
Yes.

Where was Nationals that year?
Detroit.

So you flew in with Diane ...
And Erica – Erica was my choreographer.

Was Jeff with you?
He was not there with me. Well, somebody called me and woke me up and told me that Nancy had been hurt – that somebody had attacked her.

So you were at the hotel?
I was asleep, and somebody had said that somebody attacked Nancy and that she got hurt and everything, and Erica, I think, or Diane – I don't remember ...

One of the two of them called you?
One of the two of them called me, and then Erica came over to my room to see me, and I got up, and I had called home. I was obviously shook up by that point in time and called home and talked to Jeff and told him what was going on and everything and told him I was really scared. And *(I)* basically got reassurance from him, "Hey, everything is going to be fine. Don't worry. You're ready. Just keep you're eyes open for anything weird. Just be normal." Anyway, I remember Diane wanted to go over and watch the men or the pairs or something that was going on, and she was going to meet Erica and I at the rink for practice. So, Erica stayed with me, and we went down together and over to the arena, and I was really shook up. I mean, I couldn't keep focused on what I was trying to do. My practice started out really shitty – missing jumps and things like that, and I remember I kept looking around everywhere. I was scared. And anyway, Diane – during the practice session – I mean, I was missing stuff that was really stupid, and I remember she said, "Tonya, if you don't basically pull your head out of your ass and straighten up, and don't worry and think about what you are doing, you are either going to hurt yourself or you are going to make a fool out of yourself." And so, finally, Diane got me calmed down, and I went out and redid my jumps. I don't remember if I went through a program or not. I don't remember. By the end of the session, I was skating better – still really upset.

How come you weren't at the same practice as Nancy? Were they at different times?
I think they were A, B and C *(groups)*. They put us all into different groups, and then after the short program, they put you into a draw kind of thing, and you end up in either A, B or C. I think there was C that year.

Was there any indication beforehand that something was going to happen, or was it just a normal competition?
It was just a normal competition.

So, all the girls were scared because – they thought there was a weirdo out there?
Yeah, because they said they didn't catch the person and the person was still on the loose.

Had you seen Nancy yet at that point, or I guess she was …
No. I hadn't seen her until later on. I don't remember when I saw her, but I did see her sometime later.

Did it go through your head at that period that Jeff had anything to do with it?
No, absolutely not. I mean, I had no idea what the hell was going on. I remember at Northwest Pacific – at competition – I had gotten a death threat before I was supposed to step out on the ice.

This was before Nationals?
Before Nationals – yes. I got a death threat. There was a phone call that came into the ice arena, and they told them that if Tonya Harding steps onto the ice, she will be shot in the back. And there was a whole big to-do. They got the officials involved. I told them, "I don't care. I am going to skate. This is bullshit," and they said they were taking this thing very, very seriously. They were going to move the ladies to the very end of the competition when the mall was closed, and I don't really know what transpired after that, but I remember the officials and everybody turned out to say that they didn't want to put anybody else at risk. They gave me a 'bye' *(did not have to compete to move on to next level)* from Northwest to Coast.

Northwest being the divisional or sectional *(competition)*?
Yes, it was the beginning one – it goes Northwest and then Pacific Coast and then Nationals. So, they gave me a 'bye' to Coast so no one else was involved in it. And they took me out … I mean, the police were involved and everything. They took me out the back. Oh, that's right, first of all – I had forgotten – they told me they were going to move the competition to late that night. So, the police and everybody rushed me out the backdoors and told me to go home. Just got home, and not even ten minutes later, the phone rang, and it was – I don't know if it was the manager of the rink, but

somebody called and said, "Tonya, you need to come back here. We are going to have a meeting with the officials." So, got back in the car and drove all the way out to the rink, and that's when they told me that I was not going to be skating. But anyway, to me, that was a very scary situation because I didn't know what … anything. But anyway, at Nationals, at that practice – at the very end, it started being okay. I started landing my jumps and getting my shit together. And let's see – I have no idea – at some point in time during the competition, I was still really scared. They had all this security, but it was still really kind of upsetting and scary to me, and so I had told Jeff, "Why don't you fly back here. You know maybe it would make me feel better and help me calm down." I was totally scared. I told him I went to my practice and I skated like shit. I couldn't keep my concentration. I was really afraid, and I really wanted him there to keep me calmed down and not worry so much about somebody else maybe wanting to take me out. Of course, unfortunately, at that time, I didn't know that he was the one trying to hurt everybody. I mean, there was a list, and I was on the list.

What do you meant there was a list?
When we got home from Nationals, one of my friends from a TV station called me and told me there was a list of names of people who were to be taken out at Nationals, and my name was on the list. There was mine and Nancy's and Michelle Kwan's and Tonia Kwiatkowski. There were four names on the list, and mine was one of them.

You say you were afraid because a supposed list of people had surfaced that might be attacked, and your name was on that list. Because you are afraid, you say you called Jeff, even though he had beaten you up a couple of weeks prior, but then you say you didn't hear about the list until you got home from Nationals.
Right.

So why were you afraid, and why would you call him when you supposedly despised him and he was a physical and emotional threat to you?
I didn't hear about the thing *(the list)* until after I got home. I was afraid after she *(Nancy)* had already been attacked that there was somebody that might have been there trying to attack other people, too. That's what I was saying. And then when I got home and found out that, then it make me even more of, Oh my God, you know?

You didn't have a clue beforehand that Jeff was involved in this?
No. *(Emphatic)* And he was my other half, basically, but who am I supposed to talk to? I didn't have any friends to talk to. All I had was my coach.

Did they make up the list to ...
I have no idea. No idea. I mean, I can look back now and tell you, you know, when I wanted him to come back to Nationals with me because I was so scared. That's the stupidest thing I could have ever done in my life. It was stupid. It was the most stupid thing I probably ever could have done. But because he had always been there in the past, I was feeling more safe if he was walking along side of me in case somebody tried to hurt me. I mean, my coach can't do nothing.

Your head must have really been messed up back then as far as he went ...
Yeah– that was an understatement.

I guess it was a really mixed up relationship then – for you to call him at Nationals and to have him protect you after he had beaten you up a little while before. Wouldn't you want to be away from him?
I was really scared. I mean, he was always there to protect me. If I ever had a problem, if someone ever tried to come up to me to hurt me, he would have stopped them.

But in the meantime, he – and I am only asking this because I am just thinking ...
I mean, we were getting along. Don't misunderstand me. We were getting along.

But he ...
Yeah, he beat me up, but that was old news. I was used to it. But I was doing everything I could to keep him happy so he wouldn't beat me up anymore before I went to competition. So, anyway, I had done *(the)* short program, and *(on the)* long program day, Jeff flew in before I competed, and *(we)* ate lunch, and *(I)* took him out, and we went to my competition, and *(I)* competed. *(I)* won, and then I had a whole bunch of interviews with the press. And then I remember there were officers talking to all the girls and coaches, and they talked to me, and Jeff was there with me when they talked to me. They asked when he came in, and we told them he had just got in. I

told them I had phoned him and told him I wanted him to come in. And then after that, we went back to the hotel, and they had the after-party, and we went for, I don't know, an hour, and then after that we just went back up to the hotel room and packed and got everything ready to leave the next morning. And the police people called us up in my room and asked if they could come back up and talk to me in the morning, and I said that was fine. And they came up and talked to us, and they went ahead and gave us a ride to the airport because we had missed the shuttle. So, they took us to the airport and dropped us off, and we went on our merry way home.

What kind of questions were they asking?
If I had seen anybody strange around … if I had ever seen anything like this happen before – I don't even remember. They were just basic questions they were asking.

Did you have any indication then at all … did you know … of course you didn't know until a few days later *(she had previously told me)* **right?**
I didn't know until after we got home. Two days after we got home, I knew his friend Shawn was involved. I didn't know how because they wouldn't talk where I could hear them. They would always talk in the other room, and I would try and listen, but I couldn't hear anything. Then they would turn around and say, "What are you doing?" And I would say, "I am doing the dishes" or something. Then it was the fourth or fifth day when I knew for a fact that Jeff was involved somehow, but I didn't know how. But to this day – to this day – never did he tell me that he did it – never. He always said that Shawn did it, and this other guy did it, and he was just helping them out along the way because he was, you know, closest to me. I overheard them in the living room, but that was four days after, or something like that. But everything was very confusing to me because Jeff wouldn't let me go anywhere by myself, and any time he left he always took me with him. He wouldn't let me stay at home. He wouldn't let me go the rink by myself and so my thinking was he that, you know, he was trying to protect me – to cover me in case somebody was trying to hurt me.

You didn't think he was acting strange at all?
Not really – I didn't think really – I just thought it was really strange that he wouldn't let me go anywhere.

And you weren't really living as man and wife then, were you?
No. We had separate bedrooms.

What about at the hotel *(at Nationals)*? **He stayed in your hotel room though that night – right?**
Yes.

When he spent the night with you did anything happen?
Oh, no. I mean, after competition it was just like – go back, went to the party, saw everybody, and went back and watched TV, and we went to sleep.

So you weren't together as man and wife, like sleeping together, for a long time?
No. It had been months.

I read somewhere that you had a bodyguard at the rink. Is that true?
A what?

Some guy to protect you at the rink at Nationals?
No. I never had anybody – I never, ever, ever hired a bodyguard in my life.

So that Shawn guy who was always following you around …
He was Jeff's friend. And when I came home from Nationals, he had asked him to pick us up and just kind of walk with us just so the media didn't trample me. And that was it. I mean, this guy was an idiot – moron – completely. And anyway …

When did you see Nancy at the Nationals? What happened when you saw her?
I told her I was really sorry to hear what had happened.

Where was this – back at the hotel?
I don't remember where I saw her first. I saw her parents and asked them how she was doing, and I don't think I saw Nancy until long program day. I mean, I don't remember when I saw her, but then we took the team photos, and we saw each other then, and I don't know – that was basically about it.

Did she act normal toward you?
Oh, yeah. Yeah. I mean, we were friends. We were roommates on tour and at competitions. I mean, we have known each other for years.

Did you win the short program and the long program?
I don't remember. *(She laughs)*.

Do you remember who the competitors were?
Well, there was Nancy, Michelle Kwan, Tonia Kwiatkowski, and Nicole Bobek.

So, you came first and Michelle came ...
Second.

And did Nicole or Tonia come third?
I don't remember.

When you called Jeff and asked him to come out *(to Nationals)* – you weren't living as man and wife ...
Right.

So, was it more of a brotherly thing or was it ... did you still love him up to that point?
I loved him, of course, but I was not in love with him at all.

So, you felt ...
I mean, we had been together for seven years. It was kind of like, he was the man in my life. And it was kind of like a security thing.

So even though he had been abusive to you at home ...
I got the shit beat out of me a couple of times *(after going back with him)*. That's why I went in before Nationals and trained before midnight because I couldn't wear so much makeup to cover them *(the bruises)*.

Right. Well, why then – I kind of understand because I know what you are thinking ... *(I was trying to tell her that readers wouldn't understand)*.
Well, you see, I have a security blanket of being at home. I leave home, I don't feel easy.

But back then even?
Well, yeah. I mean, I hated traveling. I always hated traveling. And even though we weren't husband and wife, we were still living together and trying to put that front on – what the United States Figure Skating Association

wanted. And it was kind of like, if he was there, it would make me feel a little bit more easy, and I have somebody to talk to. Yes, I was close to Diane, but not like that. It was like coach and student relationship. But, I don't know …

Did you have any feeling when the police were questioning you *(and Jeff)* **that they were suspecting anything then?**
No, because they talked to everybody.

So, it was a matter that they were just trying to find out what went on?
Um hm – yup.

So calling Jeff in was just a way of …
Of making myself feel better, of making myself feel more secure.

After you got back from Nationals, there was the whole media thing …
Yeah.

I remember *(watching it on television)***; there were all those people standing around at the airport.**
Oh, yeah – it was big.

When did it break that – okay, four days later …
I don't even know day by day by day. I know – God, I don't …

How did they *(the authorities)* **find out** *(that Jeff was allegedly involved)?*
Somebody said that they had talked to somebody I guess, and they called the police and told them, and I guess that there was a list of people – like a hit list or something – and one of the media people contacted me, a friend of mine, and sent me the hit list over the fax machine. I have no idea – I mean, I don't really understand anything that really happened. All I know is that … *(she pauses)*.

Okay, forgetting all that was happening – what happened to you? You get home, you're facing all this press, you got him with you, you still don't know anything, and then four days later …
It was like two days later is when things started breaking in the news, and the media or police, or whatever, was involved or whatever – that Shawn was involved – that Shawn had done this, and then somebody said Jeff was

involved, and I was involved, and somebody else, and somebody else, and I was like, well, I'm not even involved. I don't even know what is going on here. And then Diane's husband – we went to see Diane's husband *(Dennis Rawlinson)* because he is an attorney and talked to him for awhile to find out what was going on, and I guess then that Shawn was picked up, and then he – I don't know how it all transpired – anyway things just started dropping here and here and here, and then it was like the fourth day, I guess, was when I started thinking that Jeff was involved and trying to tell me what to say and not to say, and this was what was going on, and I was like, "I don't want to be involved in this. I'm not going to say that." And then when I had to go in and talk to the FBI, I had been threatened after I had heard them talking and overheard them. They tried telling me what I should and should not say. And then I went in with my attorney after we had talked – I mean, at first there were two attorneys – mine and Jeff's, but then they separated us at one point when they asked me a question, and I answered them, and Jeff ended up punching me under the table. And then when we left, he hit me when we were in the car and told me that I was a stupid bitch and I shouldn't open my mouth and all this stuff. And then I had to go in and talk to the FBI or whoever was in charge of this thing, and so *(I)* started telling them basically what I'd known, and then they asked me if I knew what hindering the prosecution was, and I said, "No. I have no idea." And they asked my attorney, "Do you want to tell her or should we tell her?" So, my attorney took a break, and we went into another room, and my attorney told me, "Tonya, you have got to be totally straight with these people. Hindering the prosecution is not telling them what you know or you don't tell them everything you know if you know something." And I am like, "I can't tell them the whole truth because if I do, I am going to end up getting the shit kicked out of me bad or something worse." So, I said, "I want protection. If I am going in there and going to tell these people what I've heard, then I want to be protected." And he is like, "Well, we will see what we can do, but you need to go back in, and you need to tell them what you know."

Had that awful thing *(the rape)* already happened? *(It was obvious to me that Tonya didn't like to talk about the attack, so I began referring to it in various other ways).*
No. Not at this point. So then I went back in, told them what I knew. They set up a couple of agents or something at my father's place, where I was staying, and I went back to my father's house, and not even 15 minutes later, Jeff walks up and breaks in the front door and comes in and say, "You're

coming with me." And I said, "No, I am staying right here." And he basically dragged me out of there and took me in the car. That's when he took me up into the mountains. And after we got up into the mountains, he stopped up on this dead end road, and then a few minutes later, a car pulled up behind us. He told me to stay in the car …

You don't have to go through all that again. I have that all on tape.
Okay.

I don't want you to get upset again.
Okay. Thank you. *(She laughs).*

But the thing is, from the time you heard the conversation in the living room … you were in the kitchen, they were in the living room, was it a day later that you went in for questioning or a few days later?
Two days, I think, or something.

At that time, though …
We had gone back and forth over to the lawyer's house.

So, when that horrible thing happened to you, you had already talked to the *(FBI)* – you had already told them what you knew?
Yes, and he found out because they called his attorney, and his attorney called him and told him what I had said.

Okay, but we are missing something here. You know how we said in the proposal that you will tell the reason why you didn't come forward sooner – I was thinking *(after she told me about the rape during a later interview)* that it was because that *(the rape)* had happened, and that's why you didn't come forward. Do you know what I mean?
I know. I can't remember day by day. I mean, literally, I have no clue how everything went – one, two, three, four, five – you know? I could not tell you what happened …

The moment that you knew …
You know, they were dragging me around everywhere.

The moment that you knew – that you heard the conversation …
Right – is when they started to bring me in and tell me what I should and should not say and everything.

Okay, so why didn't you right then – and I am just saying this because, obviously, I would be horrified or terrified, too, but why didn't you, right then, get away from him …
I couldn't.

For half an hour or something …
I couldn't.

Or phone the police?
He wouldn't let me leave – period. I mean, he would walk out if I walked out of the house. He would come out there and take the distributor cap off the car so I couldn't leave.

So, you were just afraid to say anything?
Yes – totally.

And you had good reason to be afraid because after you did tell them (the FBI) that (the assault) happened, right?
I think so. I mean, I can't tell you what happened. Really, I don't remember what expired, day by day by day. I couldn't tell you. I don't remember if that happened before hand or after hand. But I remembered that something had happened where I couldn't go in and say something. I mean, he always had a gun around – always.

How long was it between Nationals and Olympics?
A month, I think.

So, from a week after Nationals, you really didn't know what was going on?
Uh uh.

And then it was a week of just pure …
Hell.

Hell.
Yeah.

Then a couple of weeks before the Olympics, you are charged ... were you charged then with hindering the prosecution, or did they wait until you got back from the Olympics?
Ah ...

Because why weren't they going to let you go to Olympics? Do you remember it was ...
I can't even tell you. I don't know. My lawyer did everything. I was basically in the dark about everything. I guess it was like ... I don't know.

It was public knowledge before Olympics that you had learned of the thing *(the attack on Nancy)*, **but that you hadn't come forward.**
Right. Well, they had ... oh God, I just hate this.

I know. I know it is hard for you.
Well, because I don't know. I don't remember, and it just pisses me off really bad. All I know is that I had a gun in my head. I had always been threatened that they were going to take care of me if I didn't go along with their story and everything. And *(I)* could never leave, dragged me around everywhere, beat the shit out of me – was at *(the)* lawyer's house, lawyer's office, lawyer's house, lawyer's office, and him *(Jeff)* dragging me all around town and everything. *(Pause)* I don't even know anymore.

I am thinking ahead to when we are writing the book to somebody sitting there *(reading the book)* **saying, "Well, couldn't you pick up the phone and call the police? Couldn't you ..." Do you know what I mean? Couldn't you just go along with what he was saying and let them** *(the police)* **know what happened? Like, "Get over here right away because ..."**
No. I couldn't. That's why I had to tell my attorneys. That's why the attorneys separated us. And then the one attorney – mine – took me and the other one took him. And that's when I told my attorney what was going on and I was being threatened and everything.

So, you were really afraid?
Very.

But after that terrible thing that happened to you on the mountain ... wouldn't at that point you just say, "To hell with it, to hell with him, to hell with everything. I am seeing him disappear, kind of thing, and going and tell them everything he did that night?
No. I couldn't do that. I would lose everything if people knew that I was fucking raped. I mean, I was raped before, and I never mentioned it to anybody.

I know.
I mean, what am I supposed to say that it wouldn't become a total, big, huge media circus?

I think that maybe this is the way - instead of detailing in the book, maybe we should be saying just what you are saying. "I can't remember the dates" Now the reason that you can't remember these things is because ... why? It was too horrible a time? You blocked it out?
I tried to block it out completely. Put it out, you know? I mean, I have nightmares about it still.

So, these guys were hanging around the house at the time. Were you afraid of them too?
Just Shawn – the fat guy.

Were you afraid of him, too?
I wasn't really afraid of him. I thought he was an idiot, a moron, and then when things started getting – because that was the first couple of days, and then after that, he ended up being picked up.

So, you were more afraid of Jeff then?
Yes.

And were also afraid that if it came out that it was Jeff that your reputation would be like ... that people would think that you were involved?
I didn't even know that he was involved.

No, but when you heard about it – when you heard him and Shawn talking ...
Oh. When I heard him and Shawn talking, it was like very shocking, I guess, because I thought that he was, that Shawn was involved and Jeff was

trying to help him. Because to this day, he never admitted that he was involved in it to me.

Who? Jeff?
Yeah. He always said, "I didn't do anything. I was not involved in it. Shawn is a whacko, and he wanted to do this and this and this." I mean, I separated myself from him, and he would come right after me and grab me and beat me up. And there wasn't anything I could do about it. I mean, my freaking father wouldn't do a damn thing about it either.

What about the FBI agents that were sitting there that day?
They didn't do a damn thing. Nothing. Nothing at all.

Okay. What we'll do next ... I think like we said, we will just treat this like ... I don't ... you know because ...
I don't remember ... that's exactly how it should be, too.

Because I'm not a lawyer, I can't sit here and figure out facts.
No. All I'm saying is that if it is coming from me, I'm saying I remember that this happened and this happened and this happened and this happened, but I couldn't tell you when it happened. I couldn't tell you how it happened, or you know ...

The only thing that is bothering me is that in the proposal we said that she will tell why she didn't come forward sooner because something so horrific happened that she still has nightmares to this day ...
Exactly.

But we can't really say that because that happened after you went in and told them.
No. It happened before I went in and told them everything. I told my attorney this stuff and that I wanted protection.

So, you didn't go back out and tell them *(the FBI)* **everything that you knew?**
This was after. When the attorneys separated us, I had told my attorney – I had went and talked to these people, and then Jeff found out what had been said and took me up into the mountains and told me all this shit and did all this shit, and I didn't get any protection.

(Long pause) **Okay ...**
I mean, I talked to these FBI people, I don't know how many times.

When you told them, though, what you knew – had that *(the rape)* happened on the mountain all ready?
Yes. Yes.

It had happened already?
Yes.

Okay. Then we are fine. All I am thinking of is how the facts are going to look. I don't want it to be ... we can write about not remembering dates and everything else, but for the purpose of the book, you come home from Nationals ...
I have no idea of what day anything happened – of what the dates were.

Does this make ...
All I know is that I got raped. I had a gun put to my head, and I wanted protection before I told anybody what I really knew besides my attorney.

But it wasn't until after he took you up to the mountain that you did tell them ...
Yes.

That it was a day or two later?
I had told my attorney the stuff that happened.

But you hadn't told the FBI?
No. His attorney talked with my attorney, and his attorney called Jeff and told him what I had said.

Okay, I get you now.
I went in and talked to the FBI and told them what had happened, you know, what I knew.

But you had already been raped by then?
Yes.

And you didn't tell the FBI what he did to you because?
I'm not telling – I wasn't going to tell anybody.

Okay. I got you now. We're fine with the proposal the way we did it, and we'll be fine with the book. We're just ... you know, there were so many things that went on and so much happened, it has become like a blur to you probably anyway now.

It was a blur when it happened. So much happened in so little time and 90 percent of the stuff that happened, I didn't really know what was happening. I was just sitting there and the attorneys were taking care of everything.

It has been alleged that prior to the 1994 Nationals in Detroit you had called the USFSA to obtain the telephone number of Nancy's practice arena. Is this true?

No. It is not true.

It has been alleged that during this time, you made telephone calls to Nancy's arena to find out her practice schedules. Is this true?

No. That's not true either.

It was rumored that at one time, you admitted to calling either of these two places – the USFSA or Nancy's rink because you wanted to obtain an autographed poster of you, her, and Kristi for a fan. Is this true?

Yes. It is true. I called the USFSA to find out if they could get hold of her to find out if it would be okay if I would be able to send her the picture of all three of us from '91 – her, I, and Kristi on the podium because there was a sports bar in Portland that wanted it.

So, my first question about calling the USFSA to obtain her telephone number ...

That's not true.

You called them to have them contact her?

Yes, because I don't contact other skaters. The only time I would have contacted another skater would have been if we were extremely close friends where we could keep in contact and meet up.

Another thing I have – and apparently this was released in an FBI interview – a skating reporter – I am not going to put her name in the book *(I told Tonya the reporter's name),* **she allegedly said that you and she had become friends.**

Yes.

And traded regular telephone calls.
Yes.

And that you told her that you had a bet with somebody regarding Nancy.
Yes.

She said that you asked her if she would obtain the name of the skating rink where Nancy trained, and that you also wanted to know if Nancy owned property on Cape Cod.
Yes.

Okay ... what did you want the information for?
You know the skating books you get from tour? It has the nice, big, beautiful pictures in it.

No. I don't know.
Well, you get this book, and every skater is in it, and it tells where you are from and where you skate ...

You mean the books that go to the fans in the arena?
Yeah. You can *(get them)* autographed. Well, I was having an argument with somebody and bet them that I knew that I was right – that she lived on Cape Cod.

What did it matter? Did it say *(that)* in the *(fan)* book?
It said in the book that she lived where her parents were.

You mean a place other than Cape Cod?
She had a new house. Because I was on tour with her, and she was telling everybody, and at the last competition that we had done, she had told everybody that she had gotten a new house. And I was tired of being called a liar. Everybody was like, I'm full of shit and I don't know what I am talking about.

Was this on tour or after the tour?
I don't remember if it was on tour or after tour.

Because if it was on tour, you would have been able to ask her directly. Right?
No. I think it was at a competition when she was telling everybody that she had bought a new home. But the book comes from the tour. So, it was after tour – it was a different time; it was a different address and a different skating rink. And *(the reporter)* and I were good friends, and *(the reporter)* knew that she had bought a house. And I wanted to prove a point.

Who were you having the argument with?
With Jeff. Because we were going through, looking at the skating books because I always liked them, and he was talking to Shawn, and Shawn was looking at another skating book, and it said one place was here and one place was here.

Are you talking about the heavy man?
The fat person – Yeah– the stupid one.

I think she said this occurred right after Christmas in '93 – just before '94 *(Nationals).*
I don't remember when it was. All I know is that I knew I was right. *(She laughs).*

So, you mean, the book said she lived somewhere and ...
The book said she lived here, and I knew that she lived here.

Somewhere else, and so Jeff was saying ...
Jeff and I were arguing so badly about it because he kept calling me stupid. I remember that. So, I said, "I will call *(the reporter)* because *(the reporter)* will tell you that I know what I am talking about."

And did *(the reporter)* tell you?
Um hm. Actually, I think she got on the phone with Jeff and told him.

Can you see why, though, that would make people think something ... thinking that you might have been calling to see where she *(Nancy)* was so that Jeff, or whoever, I don't know who – would plan this attack on her – somewhere else other than Detroit?
At her home? I didn't have an address. I wasn't asking for no address. All I did was call somebody and say, "Hey, isn't this true – that they bought a home?"

Is it also true that you asked her for the name of the skating rink?
No. I didn't ask for the skating rink.

So you only asked her ...
I asked her the name of the town she bought her house in. And it was right outside of ... it was on some lake or whatever. And I believe she got on the phone and told Jeff.

And therefore what? That you won the bet, kind of thing?
Yeah. Because I was right. She had bought a house at this other place. I didn't ask for no address or phone number or anything like that. I asked *(the reporter)* because she knew that I was right.

And that ...
And that was it.

But can you see how it makes it look a little suspicious?
Why?

Well, right before Nationals. It is at the end of Christmas ...
Well, I don't know when it was.

Well, this woman said it was right after Christmas.
Well, how does she know it was right after Christmas? When were these questions asked to her?

I believe right after the Olympics.
Do you know *(the reporter)*?

I don't know *(the reporter)* at all.
Well, *(the reporter)* was a little bit out there. So, it could have been March. It could have been August. But the point is, though, the only reason why it would sound bad to somebody is that that's the way they think.

Okay ... what do you mean by that?
Because you know the story of what has happened, and that's why you're making it sound like I did something wrong.

Not me personally?
That's what it sounds like.

What I am doing is trying to make it sound ...

So, what you're doing is trying to make it sound like ... and you are almost like going to convince people, Yup, she did. She knew about it.

No. All I am trying to do ...

That's what it sounds like.

All I am trying to do is to clear up ...

No, but what would the people think if you put that in a book? Because people don't understand that Jeff was such a complete asshole that anytime I could be right about anything, I mean, I would do it. I didn't call up somebody and ask them for an address. I called up and said, "You know this book from tour? It says that ..." I could have been asking about anybody. I mean, it didn't even have my hometown right on it – on mine. And yet, this was just off the tour.

And so you were just trying to prove a point?

Prove a point, plain and simple, because I was so tired of him always trying to make me seem stupid and dumb and don't know anything, you know? It was just irritating to me.

Tonya told me that she was worried about how the public would perceive this information when she hadn't done anything wrong. I repeated my original question regarding whether she had telephoned to obtain the name of the skating rink where Nancy trained and if she owned property on Cape Cod, and if so, why she required that information. I then pointed out that an interviewer may ask her the same questions and that it was better to clear up any misinformation in this book. She responded:

I do not remember asking her – maybe I did – But, I didn't ask her where it was; I asked her if she would be skating at the same rink. I mean, I don't remember for sure. What I do know is that it was all to win a bet because everything on different people was different in the skating book. But I have no clue anymore what she really did ask me. All I know is that is what it was for.

And it was a bet with Jeff, and the reason was because he was always making you feel stupid. And you were with him now, not really for love ...

Yeah. At that point in time, I was with him to make it on the team.

Maybe you were a little immature at the time, too?

Well, of course. I didn't know any better about anything. I'm just trying to figure out, if we put something like this in the book, is it going to make it look bad? Or is it saying, Hey, she is doing it and is being honest, and she is just telling us. My question is how is it going to look to the public? Because if I looked at it now, it looks bad. But I really didn't do anything wrong except ask the questions to win a bet. I'm not trying to hide anything. It just that this sounds bad. It's not that it sounds bad, it's just that if people would have understood what he was like, and if I could win one bet – one little thing – I mean, it was a bet. I think it was for a quarter or something like that. Big deal.

Tonya said she would leave it up to me and Michael Rosenberg whether or not to include the aforementioned portion of the interview regarding her bet with Jeff in the book.

Now you actually weren't charged, I don't think, with hindering the prosecution until after you got back from the Olympics?

I don't think I was.

I think what it was, if I remember, was that you had told the FBI what you knew, and then the Figure Skating Association wanted to pull you out of the Olympics – wasn't it?

Yes.

And that's when your lawyer …

That's when my lawyers went in and did whatever they did to get me to stay on the team.

So you hadn't been charged with anything at that point, right?

No. I don't think so. I think it's when I got back from Olympics is when everything else transpired.

We'll talk about that the next time. That's enough for now. You don't need to get upset.

Well, the only thing – it's just – I mean, the whole situation upsets me.

I know.

But trying to give this for you to understand it and for me to even understand it – it's very difficult for me.

I know.

I can't – there are so many things that happened in a very short period of time, and I've tried basically to block it all out.

I know, and I don't like to dig too much, but I know when the book is done, I don't want anybody to say, "Oh, yeah, right," or poke holes into it or start asking questions or whatever. I just wanted it covered, and then if somebody in the media is asking you questions, you know, then it is there in black and white. Read it, and then there is no ...

Yeah. I don't think we even have to have dates or anything like that. This is what I remember happened to me. And I can't tell you when, I can't tell you how. I just remember those points. You know?

Okay, this is fine. This is good. The next interview we will do will be before the Olympics and the Olympics, and let's get that done. Actually, so much went on right after the Olympics too, and we'll just do it the same way – just what you remember. Okay?

I don't even remember hardly anything that happened at the Olympics. I mean, I remember I stayed with a friend and her husband and her baby, I think. Was that before?

It might have been before. That was after ...

That was – I think that was before the Olympics. I moved from my dad's place to my friend's house in Beaverton and then went to the Olympics.

Which friend was that?

That was Stephanie.

So, were you just training for the Olympics then and trying ...

Trying, but the media wouldn't let me alone. It was the biggest media circus I have ever seen in my entire life.

And you weren't with Jeff then?

No.

What was he doing all this time?

I don't know.

He hadn't been arrested or anything at that point, I don't think, either.

I don't know. Actually, I think he had been.

What did he go to jail for? What was he charged with?
Racketeering. Get this – he made, probably around $900,000.00. He spent $50,000.00 on his lawyer and went to jail for six months and got out.

But he went to jail for master-minding the plot, right?
I don't know for a fact. I have no idea.

In your opinion, wasn't he the one who thought of it?
He had to be because the fat guy, Shawn – he is stupid. He was stupid.

And the point is, who is going to make money off it? Jeff is?
He is.

If he is married to the National Champion and the Olympic Champion, then he is going to make the money?
Well, we weren't married.

That is true.
But we were basically living together – yes.

But he would have made …
He would have benefacted *(benefited)* – yeah. Because if he would have tried to get back together with me and make it all right, then if I would have been stupid enough, you know like I was in the past, and went back to him, he could have taken half of everything I ever made.

So, what you said all along then …
He tried to destroy my career because if I was not with him, I was not going to be with anybody else. That's what he said.

You think that was the reason that he …
Because he wasn't going to have his money machine.

No, but the original thing, where Nancy was clubbed on the knee, do you think that he planned that to further your career or to eventually make you look like you were the one who had *(planned it)* - to put you out or for him to earn money off you becoming National Champion? Do you know what I mean?
Right, I know exactly what you mean, and I have asked myself the same questions millions of times.

Okay – so you don't know?
I don't know if he was doing it to end my career – to make it look like I did it. And that way, I wasn't going to be with him – I wasn't going to be with anybody because nobody would want me after that, or he was doing it thinking, Okay, if I was to knock out her competition, she'll easily make it – no problem. Even though she is skating great, we'll take out some of the competition, so she doesn't have to worry about it. She'll go and skate great anyway. She'll make the team. She'll come home. She's so happy. We'll be back together, and we will all make the money.

We'll just say *(in the book that was intended to be the original autobiography)*, **I could not get inside that man's head to ever know what the reasoning was behind it?**
Yeah– it could have been both ways …

It could have been this way. It could have been that way. *(We could write it having you say)* **to this day, I don't know, and you know what? I don't care.**
Exactly! *(Said very emphatically)*. Because I don't care. I really don't care anymore.

All we are doing here is explaining. It is for all the people who have made their own assumptions.
Exactly – on what the media has said.

(We can say) **this is my story. This is what happened. I can't answer for him. I can't explain this. I can't explain that. I am telling you what I know, and what I knew, and that's it. Take it or leave it, but that's what it is.**
Right. Right.

You could probably remember how he *(Jeff)* **first told you or how you found out …**
I found out from a media friend of mine the day we were back, and my name was on the list, and I was like, Wait a second!

But then you probably confronted him and said, What the hell is going on here?
Yes. He went and met up with Shawn. I went with him. He comes out from

meeting with Shawn, and he says, "Shawn's involved. We have to get an attorney because he says that I did it."

Who is "I"?
Him *(Jeff)*. All along, he was saying he had nothing to do with it. You know, "I can't believe it. Shawn did this on his own. I can't believe it."

Well, why then would you be charged with hindering the prosecution?
Because I lied to them the first half hour I was in their meeting.

Saying … I don't know anything about it?
No. I told them the story he wanted me to tell them. But it was all bungled up, and it sounded like a big fucking lie. Sorry, my mouth gets really bad. Ahh.

We talked about publishing legalities, I said: We don't want to be sued. You can make some money on the book, and I can make some money on the book, but somebody could come along, and the next thing you know, we are all in court.
Right.

To prove stuff … you know?
Right. Well, everything I have said is the truth, and you know, if I had to find proof of him beating me up a couple of times in front of people – I have proof of that, and I think I can probably get it. I just have to get the people to talk.

I told her that as far as I knew, as long as we kept the story to what she had experienced and what was her opinion, we should be fine. She responded:
If I was to talk to these people and ask, "Listen, would you be willing to talk to her and just tell her – yes – that this is true, and I was there and I saw it." Then that is not hearsay. Then that would back my story, and people would understand it even more. Because one time Angela's parents came to pick me up at the house, and he *(Jeff)* tried to start a fight with her dad because they were taking me away from him.

As long as we are truthful as you and I can be, then we should have no problem. *I asked her again if she didn't mind me telling Michael Rosenberg the exact details about the rape. She responded:*
No. Because, personally, I think people need to know it. They need to know that I have been through so much shit, and that was the reason I didn't come forward.

You mentioned in an earlier interview that you "had to get yourself back in order to be able to talk to anyone else." What did you mean by that?
Because of what I went through during that time – you know what I am talking about *(the rape)* – there is no way that I could tell anybody what was going on.

You couldn't hardly think about it, let alone talk about it?
Well, when I considered suicide – you know, it is kind of hard to talk about those things, and, you know, I had dated Darren almost a year or a year and a half before I told him.

Was Jeff ever proven guilty of master-minding the plot to take out Nancy at the 1994 Nationals?
Well, he was proven guilty of racketeering.

I think most people assume he was behind it.
Him and that other guy. I would like to find out the truth, you know? I mean, to this day, I do not know the truth. I do not know the truth about all of this.

Maybe you're better not to go there mentally.
Well, I don't know. It's almost like there is that piece that has never been closed because I did not ever find out for a fact whether it was Jeff who betrayed me or Shawn or whoever. Who did this to me? You know – for sure? And still, to this day, I have no idea. And you're probably right. I shouldn't know anyway.

At some point in your life, when you are strong enough, and if there is the opportunity to find out, well, fine ...
Yes.

But until then ...
Let it go.

Let sleeping dogs lay, right?
Exactly.

Because they may get up and bite you. *(We laugh).*
It would just piss me off even more.

Okay, so you are training for Olympics and trying to keep your head together.
Yes. I had to train ... I don't even remember; I don't remember if I trained really late or not. I tried training a couple of times, and there was all this media. I couldn't get any training in – flashing of lights, you know, because *(of)* their photography and everything. I think I came in and tried to skate late at night a few times. I just don't even remember anymore.

Was your coach still supporting you?
Yeah. She was supporting me. She never believed that Jeff was ever like that. She always believed that I had hit my head on a cupboard or whatever. Who knows? And then after Jeff was arrested and said all these horrible things about me, one morning at the rink, she came up to me and pulled me aside and took me into a room and told me how sorry she was for not believing me. After all these years of me being with her she didn't believe me. And she apologized and said that she was sorry she didn't believe me and not to worry, everything is going to be fine, and just go out there and train.

How did you feel when you heard what he was saying about you, that you had been involved and you knew about it ...
That he was an asshole and he was just trying to bring me in because he didn't get off with whatever he was trying to do. I mean, he was the best manipulator there was. I mean, he could be *(Dr)*. Jekyll and *(Mr)*. Hyde. One minute he could be super nice, and the next minute he was just the most horrible person you would ever want to know. And he could manipulate anybody. I mean, he manipulated the police every time they went to arrest him for beating the shit out of me. He talked his way right out of it.

How did it feel when you heard that the United States Figure Skating Association didn't want you to go *(to Olympics)*?
I was really disappointed – really upset that I had worked so hard to get

where I was, and they were just going to take it away from me because of somebody else.

Did you ever think to try and get hold of Nancy when you heard what Jeff was saying – to tell her that you weren't involved? Didn't you want to scream at the top of your lungs, "Hey, this has nothing to do with me?"
I think I did *(scream)*. *(She laughs)*. I really don't even remember. I know that I was going to see her at the Olympics – and after all this shit had been out there and happened. When I saw her at the Olympics, I remember it was for a team photo shoot right after we had got there, and she was a little bit cold – non-receptive - towards me. But at least I got the chance to apologize to her for being involved with these people and to let her know I'm not involved with these people, and you know.

So, you did try and talk to her there?
I did try, but to no avail.

She was just kind of like ...
She was like, "Okay."

So she didn't believe you?
I have no idea.

How can you answer for her, right?
Um hm.

So then what? You just got on with ..
Like I always ... it hurt my feelings because we had been friends for so many years.

Who did you room with at the Olympics?
I think it was just me.

Did you stay at the Olympic Village?
Yes. I had my own dorm room. I think I did. I had my own dorm room, and then my father and Stephanie and her father and I think her husband, too, I can't remember if he was there, too— I think he was, and 'Inside Edition' had got a house and paid their way to be able to be there with me, so I got over to the house. I didn't get to go anywhere by myself. I was

always driven by, I don't know, kind of like security people or something, everywhere I went, and they took me over to the house to see everybody. But I always had to stay at the dorm.

How were the other skaters toward you – other than Nancy?
Well, I think they were okay. I mean, I couldn't tell you. I don't even remember. I mean, everybody seemed to be nice to me – Surya *(Bonaly, who came fourth at the 1994 Olympics)* and Oksana *(Baiul, Ukrainian and World Champion and Gold Medalist at the 1994 Olympics)* and all the other skaters, I'm pretty sure they were all pretty nice to me, you know. But ...

Do you want to talk about the Olympics now?
I got to go.

We discussed when the next interview would take place. Then I said, **All right. I hope I haven't upset you. I didn't mean to.**
Oh, no. It just really upsets me that it is so confusing to me.

That's fine. We'll say all that in the book, so don't worry about that. It's just I hate bringing up bad memories for you, but ...
We've gone and done it, and I don't have to do it no more.

That's right. That's exactly right. It's the last time you have to talk about it.
I mean, yeah, the people are going to be asking about it and shit like that when it comes out, and it's like, Hey, you know what? All this shit happened to me. You can believe it or not. I don't care. I'm putting it behind me. This is the closure of my past life, so I can start fresh and have a new life.

(10)

Making Television History –
Skating at the Olympics

"I wanted to go out and show everyone that I deserved to be there and that I was one of the best skaters in the entire world."

While I was transcribing the tapes, I realized that because of the circumstances surrounding Tonya during the interviews conducted in 2001, we had not fully covered the 1994 Olympic Games, and she agreed to provide me with the following interview in January, 2007. As in parts of the rest of the book, some of her earlier comments have been inserted for the sake of chronological order.

Previously, we had only discussed a small portion of the 1994 Olympics. What I would like to do now is go over your whole experience at those Olympics. I know it is probably a little difficult thinking back on all that now.
Oh, yeah. *(She laughs).*

What frame of mind where you in prior to leaving for the Olympics? Do you believe you were prepared, or had the media frenzy interfered with your mindset, your focus, your training?
The media definitely changed my mindset. It was totally involved, and training was very difficult. You know, having people flashing cameras in my face when I am trying to do my jumps, and it made it really, really hard.

Right, so even the practicing must have been ...
The practicing was probably the worst, besides everybody trying to follow me everywhere.

Do you believe that had an effect on the way that you skated at the Olympics?
I think it had a little bit of an effect because my frame of mind was off. The training was off prior. Once I got there, it took a couple of practices to get my mind going again and focusing. But I'm not going to blame anything on the media and all that. It was just a real difficult time.

You said that the other Olympic skaters treated you well, but were you feeling apprehensive at all, or did any of them make you feel unwelcome, or did anything at all like that go on?
No. Un uh. I mean, everybody treated me pretty well. I stayed to myself and tried to focus on me – trying to keep myself in line.

At that time, were you worried about what was going to happen when you got back *(home)*, or were you just focusing on …
Well, everything, you know, was just turmoil, so I was probably thinking about what was going on back home – what was going to happen – but I really wanted to just focus on my skating, and you know, yeah, I make the mistake in the short program on the combination with the turn in between, but it was a nice skate. And then for the long program, with the lace breaking and stuff – I mean, I had come down out of the last jump I did – the triple Axel – and sliced it when I came out, and didn't know it until … I always tighten my skates up, just to make sure everything felt good, just before I went out, and when I had tried to do that, that was when it broke. And trying to put it back together, and knowing that I only had so much time to do this – it was just – at that point, I completely lost my focus. So, when I stepped on the ice *(for the long program)*, knowing that lace was not going to hold me, it was like all … everything I had just gone through and all the hard work that I had put in to make it one more time was gone.

Just before we do that *(talk about the competition)*, did you get there pretty close to your performances, or did you …
I don't even remember. I know it was a couple of days before.

Did you practise at all with Nancy, or did you watch any of her practices?
We were on the same ice a couple of different times, but I am concentrating on me. I am not concentrating on her or anyone else. The only thing you really had to watch was making sure that you don't run into somebody or things like that because everybody skates differently.

Who did you feel at that competition – at that Olympics, was your biggest competitor?
Wow, I don't even remember. I have no idea. *(She laughs).*

You weren't thinking – Oksana Baiul at the time?
No. No. I watched her a lot of times because she was such a graceful skater. It was amazing how graceful she was. She was like a little ballerina, yet she could still do the jumps.

You competed the short – the technical program – on February 23rd at the Northern Lights Hall in Hamer. Did you have any idea that tickets were being sold outside the arena for $2,000.00 a piece? That was ten times what it was worth. Did you have any idea of how much the world was focused on seeing you and Nancy on the ice together?
Well, I figured it would be one of the most watched things just because of all the controversy going on, but I think that is pretty cool that that many people wanted to see how well I and Nancy and everyone else would do.

You don't think they were tuning in to watch and see if there would be any conflict?
Yeah, I'm sure they probably did. *(She laughs).*

And then what happened, from what I understand, a lot of people who may not have been interested in the sport before became interested after that.
Exactly, and that was because of the controversy.

Take me through that first performance – the technical program. I think you placed tenth after that. That would leave you out of the medal contention.
Well, it also depends on how everybody else does. I've always said that it's not against the other skaters, basically, it's against yourself because you have to go out, and you have to perform the best you possibly can, and it's up to the judges where they put you. I started the program, did the triple Lutz double toe combination, and I did a turn in between the triple and the double. And then I had done the other double and the footwork and everything, and then the double Axel. I mean, I was happy with my performance, but I knew with that turn in between, there would be deductions.

Do you think that nerves played a part in that?
Probably a little bit. Skating to me is basically a luck sport as well. It's all about your mind and everything else because everything plays a role in it. You can be perfect for a whole month doing everything exactly perfect every

time, and then you can step out on the ice and nerves – your boot just does-n't feel right, your dress might be going up your rear, the beads are scratch-ing you, or it doesn't feel good, or you just don't like the feel of the ice. It's slippery, it's slow, it's hard. I mean, you just never know.

So, even if the media (frenzy) hadn't happened, all those other things come into play anyway?
Yeah.

So you have that, plus everything ...
Everything plays a role.

Nancy placed first at the end of that technical (program), and cameras showed you applauding her performance. What where you really feel-ing inside, though? It was polite of you to applaud, but ...
Well, I mean, she deserved it. She went out, and she did it.

So that whole thing of the media trying to make you look like rivals or whatever ...
You know, I just don't understand why they have to ... why the media always has to say 'rivals.' We're all competitors. Not just me and Nancy – every single skater is competing against each other to go out and show the best performance that you can. I mean, it is not a Tonya and Nancy com-petition.

But I guess because of what happened prior to ...
Exactly.

That's what it was played up as. All right ... the days between the tech-nical and the free program, what did you do? Do you remember now, or is it too far back?
I remember doing the practices. Oh my gosh – just hanging out, doing almost nothing, I guess. That's all. I don't really remember. I remember I did a couple of fittings on my costumes.

Pretty much focusing on your skating?
Yeah, I think that was just about it.

You didn't know then that you were out of medal contention? What I wanted to ask was, did you feel that it was all over and if you wanted to leave, or did you just decide to go out and do your best for the final performance?

I wanted to show the world that I deserved to be there.

Even though you ... deep down, did you think that you could place in the top three?

I didn't think that the judges were going to give it to me even if I could have.

Really? Did you feel that way before you went in?

Even if I had gone out and done a perfect, perfect program, and everybody else made a whole bunch of mistakes in front of me – I mean, there is always that possibility. Every person in front of me falling a couple of times and me doing an absolute perfect program with a triple Axel – there is always that possibility that I could have placed third, but I didn't really think, after the short, coming in tenth, that I was going to be able to medal at all. But I wanted to go out and show everyone that I deserved to be there and that I was one of the best skaters in the entire world.

I don't remember the actual performance. Did you do a triple Axel?

Ah ... *(She laughs).*

What?

I don't remember. I think I did it and fell out of it, or fell, or I popped it. I don't remember.

So, you didn't feel that way before you went into the Olympics, but after the technical program, you felt the judges were not going to ...

Well, I felt – I felt that way probably even before I went. But if you go out and do perfect, then if you didn't get the marks, then there would be – you know, when they pre-judge you, type of thing.

So, your intention of going there then may not have been ...

Was to prove that I deserved to be there – that I was one of the best, and I was going to show the world that I was one of the best.

February 25th was the day of the long program. You were eighth – getting ready to skate – in the lineup. Take me through the beginning of the program that ended with the broken skate lace.
Well, I had went to tighten up my laces, and it broke. So I tried to tie it back – couldn't.

Prior to going on the ice, the lace had broken?
Right – after the warm-up. And then they gave me so many minutes to get out there, and we knew that it was not going to hold, but that I had to go out there and at least try. But I knew that there was just no way. I mean, I had several holes undone – only a couple of eyelets done *(tied)*. It was so sloppy that if I had even tried – I mean, I thought, well, at least I have to go out and try, but I knew that once I *(unintelligible)* on that Lutz, I could break my ankle or something.

Didn't you have time to change the lace?
Afterwards.

No – you broke it during the warm-up, and you were eighth out to skate. Wouldn't you have time to change the lace?
No, because I was in the second warm-up. I think there was only one person, or two people, before I had to go out after the warm-up.

So being eighth in the lineup doesn't mean ...
Right. There wasn't eight of us on the ice – or four of us out on the ice. I can't remember. I think there was six of us on the ice at each time.

And so you were second going out?
I think I was second or third – something like that.

But you didn't have time to change it?
No. And so then they gave me time to get a lace.

You were crying – I remember that distinctly.
Oh, yeah.

You put your foot up *(on the board)* to show them *(the judges)*.
Right. Right.

Where you really upset?
I knew that I had lost my chance. But trying to get another lace to fit –
when we got one, it turned out – it was like 20 inches too short. But in the
midst of all of this, the judges had announced that they were going to allow
me to fix the lace – to get a lace that fit – and then put me last.

Isn't that something your coach would bring along – extra laces?
Well, you would think so. We forgot. *(She laughs).*

**After the performance, apparently when you were asked about the bro-
ken lace, you told reporters that maybe somebody didn't want you to
skate. What did you mean by that comment?**
God, probably. I don't know. I don't even remember what I said.

You didn't mean a rival or somebody …
I have no clue what I would even be thinking at that point in time.

**Did it go through your head that maybe somebody tampered with your
laces?**
You never know.

Are you thinking another skater or …
You just never know. I don't even remember saying that to reporters. I have
no idea.

Looking back now, do you think somebody tampered with that lace?
I doubt it.

You just think it was something that happened coincidentally?
Where it was sliced, I had a big, huge slice across the toe of my boot.

Which means?
I came out of the jump and sliced it. And that had happened lots of times.

On your warm-up?
Yes.

That's true *(that it had happened many times)*. People thought …
Look – let me say this. People have said I have had so many problems with

either laces or a blade or whatever. I have known other people that have sliced laces or broke laces or broke a blade at practice or whatever. People have to remember that when I went to these training camps and they did all these things – you know, bio-mechanic stuff – I was coming down on one foot with 400 and some odd pounds of pressure – on just one foot. And then I am jumping with my feet up in the air, over three feet high. You know, things happen. Things are not, you know, non-breakable.

There were a couple of incidents. For example, at the '93 Nationals, your dress strap broke, and, again in '93 at Skate America, one of your skate blades came loose. So, these are all just coincidences then?
Yep. It happens. Like I said to ... you have a blade that is hooked to a bottom of a boot that is made out of wood with screws, and with that much poundage of pressure coming down on a jump – you know, if you are off and you come down, you know, wrong, anything can pull a blade loose. I mean, I checked my blades every single week. I was always making sure they were tight. I sliced laces in practice quite a few times because my feet were so tight in the air. I jumped so high and so tight that when I came down – if you're not exactly right, things are going to happen.

After you got the lace repaired, you were going to skate last. What did you do while you were waiting? Didn't that make you really nervous? Were you watching the other skaters or ...
No, no. I never watch the other skaters. You concentrate on yourself. Let's see – just kept trying to keep warm, keeping my body in check – jump around, things like that, trying to keep yourself warm, trying to keep ready, focused. Going through the program in your head. Going through the jumps in your head – all that kind of stuff. But, it is very, very hard. When you look at it, okay – in between that, I just blew it, you know? It was very hard just trying to keep focused. But just keep thinking to yourself, I deserve to be here. I want to show everybody what I can do.

Now on your long program, you completed four triple jumps, and you ultimately placed eighth. Were you satisfied with that performance?
Yup, I was actually satisfied with my performance. I went out there and did the best that I could, and that is all that anybody could expect me to do. And another thing is, too – I don't really care what other people think. If I'm happy with my performance, then that is all that matters.

And actually it wasn't a bad skate.
No.

If you had placed higher in the technical program, who knows?
Who knows?

How did people treat you after the Olympics? Did you go home immediately, or did you stay for the Closing Ceremony?
Ah, I don't even remember. I know I didn't get to go to the Closing Ceremony.

You probably headed right home?
Probably.

How did you feel on that plane ride home? Were you glad that it was over? Were you disappointed? Did you feel like you had failed? How did you feel?
I don't know. I have no idea.

You mean you don't remember or ...
I don't remember.

Or was your mind such that ...
I just don't remember.

Were you worried about going home?
I don't know. I knew that when I was at home, everything was going to snowball into whatever was going to happen.

When you got home, did those legal wheels start turning right away?
I don't remember. I don't remember the days, the dates of what happened here or there. I don't remember at all. I just know it came down to me getting charged with hindering the prosecution.

How did you feel when they took your medal away – I mean, your title (National) – in '94. That must have been devastating.
It hurt me. It still hurts me to this day because other skaters have done horrible things and didn't lose their title and are still skating to this day – didn't get reprimanded by nobody.

Who? What do you mean?
Other skaters – oh God – Nicole *(she said the last name of the skater)*.

You mean when she *(allegedly)* broke into that house?
She broke into another skater's house, ruined her skates, her costumes, and stole money.

And nothing happened to her?
Nothing happened to her, and she got to keep her title.

And she was a U.S. Champion.
Yes, and they didn't do a damn thing to her because she had money and because it was the first time she had ever been in trouble. Well, what about me? I had never been in trouble with the law before.

How did you hear that your National title was taken away?
My lawyer.

What did you do – cry?
Yeah, and I said it wasn't fair, but at least I know in my heart that I won and that I earned it. I went out there – I was the one who had to step on that ice and pull my shit together, and I'm the one who had to do that.

Did it bother you after the Olympics that Nancy was given so many accolades – riding on floats in Disneyland – while you're attempting to defend yourself and really having your life fall apart?
Well, that's what life is all about. She deserved what she got. She went out and skated great, and I thought that was really cool. And, yeah, I was disappointed that, you know, I lost everything, but that's just life. You just got to pick yourself up and try to keep going.

No bitterness?
No. Un uh.

Not toward Nancy then – no bitterness towards her, but bitterness about what happened to you?
Yes – just disappointed that everything fell apart. Looking at it now that I am older and wiser – that what an idiot I was for listening to other people and just, you know, all those years of hard work – gone. And then thinking

to yourself, Okay, if I haven't got my skating any more, now what am I going to do? I didn't have a college education. My skating was my whole, entire life. And I had planned, after the Olympics, of being able to continue skating and do ice shows and, you know, pro competitions and things. I mean, that was my goal.

You said at the beginning of the statement that you just made that you wished you hadn't listened to other people. What people?
People from the Association that got involved prior to the Olympics, telling me what I should and should not do.

You're referring to staying with Jeff or going back with Jeff?
Yes, yes, because that is totally not fair. People should stay out of people's personal lives and judge the person on their skating ability – not what they wear, not how they talk, not how they act. I mean, if somebody – I consider myself a hick girl, you know, because I like the big rigs and the hunting and the fishing and all the outdoor stuff. I don't go shopping all the time and go get my nails done all the time. I just throw on my *(unintelligible – probably means jeans)* and my boots and my t-shirt or sweatshirt and go, and I really don't care what other people think of my … of how I dress. That's how I was treated. I was told to do one thing, and if I didn't do it, I probably wouldn't make it.

And you were so fearful of these people – this Association …
Yup.

The United States Figure Skating Association?
Yup.

That they could ultimately take away …
Take away everything just because I didn't want to listen.

When Nancy was on the float in Disneyland – I don't know if you remember this – the microphone picked up her using some colorful language saying that she didn't want to be there. Do you remember that?
I remember that.

A lot of people were offended.
I was offended. Come on. If I got to ride on a float with Mickey Mouse, that would be – Oh, yeah! This is like the coolest thing. And for her to make comments like she did, I was just like, I just can't believe she would say something like that.

So, you can understand why people were offended by that?
Oh, yeah, I can understand. It was like I said, I would be so thrilled to just have that opportunity to ride with Mickey Mouse or any of them. It could have been Tigger. It could have been anybody – I would love to be there.

Just to be in the parade?
Yeah– just to be part of it. So, I thought it was kind of rude.

Now she went on to fame and success in professional skating. Your career pretty much came to a standstill. You are banned from amateur competition. You're stripped of your National title. You are unofficially banned from professional shows and competitions. How did you get through that emotionally, especially knowing that the whole surge in the popularity of figure skating came about as a direct result of your alleged involvement with the attack on Nancy? Do you understand what I mean?
Yeah. It was devastating. I mean, there was lots of times that I didn't leave the house for long periods of time. Linda and Greg Lewis have been a very big part of my life, and she was there every single day for me. I mean, she never had children, and they basically, to this day, have adopted me as their daughter. They think of me as their daughter – unconditional love, no matter what has happened in my life. From that day until now, they have always been there. If I make a mistake, they help me pick myself back up and keep going.

But didn't that at times make you want to ...
Hate myself.

Sorry?
I hated myself. I have come to realize over the years that no matter what mistakes you make, you are always going to make mistakes; you just hope you get on the right path. And then if you make a mistake, hopefully it's not going to be too bad that you can't recover from it. I mean, I have made some pretty stupid mistakes in my life, but I look at it as – not as an excuse

or anything, but I always look at it like I really wish I had a better upbringing – not money and stuff like that, but guidance – guidance on life and things. You know, how to choose which direction you are going to go and not be so naïve with people. I always wanted ... I mean, I never had friends hardly at all growing up – moving around so much. I was always looking for approval. I always wanted to try and make everybody happy – wanted to have friends, you know? And when I had money, of course, I had friends. When you don't have money, the people that are not your real friends, they are not there. They don't care. They just want to be there – yeah, she's my friend, I like her, but I'm going to go the other way now. Looking back, I have made some very good choices in my life, too, with people, since that time – learning and, you know, not trusting people and really starting how to learn how to read people. And now I know these days, right now, who my real friends are. And like I said, Linda and Greg have been there for me, and they will probably be for the rest of my life.

Do you believe, Tonya, that if you had won the Olympics, or if at least you earned a Bronze or Silver medal, do you think you would have been treated the same way when you got home? Do you believe you would have been stripped of your National title and the Olympic medal and been banned from skating, or do you think you would have been allowed to keep skating?
I really don't know how to answer that. I mean, that is not up to me. I mean, I would hope that, ah ...

But looking at it objectively, if you had brought home that Gold medal or one of those medals, do you think they would have treated you the same way?
I don't know. I really don't know. It's really hard to say. You can look at it from two different ways. Well, yes, they would have let me continue skating because I am one of the Olympic medalists and then I went and proved myself – not being involved in that *(the scandal)*. But, yes, I got *(charged with)* hindering the prosecution, but what a lot of people don't understand – there are a lot of people out there who think I did this.

Yes. It is almost like the myth that goes around now *(as if she had actually been the one to club Nancy on the knee).*
Exactly. But I would have probably still got hindering the prosecution because I did that, but I may have been able to continue skating. They may have said, I can't compete amateur anymore, but they would have ... I

would have been able to do the pro skating shows, the pro competitions, and things like that. I don't really know. I was judged by what the media was saying, by not only the judges, but everyone – all the people as well. It is just – even today, it is really hard for me to talk about it and look back on it. I mean, you can't change the past. You will always remember it, but you try to move on and make something better of your life.

Okay, I think that is good for the Olympics.
I was going to say one more thing. Even after the Olympics and after all this stuff had happened to me, I believe I have been treated totally different than how they have treated other people. A girl who won after me – it was like a year or two later – had gotten in trouble ...

Who? Nicole *(I mentioned the last name of the skater)*?
Yes – who had gotten in trouble, but she got to keep her medal. She continues to skate – I don't know now, but she continued to skate. She was allowed to do everything that she wanted to do. Why wasn't she not allowed *(to participate in shows, etc)*. when she was the one who actually did it?

It is interesting. That particular Olympics, the girl who won the – I believe she brought home four or five gold medals for Canada in the triathlon, you know, the shooting and the ...
Yeah, right.

She has just now been arrested in the United States for allegedly taking her daughter there when she wasn't supposed to. One of the figure skaters, a male figure skater, who won a Bronze medal at those Olympics, has now been banned from coaching in Canada for a year for things he has been doing.
Um hm, and look at Oksana Baiul.

Oksana Baiul was arrested, was she not, for drunk driving?
Right, drunk driving, and she almost killed somebody.

These *(athletes)* **were all from the 1994 Olympics.**
Yeah. All these people got to continue skating and made millions or whatever. They still have respect. They still get to step out onto the ice and get respect.

And you don't?
No.

(11)

After the Olympics

*"I was flat broke. I had nothing. I had already lost my career.
I mean, what was I supposed to do?"*

*I had called Tonya the previous day for a scheduled interview. When we
spoke, she told me she wasn't feeling well, and she sounded despondent
about several matters. We rescheduled the interview for the following
day. When I called her the next evening at the arranged time, she began
talking immediately, relating a story of what had just happened to her.
I asked Tonya to wait until I turned on the tape recorder where she then
picked up where she had left off.*

... she *(referring to a woman whose life she saved a few years previous)* was in
the bar, and she was playing video poker, and I went in the back room to
play video poker with Mom *(Linda Lewis)*. She *(the woman)* fell off the
stool, and she collapsed on the floor, and I gave her CPR.

And tonight ... what happened?
Tonight I went to a restaurant with my friends ... a man came over and
asked me if I was Tonya Harding, and I said, "Well, yes I am." And he said,
"Well, I own this bar – this restaurant, bar, and I wanted to thank you for
saving my mom's life. And I said, "Your mom must have been the lady that
was in the *(unintelligible)* where Mom and I *(unintelligible)*. He said, "Yes,
and I wanted to thank you." I asked him, "How is she doing?" Because I
had tried to contact her – that was two years back, to find out anything –
how she was doing, and no one would give me the information. And I guess
she ended up passing away a couple of years ago. When Darren worked at
this place *(unintelligible)*, the guard that walked around was, I guess, her
brother. And I mean, totally small world, small world. And I had talked to
him, and at that point in time, she was still alive.

Right, and tonight he was telling you that she passed away?
Yeah.

When did this happen originally?
I think it was in '96 or the beginning of '97 because it was before I had sold
my house, and I sold my house in March of '97.

What a coincidence, seeing him tonight.
Yeah. It was really cool, you know? *(He)* invited us back, so we could come in on the weekend, and said that if we called ahead of time, he would save us a table.

Oh, nice.
Very, very nice man – yeah.

Had you met him before?
No.

So, all this time, he probably knew who you were and didn't know how to get in touch with you to thank you.
Uh huh.

Isn't that amazing?
It is – very amazing. It's a small world. I mean, all this time, you run into people and they are connected with somebody else that you know.

You are sounding much better today.
I am feeling much better today. Mom and I prayed together, and we had a small bible study between her and me and my friends, John and Mike, my mechanics, because they had to come over to fix Mom's car today because it died on her this morning, and I had to save her. And so, I jumped the car and brought it down here, and they came over to fix it, and we ended up having a small bible study. And right before they got here, Mom and I prayed, and that both of us – saying, "God, please take these bad toxins out of our body. Make us be able to breathe better, feel better, and stop the devil from trying to come in and ruin things that are going on. Make everything better. Take care of us. Take all of the weight off of our shoulders and take care of this for us because it is getting to be too much at this point in time." And I swear that within ten minutes, I could breath, and within 15 minutes, Mom's nose was cleared up, and she was feeling better. I swear to God on everything Holy. I could not believe it.

And mentally you sound relieved – or lifted.
I just *(sounding in awe)* – I have no idea because last night I was just …

I was worried about you last night.
Well, I can promise you I would never do anything bad, you know? Because

I know that God has something in mind for me. I was just so tired of all the bullshit and feeling like the devil just pulling me down, down, down. For something ... today, when we prayed, it was just – I don't know, I feel better.

So it's working already?
Definitely – I couldn't believe it. Last night, I was able to breathe. I got a pretty good night's sleep. And this morning, I got up, and it was a little stuffy after I blew my nose, and then after her and I prayed – she got here and when I saw her, she was still stuffy and felt like crap, but felt better when she was out in the fresh air. And then when she got here, and we were talking and when we prayed, and then it was just, I don't know, I don't know. God is listening to things. God said He will never give us anything – give us too much that we can't handle. I don't know.

He will never give us more than we can handle.
Exactly, and all of a sudden I felt this big weight ...

It's all for lessons to be learned. I believe you are going to use it at some time in your life – these lessons or whatever it is we go through.
Definitely, so I feel like, spiritually, He has taken care of me. He has let me know that everything will be okay.

Oh, I'm glad. I'm really glad because you sound so much better.
I feel much better. I mean, it was just whoa! *(She laughs)*. It was just one of those days that you feel you want to ...

You just move on to the next phase.
Yeah, like you want to give up on everything, but then you put your faith in God and say, Hey, this is getting to the point where it is just too much for me to handle. Please help me.

I told her a story about someone I knew who thought he had wanted something, but it didn't happen, and how I believed that everything happens the way it is supposed to and how life unfolds the way it is supposed to. She responded:
Exactly. Exactly. I mean, I believe that. It's like offers that come in. We have them – done deals, and then something happens where I don't do it after all.

It gets frustrating?
But then you look at it, and it's like, there must have been something wrong with it or it couldn't have been good for me because if it had been good for me, it would have gone through.

I told her that I told my friend he would probably be grateful in time about his disappointment because most likely something much better would take its place that wouldn't have happened otherwise. She responded:
Exactly, and the way I look at it, too – Mom and I were talking – for everything to be hitting us so hard and everything around us to be so bad, there must be something really good coming up.

Tonya asked for me to hold on while she let her dog in the house. When she came back to the phone, I asked: **Is he okay? I was worried about him, too, last night because you were saying he wasn't getting enough to eat. Is he okay?**
Yeah. He's eating fine today. He's eaten five times.

How do you spell his name?
Koda, but when I talk to people, I tell them his name is Dakoda because he won't respond to it except from me.

You've had him awhile now?
He turns three November 20th.

And he's your real baby?
Oh, yeah. He's my protector, though.

What kind of dog is he?
An English Mastiff.

I've seen pictures of him. He is such a beautiful dog.
He is. He's like a baby, though.

Is his color gray?
No, his color is like my hair – blondie color with a black mask. *(She talked about seeing a movie with a dog in it that looks like Koda).* When we were talking about getting a puppy, we were talking about getting a Hooch – 'Turner and Hooch' *(as in the movie),* and we were told that was a Mastiff,

and so when I saw Mastiff in the paper, I went and looked at it, and of course it was a puppy, and you know, I can't turn down this one. So we got him, and it turned out he was an English Mastiff, and the 'Turner and Hooch' dog was a French Bordeaux. But I am so glad we have him – I have him – because he is my protector.

How much did he weigh when you first got him?
Oh jeez, I don't know. He was under 20 pounds.

And what is he now?
Two fifteen. I have a table, my front room table, and the bottom of the table is probably, I don't know, is 10 inches tall. He used to sleep under the table when we first got him, and now it is just funny because he stands up to my waist. His back is to my hip bone, and his head is up in my boobies. *(She laughs)*. When he stands up, completely straight without hunching or anything, when his paws are on somebody's shoulders, he's up at 6'6" or 6'7."

Is he really gentle with you?
Oh, yeah. He can get rough when he gets playing because he is so big. He can knock me down.

But he never bites you?
He doesn't bite people. He doesn't like it if people stare at him, but what dog does? But he's never bit anybody. He's nosed two people when they were staring at him face to face, but he's never bit anybody. He thinks he's a Chihuahua. I mean, he took over my bed. He took over the couch, the loveseat, and everything else. And when I'm gone – if I'm gone for any length of time – a series of days – I'll leave him in the back room, or I'll leave him in the house if I'm only going to be gone for a couple of hours – he thrashes things – like the towels. If I have a pile of towels in the back-room, getting ready to do laundry, he'll spread them out all over the place and make his little bed. And if I don't put a chair in front of my bedroom door and close the door, he'll be up on my bed. And I can have my bed perfectly made, and he'll literally pull the covers back and lay down under the covers with his head on the pillow. Literally, he will pull them back so he can sleep on my pillow.

Tonya told me about some favorite pictures she had of the dog, and we then discussed photographs for the book. She was worried because she didn't have any baby pictures, but had a few of her childhood and early skating years. She knew her father had a picture of the two of them, and she was hoping to obtain it for the book. She then said:

I've actually been getting closer to my father again. I mean, even though the respect level still isn't there because of everything he has done.

I know, but he is still your dad.

I love him, and he comes in and he sees me, and you know, he's my dad, and he's not going to be around forever, and you know, I do enjoy his company. Sometimes he can be, you know, that stubborn old man.

We continued to discuss photographs and where we could obtain them. I then turned her attention to the current interview, which was to cover what happened after she got home from the Olympics.

It's so blurry to me about a lot of the things.

Try to remember as best you can, and don't worry if it's in the right order.

Let's see, well, I went through the court thing and all that. I got sentenced 500 hundred community hours – community service hours, and I ended up working at *(unintelligible)* senior's center – cooking meals, being able to feed the people, and all that, and I really enjoyed that. It really helped me to see a part of the world basically that I had not even known existed. Being able to give these people, these elderly people that come in, and also for meals on wheels, where you take it to the people at their home – this was their one meal that they got a day. And I had no idea, and for me to be able to feed people – first of all cook it, and then serve it to them and be able to put a smile on their face, was, I don't know, it was just very ...

It was okay *(for you)* that you were doing this then?

Yeah.

It wasn't like punishment?

I didn't mind doing it. I didn't mind doing it at all.

Where you charged any money?

Oh, yes. I got charged a $100,000.00 fine, a $10,000.00 fine, and then I had offered to do a skating show or something like that to raise money for the Special Olympics. Well, I never got to do any kind of skating show, but I still had to pay that $50,000.00. I gave $25,000.00 up front first and then …

Who did you have to pay that to?
I have no idea.

The government – is that how …?
I don't know how it went.

But it wasn't to the skating association was it?
No. No. The money went to pay my lawyer, and then it went to the Special Olympics.

How did you feel when you knew for sure that you were going to be banned from sanctioned competition?
I didn't care. I gave it up. I told them I'm willing to give up my amateur status, and then after I gave up my amateur status, then they banned me afterwards. But anyway, I gave $25,000.00 to them *(Special Olympics)* first, and I worked for them for a week at their warehouse and ended up not being able to continue doing that because the diesel exhaust around there was so bad, and it was so dusty in there that I was getting migraines immediately.

Which warehouse was this?
It was for the Special Olympics.

Was that part of the community service?
No.

You were just going to do that *(on your own accord)*?
Yeah. But then I never got a thank you. I never got anything from them. Nothing. It was just like, okay, give us our money and see you around. Well, when I didn't feel like I had got anything back from them – when I had worked at *(unintelligible, but most likely the senior's center)* and realized how, you know, they needed new pots and pans, they needed to be helped to pay for food, and all this stuff for these people, and so I wanted to donate the other $25,000.00 to the senior's center. And I had to go into court, and they *(the Special Olympics)* were like, "Oh, well, we've already planned on this money," and da-da-da-da-da, and so the judge made me give the money to them anyway – made me give the $25,000.00 to them.

Where did that $25,000.00 come from?
Money that I earned and things like that.

So, that was part of the deal, then, to pay out …?
Yes.

From the $100,000.00 (fine)?
No. I got a $100,000.00 fine, and then I got a $10,000.00 fine, and then I offered to do a skating thing to raise money for the Special Olympics for $50,000.00. But when I didn't get to do any fundraising to do this, it came out of whatever monies I had made. But I never saw a dime of any of the money that my name made in '94. Not a dime, and to this day I am still paying off on taxes from that money that went into a trust account with my lawyers' names on it.

What money were you earning in '94?
Well, it was like from the interviews and things like that. All that money went into a trust account, and then it paid my lawyers, and it paid everything else, too.

I guess your legal bills were high, too?
Oh, yeah. I mean, I easily spent – my name made this money basically – I easily spent, with the fines and everything else, over a million dollars.

Legal (bills) as well?
That was including that, yes. I had to pay the taxes on it.

How could you have spent a million?
Well, because, supposedly, it came out to like $900,000 and some odd thousands of dollars for my attorneys to prove that I was not involved in that (the attack on Nancy). If you really think about it, my name made about $940,000.00 in the beginning of '94. I never saw a dime of it. It went all to the lawyers. But I said all along that money isn't the issue, and if it took $940,000.00 to prove that I wasn't involved in that, then, hey, that's what it took.

Where would you get (the figure of) $940,000.00? What do you mean? I don't understand.
My name made it. I did interviews, and people paid big money for those interviews, and it all went into a trust account at my lawyer's office with my

name on it. And I could never access that. I could never get any of that. It went all to them. $940,000.00 went all to the lawyers.

They said that was their fees?
Oh, yeah. They went through all of it. I had to hire private investigators to go to try and find these people that were lying.

About?
Well, there was a man who was working supposedly at the hotel at Nationals and said that I came up and asked him for Nancy's room number. And that was not true. I went up to the front counter and asked the man if *(she gave me the name of a reporter)* had checked in yet. And she was in charge *(worked for)* of 'Blades' magazine. She wrote for them and stuff. And that's who I asked for, and I asked if she checked in yet. I had to hire a private investigator to go find this person who worked at the hotel and finally got him to confess that that wasn't true – that I never did that. And that cost me almost $20,000.00 to send the private investigator back east. And I'm still paying today. I'm still paying the taxes on the money that I never saw. I had to sell my house to pay the taxes on the money that I never saw. And I'm still paying it. I still owe about 40 grand because all along it's just like penalties add up and add up and add up. And I end up – sold my house, and $98,000.00 of that went to the Federal.

Income tax?
Yeah. And I think it was $25,000.00 or something like that – no the $25,000.00 never got paid – that's right. And I paid off my home loan, and that left it even.

So, a $100,000.00 fine ...
Yup.

$50,000.00 for the ...
Fine – for the Special Olympics.

And $900,000.00 for legal fees?
Basically, yeah, and $10,000.00 for the State.

$900,000.00 for lawyers?
Supposedly, yes. I never saw a dime of that money – never – not one dime of it. It went into a trust account.

Wait a minute; I may be mixed up – you mean you earned $900,000.00?
Yes, my name did.

Your name earned $900,000.00. How much do you figure your legal fees were, though?
Well, that's what they said it was.

So what you are saying is that you earned $900,000.00 in appearance fees, interviews, ...
Right, during all that time.

It went into a trust fund ...
Yes.

And the lawyers claimed it, saying that's what our ...
With their name on it. It was at Bank of America – was their offices; it was the same building. They opened a trust account with their name, attached with my name on it, and they took – the money was all gone. I didn't see a dime of it. Yet, I had to sell my house. I lost everything because I had to pay the taxes on it, and to this day I am still paying taxes on money I never even saw.

Money that you supposedly earned and you never saw and the lawyers said it was their money because that was their legal fees?
Because they proved I was not involved in the Nancy Kerrigan attack, that the only thing I did was hindering prosecution.

Did you actually get a bill from them saying $900,000.00 legal charges?
There were so many papers, so much crap, that I can't even tell you how it all came down. I have no idea.

You had to sell your house. You had been in that house how long?
Three years.

It was a nice house?
Yeah.

Where did you go when you sold the house?
I lived with a friend and with another friend, and then I lived over at Mom's *(Linda Lewis)* house, and then I finally got into a place of my own, and then …

Let's go back to '94. So, you have done all your community work …
Well, it took me a year to do my community service and all the other stuff and everything. But at each place I worked at, though, I got raving reviews, and I made a difference in people's lives, and that's what was important to me. And I learned so much; it was fine for me to do that.

Did you miss skating?
Yes and no. It was really hard. It was like *(I couldn't)* go into the rink – go anywhere without somebody saying something nasty about me.

Would they say it to your face?
Oh, yeah.

So it was the other people bothering you more than missing skating?
Right.

What kinds of things would they say?
Oh, you name it, you name it. "Oh, my knee – why don't you take … and break my leg with one, and we'll see what happens." I mean, it goes – ugh, anything you can think of that had anything to do with knee bashing or anything like that – you name it, I got it. And so I really put myself in a little shell and didn't really do much. Then, finally, Easter Sunday of '95 is when I became a reborn Christian.

And how did that happen?
Well – Linda and Greg – we went to church, and they gave me my cross, and we had the pastor pray over me, and basically *(it was)* like a christening almost, and *(the pastor)* introduced them as my godparents. And so from that point on, they were my godparents. I became God's child, and now they have been the best people in my life – my whole entire life.

You hadn't been particularly religious before you met them?
Well, I believed in God.

But you hadn't been to church a lot?
No. I didn't realize – about the right things and the wrong things, you know. I mean, in '91, I believed in horoscopes and all that stuff. I thought, you know, my horoscope would say, you're going to do good and this and that and other things, and I realized later on – I mean, I have my bible sitting here right now on my table, you know, and I read it, and I realize that horoscopes and psychics and things like that are mediums. People who tell the future – it's not true. You know, that is out of the pit of hell. *(She laughs)*. And I learned really a lot.

What religion is it – reborn Christian?
I am a Christian, yes.

A born again Christian? So you believe this has been a strong foundation in your life – getting you through the hard times?
Yes, I do. I have seen things that make me 100 percent believe. I pray every single morning. I pray every single night when I put my head down. I pray every day when I'm driving around.

So you don't necessarily go to church on Sundays, but you pray on your own?
I go every once in awhile. When I find a good church, then I do go. All of us were going to go last weekend, last Sunday, to the church right across from John's place, but we have not been getting up early enough to go. *(She laughs)*.

We talked about praying on your own, and she responded:
That's right. When we talked today, it was almost like a small bible study. We have decided that we are going to do bible studies once a week on Thursdays. And it is good for me.

It is a positive thing.
It's a positive thing, and its cleansing, and you learn things. One of my favorite sayings is, "No weapon formed against me will ever prosper, and every tongue that rises up against me will be consumed." That is my favorite one of all of them because there is always somebody's tongue that rises up against me, but I don't ever have to worry about saying anything or doing anything because I know that He'll take care of it.

Okay, so back in '94, you had met them *(Linda and Greg)*, **but you weren't that close to them** *(at that time)*. **When did you meet your second husband?**
I met him through friends.

In what year?
The beginning of '95. We saw each other on weekends with all our friends for awhile and then because I had been seeing that guy Doug for awhile.

Which guy was that?
Doug was my boyfriend for a year and a half after Jeff. Jeff was my first; Doug was my second.

Were you serious?
Linda – my other friend, Linda – it was her son.

Was it a serious relationship?
Well, yeah; we ended up being together for a year and a half.

What did he do?
He was the assistant manager in the warehouse of *(she gave me the name of a department store)*.

What split you up?
We just went two different ways.

Did you actually live together?
Yes.

In your house?
Yup.

The split-up wasn't violent or upsetting?
No.

It was just drifting apart?
Yeah. Anyway, Michael *(her second husband)* and I were just seeing each other basically as friends for awhile, and then we started dating, and then we ended up getting engaged, and then we ended up getting married. And

everything was great before, but then right after we were married – a couple of weeks later – we were in the kitchen at my house, with my father
there, and he came in the kitchen and was tickling me, and I had not had
my coffee. I was just kind of wanting to wake up, and he tickled me to the
point where I was like, "Please stop. Don't do this." I said it so many times,
and finally I said, "Listen. I've had enough." Well, he turned around and
back-handed me right in front of my father. I told him, "You touch me
again, and I'm going to grab you by the balls and put you to the ground."
So, what did he do? I turned around to get my cup of coffee, and he comes
over and grabs me. I dropped my coffee cup, breaking it into the sink. I
turned around, grabbed him by his balls as hard as I freaking could – put
him to the ground. He had tears coming out of his eyes. And I said, "You
ever lay a hand on me again, your ass is out of my house, and I'm going to
file for divorce." Well, that lasted for a little while, and then he got upset
with me one day, and I ended up going upstairs – I was going to get something and leave, and I said something, and I ended up falling down the
stairs, and I told him, "Get the fuck out." Well, he didn't, and I left, and I
went to come back, and he had locked me out of my own home. I came
back with Mom and Dad, well, Linda and Greg, to get my medicine
because I was staying with them. He wouldn't let me in the house to get my
medicine or my skates. He threw my medicine out the window at me. So,
finally, I called the police and had them come, and then he jumps in the
back of my truck so I couldn't drive away, and the police said, "Well, there
is nothing we can do about it. And, if he happens to jump out and accidentally hurt himself, it's basically attempted murder." So I ended up letting
him take my fucking truck. And so he took it and ended up putting 20,000
miles on my truck in, what was it, five months before I got it back through
the courts.

You filed for divorce from him?
Yes, I did. I went through counseling, though, for a month with our church
with the pastor. I went several times – went to church every Sunday – nope,
didn't work. I've had enough. I don't deserve to be treated like this. I was
treated like this too much. I'm not doing it again. Now that it's over – good-
bye.

Were you seeing him during the counseling period?
Yes. Yes. We did it together.

What did he do for a living?
Well, he was a mechanical engineer. And he had been in the navy, and he worked for a company called *(unintelligible).*

Was he your age?
He was four years older than I was.

What about Doug?
He was a year older. Not even quite a year. And anyway, he *(Michael)* had broken his back and had back surgery, and he was going to be going back to work, but he ended up having so much pain, he had to have back surgery again. Then I found out – right at the same time that I told him never to touch me again or I am going to divorce you – I found out that he *(might have been)* defrauding the government with money about claims on his back, and that was one of the things that sent me to divorce because I was not going to get involved in something like that.

You'd had enough trouble with things …
Well, yeah. I am not going to go through this. Yeah, I married him, but you know what? It's better for me to get out of it than stay in it because I went through that once for seven years. And you know, people can say what they want to say, but, hey, I deserve to be treated with respect, love, dignity – have somebody be proud of me, stand by me no matter what, and, hey, that just wasn't going to happen.

It has been reported that you were the victim of a kidnapping attempt. Can you tell me about that?
It was a long, long time ago. I remember it was at my Milwaukee home. I left my friends and went home. I wasn't feeling well. I had a headache. I had left something in my truck, and I went to get it, and somebody was trying to steal my truck, and I told them, "Hey you can't do that" – whatever, I said, I don't remember. And the next thing I know is the guy is shoving me into the car, telling me that I am going to drive him to someplace – whatever.

How did you get away?
I ran my truck into a tree in the middle of nowhere, and he hit the windshield, and I jumped out and ran and hid. It was really dark out. He went looking for me and passed me, and I jumped back in the truck and got out of there.

Was he ever charged with anything?
They didn't find him.

What made you get back into coaching? You really hadn't been coaching before this. What made you ...
Well, I had coached back in '90, '91, '92.

Just sort of off and on, though, right?
Yeah, then I came back and taught for a couple of months – I couldn't really tell you when. I don't even remember. Then it just all faded out again, and then it came back – just up and down for several years. Coming up this year *(2001)*, I think it is April or May, it has been two years that I have been teaching now.

And are you still teaching now?
Off and on. I haven't taught for awhile because I have had so many problems, but I still have my kids, and they want me to be in there, and they said when I am ready, give them a call and come in and do it. They still want me no matter what.

This would be good for you to get back into. You should be doing that full-time.
Absolutely. I love teaching. It gives me a feeling of satisfaction to be able to see the smile on my kids' faces when they accomplish something. I mean, it is remarkable.

Is this a goal for your future – to do this full time?
I want to teach. That's my – that's the thing I want to do with the rest of my life. Like Diane – she did Ice Capades for three years, and then she went into teaching, and that's what she does. Well, I have always looked up to her. She was like a mentor to me when I was growing up, and I have always wanted to be able to be like her, you know? Be successful on her own, and then be able to have a man that comes into her life just adds to the joy of it. Teaching is wonderful. I love it. I'd like to be able to go out and do appearances, commercials, whatever to be able to make a living, to be able to teach skating also. But if I keep hurting myself ... every time I hurt myself, it's like I am just going back to start teaching and then, boom, something happens, and I can't do it. *(She laughs).*

Well, you will get there. You'll get there again.
Oh, I will, definitely.

Tell me *(more)* **about the** *(outcome of the)* **'Penthouse' video. You already told me what was on the video.**
It was my wedding night. I knew the beginning part, but I didn't know that there was anything, actually, you know, physically going on in it.

When did it come out in 'Penthouse'? Was it '94?
Yes. It was in June or July, or something like that. Actually, it might have been earlier than that. It might have been April or May. I don't even remember now.

How did you learn about the 'Penthouse' issue?
The lawyer calls me.

Whose lawyer?
His lawyer – and calls me and told me they have this video, and 'Penthouse' has got a copy of it, and I need to know what I want to do, and would I like to come down to see it. And I am like, "What video? What are you talking about?" And when I got down there, he was sitting there with his attorney, and I was just like, okay, great, okay. He was there and just smirking. Just had this dirty, little smirk on his face, like – hah, hah, hah, I've ruined you completely now. So, I took the tape – they gave me the tape – I took it in a room, and I started to watch it, and I'm like, Oh my God. I started bawling. I was in tears.

Did Jeff deny sending it there?
Yeah, he was like, "I didn't do it."

What was he at the lawyer's for?
Because he was on the tape.

He is on the tape, and he has decided that ...
It was part his.

So he was going to sue them?
He was going to sue them on top of me suing them for this thing. And they said, "Well, we're going to do it anyway because we've got a copy." It was his way of making money.

Do you know in your heart that he sent it?
I don't know. I have *(heard)* so many shit things now that it is pathetic. I have heard that he did it. I have heard that he was in cahoots with *(another man)* – that he stole it and sent it in. And I heard, oh God, I have no clue who did it.

But you think it was him?
Most likely – I mean, he made money off it, too. He made exactly the same amount of money that I made off of it.

So he didn't give them permission to use it? They were going to use it anyway?
Well, supposedly. That's what he says. I mean, I didn't do the contract with him. It was totally separate. I contacted my attorney and had him come down. And my attorney came down the next day. And him and his attorney, and me and my attorney, sat there and talked about it. And he was like, "Oh. I want to accept this and da, da, da." It was a way that he could make money off me and ruin me at the same time.

Was there any way you could have stopped it?
I tried. They had a copy of it, and they already had it going to print.

So your lawyer recommended to settle with them?
Well, it was either that or go to a full force lawsuit – court. It would be in the papers. Every single person out there would know. He recommended to me – I mean, we bickered about it for a couple of weeks ...

Who – you and the lawyer?
My lawyer and 'Penthouse,' bickering back and forth, trying to stop it and all that stuff, but you know, they were going to do it anyway. So, my lawyer told me, when finally we got an offer that came in that was better than the last one, not insulting, he said, "You know what? You probably won't get any more out of this if it was a lawsuit. And it will cost you this much to go through a lawsuit. So it's probably better that you accept this so we don't have to go to court and do all this." I'm like, okay, I can't stop it, so at least be paid for it.

Do you wish now you would have stopped it?
Oh, yeah. Damn right.

No matter what the cost?
No matter what the cost, I would have gone to court, and I doubt I would
have been able to stop it, even then, but they sure as hell would have had
to pay me a hell of a lot more money than they did.

**So, I guess you thought it was just going to be the still pictures and that
you had no idea the video tape was going to be roaming around until
this day?**
Yeah. Right. The money I made off the magazine – that's how I bought my
house. I totally gutted that house and remodeled it and painted it. I mean,
I put all my hard work and effort into it. Got myself onto my feet, and then
to have it taken away from me all again.

Do you mind me asking how much you made on that *(the magazine)*?
They offered $200,000.00 down and then just whatever so much a month
from sales for so many years.

Did that have to be split between you and him *(Jeff)*?
No. It came out to $400,000.00 for both of us and then so much from the
sales.

**You had said that you had gone into the room to change and that he
must have set up the camera, but an article on the internet – I haven't
seen the video, nor do I want to see it – but it says that you were in your
wedding dress.**
When I walked in the house - yeah.

But not in the bed, right?
No.

It says "a topless wedding dress."
No, my top was down on my wedding dress – I was being cute coming in
the front door with our new video camcorder, and I showed him my butt
and stuff, and my leg thing *(garter)*, you know – that you wear? You know
– just being cute. I mean, it was our wedding night.

The video wasn't of you in the wedding dress?
No. The video was in the wedding dress at first, and then the sexual part
was after that. I went in, and I put on this little nightie thing that I had got,

and I guess he put a camera in the closet or something because I sure as hell didn't see it sitting there.

So, the topless wedding dress they are talking about – that's nothing then?
There wasn't a topless wedding dress – no. I was topless because I took it down.

You were clowning around?
Yes.

And I guess that's like –so what? It wasn't something you were expecting the world to see?
Exactly.

Even if you had done the whole video tape thing ...
That would be so embarrassing.

But even if you had, it would be something that you would think only your husband and you would see – right?
But I mean – no – I am so prude.

So, it is something you never would have done anyway?
No. No. No. No. No.

You are a prude?
I am definitely a prude. If my shirt is too low, I am always tugging on it. Or if I think something is showing, I will fix it all the time. I mean, I wear turtlenecks probably 80 percent of the time. I don't wear any – hardly ever anyway, I'll say – I don't want to say never, but hardly ever do I wear any miniskirts or anything like that. Usually, it's long skirts or three quarter length skirts. Nothing – hardly ever anything too suggestive at all.

And you've always been that way?
Yup. And I think it is probably because of what I've been through. Of being molested as a child growing up – being raped, and people always telling me, you're ugly and all this stuff. I've always covered up.

In the book *(I gave her the name of the book)*, **it mentions a costume you had that the USFSA said was too skimpy.**
That was my '94 Nationals program dress. I did it with purple – with a very deep V with flesh colored material right in the middle, and it had this gold trim that went across that on the V. There was nothing showing.

I saw a picture of it. I didn't think there was anything wrong with it.
But they thought it was too risqué. Too risqué? Come on. Look at what the girls *(female figure skaters)* are wearing.

So if you are on the ice, it is a different thing?
The girls – what they are wearing nowadays – you should see it. I mean, I couldn't believe it. People always bitched about me and my costumes.

They would find something to bitch about?
Something – nothing was ever good enough in the skating world for me. I mean, I would try and try and try, and bend over backwards, and it would never help. I mean, because of one person, I won Nationals? And the other person fell twice?

Say that again. What do you mean because of one person?
The judge – one judge at '91 Nationals gave me a 6.0, and that is the only reason I won Nationals, and Kristi Yamaguchi fell twice. And I did a perfect program with a triple Axel, and the other judges were going to put her first.

Did you ever have any fancy designers make your costumes?
There was one lady that – the maroon dress – the Olympic dress – was a big name lady. And she made that one and the turquoise one that I wore in October at the *(ESPN)* Championships.

Did you have that costume for awhile?
I had it since '94. She had made the maroon one for Olympics and the turquoise one for Worlds. I didn't go to Worlds, but I got the costume.

I guess up until that time you couldn't afford to have big designers?
No. Usually somebody else locally made it. I mean, Jeff's sister actually made a couple of my costumes because she was a seamstress. And she was out of work, so I said, "Hey, how about if you make my costumes for me?"

And so she made two of my costumes, or three of my costumes, for me. She even fixed my boots for me because one of my eyelets had fallen out, and she had to fix that for me. And then I started to get – almost like shin splints, but on the sides on the outside, and I had to cut my boots down lower, and they had to be sewn up around the top – a rounded type on the top, so it wouldn't dig into my leg, and she did that also. And then after that, when I started ordering my boots, I just had them do the rolled edges and lower anyway.

So, everything *(after the Olympics)* was *(happening)* at once. You settled with 'Penthouse.'
I settled out of court with them.

But you *(basically)* allowed them to print the pictures, right?
Well, they were going to do it anyway. They already had it in print. I mean, ready to go out in their magazine, ready to be sold. They were going to do it whether I said, "No," or not. Because by the time – if I had have gone through court – by the time all that would have happened, they would have already been out anyway. And so, instead of going through all the legal cost time and the publicity – I was trying to keep it as quiet as I could because it was so embarrassing.

How did you feel then when this came out?
Oh my God – humiliated, embarrassed – didn't want to be around anymore – didn't want to deal with it. Having guys gawk at me and make rude remarks and gestures.

Had you seen the pictures before they came out?
When I went to my lawyer's office – my lawyer had called me and said, "You need to come down here," and I went down there, and he had the video, and he said, "This is what they have. They already have it ready to go out. They have taken stills from it, and it is already in print and ready to go." And when I saw it the first time, I watched about ten seconds of it, and I ran to the bathroom, and I was puking for about half an hour.

The video supposedly belonged to Jeff, right?
Supposedly.

So, it was coming out, and that was it? But couldn't you have sued 'Penthouse'? Couldn't you have turned around and said …?
Yeah, but then it have been a big thing in the media – big, big, huge scandal and publicity thing I didn't want, and I just wanted to try and keep it quiet and all this shit. And at that point in time, I was flat broke. I had nothing. I had already lost my whole, entire career. I mean, what was I supposed to do?

Because you got all these legal bills and you've got everything else?
Yeah. So I ended up settling with them out of court.

Figuring it would be quiet?
Yeah. Oh, no. After it all came out, then it all came out.

Do you wish now that you had tried to stop it?
Yes. Well, I had tried to stop it, but it was already in print, so there wasn't anything I could do. The dockets for court were six months out at least. It would have already been out by the time I would have been able to sue them, but now, when I look at it now, as I'm older – back then, when you flash a whole lot of money in front of somebody who doesn't have any, and you know.

You wish now you hadn't taken the money, and …
Yup.

And had said, I don't want these printed. I'll sue you, whatever?
Well, I said I didn't want them printed, but it was too late for that anyway.

Right, but if you had to go back and do it again now …
If it was happening to me right this minute, I would tell them, "You go ahead, and I am going to have my attorney sue your ass so quickly, you won't even be able to wipe it."

Then if it would have come out, it would have been against your permission.
Exactly.

They wouldn't have thought you were a part of it.
It came out that way anyway. It was against my okay. Now I look at it – but you can't, you can't just look back and say if this would have happened, or

this – that "what if" kind of thing. It does nothing. You make mistakes, and you live with them, but you learn from them, and you don't make the same mistakes again.

If you could change anything in all those years, what would you change?
I think the things I would have changed is that, hopefully, I wish I could have grown up in a stable environment – home, loving family, that I wouldn't be wanting to be loved by somebody so much – wanting to have affection of some kind.

That you were willing to settle for what wasn't a healthy relationship, but because you're starving for affection ...
Exactly.

You're settling for these – not nice people.
Deadbeats. I wish I wasn't so naïve. I always wanted to believe in people, but obviously, nowadays, I don't believe it until I see it. I don't trust until they earn it, and I wish I was the person, back then, that I am now. My life would have been a lot different, but ...

It's for reasons, though?
Yeah– everything that has happened to me has happened for a reason, whether it be super, super bad, whether it be good or just in the middle.

So, your regrets then ...
I regret being young, naïve, and just not having the life that a lot of kids did.

Do you look at this now as you are older and think, yes, it was my environment and the way I grew up, but also isn't a big part of your insecurity that you had back then, your lack of confidence, whatever, doesn't it also have to do with the skating world as well because of the pressure they put on women or young girls to look good, to be a certain way?
I think so. I think it has to do with all of it, you know? I mean, it's like they all expect you to be a certain way, act a certain way, dress a certain way – all of it.

So, if you're not going home and getting the build-up, the confidence build-up – 'Oh Tonya, you are a beautiful little girl,' and this and that, you don't have the strength then to even face it at the rink then, do you?
No.

You just go with the flow, and if they are telling you to stay with this idiot guy because he is good for your career, you do it, right?
Yup. Yup.

Did you see any other women around you in skating – were there things like eating disorders and anxieties?
I really didn't pay enough attention to that.

You were going through enough of your own – not eating disorders, but problems?
Yes. I just kind of stuck to myself and always did the best that I could because I wanted to be the best. And I always worked really hard. There were a few different times in certain years that I let myself go and gained weight or something, but I was always told through my whole life that I am fat and ugly and am not going to amount to a hill of beans. You're stupid – you know?

You don't think that now do you?
Absolutely not, but back then I didn't love myself.

And you do now?
I love myself, and that is why I have the opportunity to love other people. And you know what? I have friends and family that love me, and I don't need sex. I mean, I haven't had sex in – I don't know how long.

So many women say this.
I just want people to care about me and respect me and to be able to go out and have a good time and just take care of myself.

Do you want children someday?
At this point, un uh. No.

It's enough to look after yourself?
I got my dog. Let me tell you ...

But if the right man came along and *(it was)* a strong relationship …
The only way that I would ever have children – a child – would be if I was married and financially secure, knowing that our bills would always be paid for each month, and we both agreed 100 percent and wanted to do that.

And also *(after being)* a long time into the relationship, where you know it is going to last?
Yes.

***(I told her the reason I never had childre, and then said,)* People like you and me tend to put all our affection into our animals.**
Exactly. He is enough kid for me, let me tell you.

What other things happened during this period?
I skated at the hockey game in Reno.

Tell me about that.
Well, it all turned out great.

When was that?
That was the beginning of '97.

And what happened?
I went to Reno to skate at the beginning or half time of the game. I went down there, and at first it was kind of a 50/50 thing with the crowd, but by the time I got done, it was a standing ovation, and I was supposed to go to a dinner afterwards, and I was signing autographs, and they gave me a half hour or 45 minutes to do that, and there was over 400 people in line, and I ended up staying over two and a half hours and signing every single one of them. Out of all them, there was only one person who came up and stuck a piece of metal in front of me and asked me to sign it. The security people grabbed him and took him off – bam – that was it.

Was he being an idiot?
Well, he wanted me to sign a piece of metal – a metal bar.

Oh, I understand. *(A reference to the weapon that was used on Nancy).* Was this the first time you had been in the public eye since all of this had happened?
Yes.

So, it must have felt good to have 400 people standing there?
Definitely.

Did it feel weird when you first came out and were getting that mixed reaction from the crowd?
Well, yes and no. *(She laughs)*. It's kind of hard to explain. I mean, I don't remember how I felt, but it was a little scary, exciting, you know, all of it at the same time.

You made a movie too, right?
I did a movie down in L.A. in '94 and it was a 'B' rated movie, but let me tell you, I have a lot of respect for actors and actresses. It is hard work – very hard work.

What was the movie called?
'Breakaway.'

Is that something you would want to do in the future?
Oh, I wouldn't mind, you know, if it was a really good movie and it had good taste to it and everything.

Did it *(the movie)* go on TV?
No. It went straight to the videos.

It wasn't like a porn thing or anything?
No, no, no, no – no.

What type of movie was it?
It was an action movie. I owned a restaurant, and my boyfriend in the movie was supposedly with the mob, or something like that, and at the end of the movie, they killed my boyfriend, but he had stashed money, and I had found it, and I ended up spending it all on a desert island. *(She laughs)*.

Do you get tired of this tough girl image?
Yeah, I do. I do. You know, people just see me on TV, and they see all this crap, you know. If they believe it, they believe it. But the people that don't know me, and then do meet me and get to know me, are totally the opposite.

But you know when you did *(the show)* **on TNN, introducing 'Bad Boys Week,' does that bother you?** *(Tonya was dressed in leather and posing with a motorcycle).*
But that was done as a tongue-in-cheek.

So, you don't mind doing that as tongue-in-cheek?
Yes, I had a bike sitting there, and, yes, I was wearing leather, but it was done in very good taste. It was wonderful. I loved it. The people absolutely loved me. They said they never had a person so good to work with as me. They were calling me the 'one-timer' because I got through it so quickly. I did it one time and got it right.

So you can laugh at yourself in a way?
Yeah.

Because you understand that some people have this image of you, and you don't mind laughing at yourself, but that's not who you are?
I mean, hey, people are going to believe and look at it the way they want to, and they have their own opinion. But if people were to meet me and get to know me as I am – as a person, not as the media portrays me, people would really like me. I mean, people do – people like me when they get to meet me.

(12)

The Hubcap Incident

"Stop making accusations about me.
You don't know me. You don't know my life."

In February 2000, Tonya was charged with assault after an argument took place with her boyfriend and she supposedly threw a hubcap at him. Eventually, the charge was reduced to disorderly conduct and malicious mischief. As noted in the introduction, it was decided the comeback theme of the original book would obviously have to be changed, and in the summer of 2000, we decided to rewrite the proposal to reflect her current experiences. Following is the interview that took place in that regard.

The first thing I want to do is talk about how we can change the proposal because the first one ended in West Virginia *(where she made her professional skating comeback),* **but obviously a lot has changed since then. At the end of that proposal, you were talking about going back into skating, and now you are not talking that way. I can write about the changes, but now I want to know why you want to do this book.**
Basically, I want to teach skating, and if I get the opportunity to do an exhibition, appearance, or something like that for skating, then that would be fine, but I would rather do different things with my name basically, like TV hosting, radio hosting, you know, appearances, motivational speaking – those types of things.

You expressed a desire, awhile ago, that you wanted to get out of the limelight, but your name is obviously out there, so you might as well, use it to do good things.
I have to make a living somehow.

So, are you saying that it is impossible for you to make a living in other ways?
Yes. There are other ways like TV hosting and appearances and things like that because people use my name to bring the public in. I sign autographs and things like that, and those are the kinds of things I do to make money.

If you were to take a normal job ...
I can't.

Why can't you take a normal job? What happens?
For one thing, I work well with people, but people do not want me working for their business.

Do you think it is prejudice?
I don't know, and I also am not going to work as a waitress. I do not have any other types of skills except for like painting houses, things like that. You know, I never went to college and got a college education because skating was what I did. And I sure as hell am not going to work for seven bucks an hour – not when I make $60.00 an hour teaching.

And people won't let your name go away ...
People won't let the past go away.

So, why not use your name to make a living and to also bring good?
Exactly, and there is a possibility that we may have a skating video come out hopefully by Christmas. I don't know if we will make it or not, but it will be 'Tonya's Top Ten Skating Hints.' And it will have me doing a short exhibition now, and it will have the pro championships and me teaching a kid or something, and at the end, it will say, 'Keep your eyes open for my next two or three videos – skating instructional videos,' at the very end, and of course, my book.

Why do you want to write this book?
I want people to understand me and not make decisions ... rash decisions on who I am and what I am based on what they hear. I want to set the story straight about my life, about who I am, and it is a closure for me. I am closing the door from my past life.

When this book is out – published, you know you will have to talk about it (your life) if you are doing interviews?
Right – I know that. Once that's done, it's done. I am not ever talking about it again.

It is serving as a closure to you, as a way of kind of purging your soul to get rid of the past ... start anew? This is the way it is, a clean slate, my story, the way I see it? It's out there for you to believe or not to believe, but now it is gone from me?
Right. This is my book. This is coming from my mouth, from my heart, and nobody can take that away from me.

It may take away some of the prejudgments that people have, even if they don't know anything about you, but hear about you in the media.
They hear what they hear on the media, and they believe it. And this is coming straight from my mouth. It comes out and says, "Hey, this is me. This is who I am. This is what I went through my whole, entire life. Stop making accusations about me. You don't know me. You don't know my life. You don't know what I've been through. Maybe you can understand me better and know what I've had to go through my whole life."

Now it is *(in)* black and white. This is it. It is out here. Do you want to read it? It's here to read. Right?
Well, I mean, people are going to read it because they want to know. But I want people to read it so people will know me, and understand me, and not just the media – placing their judgments on me from what the media has said because the media never gets it right.

I reminded Tonya that I had formal interviews with her from earlier in the year and that, although we had spoken many times since, it was usually on an informal basis where the conversations were not taped. I requested to be brought up to date as to what had happened to her since the car accident. She responded:
After the car accident, with the situation with Darren *(the hubcap incident)*, I took full responsibilities for my actions, even though my actions were based on medications and alcohol mixed together that caused a blackout. It was a very hard time for me. I lost everything, including my best friend ... my lover, and now I am happy to say that we have been working our problems out like any normal, human person has. We have worked our problems out. We are seeing each other. We are together. We may not live together at this point in time, but we may in the future. He has talked about moving in with me.

It's open. It's a possibility?
Yes.

As far as you accepting responsibility for what went on ...
I got disorderly conduct and malicious mischief. That's it. No domestic violence. No assault charge. Nothing. They were all dropped. I took full
responsibility for everything. I went to jail for three days, and the public
humiliation from this whole, entire thing was very hard. I hit rock bottom
again. I had two nervous breakdowns during the time that this had happened. Let's see. So, once I hit rock bottom again, I decided, well, this is it.
Time to pick myself back up again and turn my life back around again and
keep going forward and not give up.

And you served how many hours of community service?
Eighty.

**Eighty hours of community service, which entailed office work, yard
work, right?**
Just put in 'miscellaneous.'

What about the classes you have to go to?
Right. The judge decided that I needed anger management. He thought I
had an anger management problem because he thought that ... he was pre-
judged *(believe she meant prejudging)*. He took what happened in '94 and
put it on here and did nothing. He did not go along with anything that the
district attorney had gone with. He threw it all out.

**But the last time I spoke to you, you said you were learning things from
these anger management classes.**
Yeah. Definitely. I definitely learned a lot. I mean, it has been very good for
me, and I have learned that I don't have to take shit from anybody. I can be
assertive without being aggressive. And you know, it has been pretty good.

*I commented that her experience, when written in the book, may help
others who have similar problems.* **What comment did the judge make
to you?**
He said – when they *(her attorneys)* said I was going to teach ice skating lessons to underprivileged children that couldn't afford it and I would do
(teach) 100 kids in a year's time or whatever, and the judge said that I am

not a good role model and I will not be doing that. And then when he asked me – he didn't even look at anything – he was just sitting there with a smirk on his face the whole time – he didn't even look at the stuff, and he asked me if I had anything to say, and I just told him that I was sorry that this had happened, and I was embarrassed, and I am taking full responsibility for my actions. And he said, "So, is that what you said to the judge in 1994 also?" Totally prejudgment. He was trying to try me for 1994 when all it was, was hindering prosecution.

What did you say to him?
I didn't say anything. My lawyer grabbed my hand.

And that's when ... three days in jail?
Yeah.

Was that supposed to be if you plead guilty to domestic violence ...
To assault or domestic violence – yes, but I didn't.

So you never plead guilty ...
No jail time was supposed to be done at all.

Now, this was already set up between the lawyers I guess?
Right.

In the book, will you be willing to talk about what happened that night with you and Darren?
I don't know what happened.

To the best of your recollection or what people told you?
I don't know for a fact what happened. Period. All I know is, I drove up; I got out of the Jeep. He had made a comment that his bike was more important than I was, and I saw the bike sitting there. I picked up the center cap to the truck wheel, and I threw it at his bike. And the next thing that I remember is that I was on the ground, and I thought that he was holding me down, and I told him to get off me, and I punched him in the face to get him off of me. That's all I know.

Do you remember calling the police?
I didn't call the police. I called my mom *(Linda Lewis)*, and the police were on the line – because I don't have a vehicle.

Oh, because you were going to leave?
Yeah. I was going to have Mom come and get me.

So, who called the police then?
Darren did. I did not call 911. He called the police station to ask them what he should do.

Oh, I see.
And the police took it upon themselves to come out to our house, and then they arrest me, and they don't arrest him when he has alcohol on his breath, my hands are bruised, and I am freaking out. They took me instead of him because he had a bloody nose.

You were on medication then?
I was on – I had taken Percodan the night before.

What's that for?
Painkillers for the surgery on my foot from my car accident, and I had been going to physical therapy for my back because I had a dislocated shoulder, a strained neck, and vertebrae that were out of place, and I had taken Percodan the night before, which is Aspirin, and I am allergic to it.

You didn't know that?
No. The doctor prescribed it, and the pharmacy filled it, and I picked it up, and the pharmacy had it right on their screen that I am allergic to Aspirin, and they gave it to me anyway.

What other medication were you on?
I take Zoloft for clinical depression.

Do you still take that?
Yes.

And how long have you been taking that?
Since 1996, and that day I had taken 750 milligrams of Hydrocodone, my Zoloft …

What is the Hydrocodone for?
It's a codeine. It's a painkiller. They gave me two different kinds.

This is all for your surgery and back problems?
Yes, and the Percodan makes me sick to my stomach, so I took the Hydrocodone that day, and Mom was with me – so 750 milligrams of that, plus 800 milligrams of Anacin, which turned out to be Aspirin, and my Zoloft, and then four and a half hours later or four hours later, I went and had three beers with Darren at dinner. But I didn't eat any dinner because I was playing video poker, and I wasn't hungry. And as soon as we left, I guess, was when I started going berserk. And I have no idea.

I can see why. That's a lot of mixed medications. But they should have told you ...
But the pharmacist never should have prescribed *(given)* Hydrocodone or Percodan knowing that I take Zoloft. The two medications do not mix. You are not to take them together, ever.

There was talk for awhile of you maybe suing the pharmacy or the doctor.
I thought about that, but I don't have the money to do that kind of stuff.

Maybe it's just easier to let it go, right?
Yup.

You have sure been through the grind.
Yeah.

Okay. What else about that time? You know, other stuff we can talk about in more detail later on – what you've done this year ...
I haven't done anything.

What was it like to be in jail? That has to be horrible.
It was the second most horrible thing that I have had to go through.

What was the first? Oh. I know what the first was *(the rape)*.
Yeah. And I will tell you, I am never going back. I am never going back to jail. No, ever, never, because they wouldn't give me my medicine while I was in there. I had a nervous breakdown while I was in there – panic disorder, panic attack – major league. And I was in this little, teeny, tiny room by myself, which was better than being with everybody else, but it was the worst 72 hours of my life, besides the other. But if me going through all this

crap that I have been through in my life – if I can help one person through life – don't make the same mistakes that I have made – you're human, you're going to make mistakes, but think before you make your mistakes. Don't go the same route that I did. And if I help somebody out, I guess it's all worth it.

I heard you when you were on Larry King saying that the sink ...
The sink and toilet were connected.

And you had to drink out of that sink?
Yes.

Would they let you wash your hair or anything?
No. I got to go in, and there was one bathtub – one – and that was where I got to take my shower, and I was disgusted by even taking a shower there.

You mean it was the one that everybody else used?
I guess. I sure as hell didn't see anything else. I didn't wash my hair. I got to take a bath, basically, but I didn't take a bath – I just washed myself up – once.

What did you do there? Were you allowed to read? Were you allowed ...
A couple of people who worked there brought me some magazines and a book. And I looked through the magazines, and somebody brought me some cards to play with, but mostly I tried to sleep the whole time away. And I cried 99 percent of the time. It was horrible. I slept on the floor.

Why did you sleep on the floor?
Because that's what they gave me to sleep on. They gave me this little, tiny mat that goes on the floor, and you sleep on it – two feet. You don't get a blanket. You don't get a pillow, nothing.

So, no music, nothing?
Nothing. Absolutely nothing.

You were allowed to phone Linda, weren't you, once a day?
I got to make a phone call once a day.

And you called Linda?
Yeah. And I called Darren once, too.

When you went to do community service, I remember seeing pictures of you at the … (cemetery – in 'People' magazine and other media).
Yeah. I worked up at the cemetery helping them to get ready for Memorial Day, and it was really – it was pretty interesting getting to help out and stuff. They had me planting flowers and things like that. At first, they had me working the weed-whacker thing. It was too heavy for me, so they said we'll have you plant some flowers. Well, I ended up planting flowers, but they had me in the baby section, and so it made me cry.

And you had all the media standing around, too, right?
Only when I was weed-whacking, and they were all gone after that.

They got their pictures?
Yeah.

And when you said that you lost everything because of this, wasn't that Ice Capades deal going through?
Well, the week after this all happened, the 'Globe' article came out – that Darren had done – and the 'Globe' altered the photograph, on purpose, deliberately, to make me look bad. And they finally turned around – the day that I did the cemetery thing – interviews were there – press conference – and they admitted on television that, yes, they did alter the photographs. I am in the process of suing them at this time because when that article came out, I had a nervous breakdown because it made him look like I beat the shit out of him. I mean, they did this on purpose to me. And that's when I lost an Ice Capades contract for eight months and a radio program show for a year, and no one would ever want me again for their skating shows or anything like that. People just didn't want to deal with anything with Tonya Harding because she is such a bad person.

After you worked so hard to get your image back …
The media screws me over every time. They do not go with the facts. They make assumptions, and they go out and say whatever the hell they want to, to make someone listen to their story.

Why did Darren do that Globe article?
The same thing with 'Inside Edition' – they were going to do it anyway – they offered me (him) money. Yeah, put a little bit of money in front of anybody's face, and they usually will jump on it.

You know what, Tonya – that's right because we are all just human, aren't we?
No, no, we're not. I had a deal to do a new rock video where I was going to dance in the video, and the contracts were almost completely signed. Everything was a go, and two days before it was all going to be signed and going, they changed producers, and the producer said, "There is no way that Tonya's contract is going to fly. We have full rights on how she dresses, how she does her hair, how she dances, and everything," and they wanted me to show titty and ass. And I said, "You know what? Your money and your video is not important to me for that."

Good for you.
So, I lost three grand that I was going to pay my rent with and my truck payment with this month, coming up right here, because I'm flat broke again.

I told Tonya how I had been offered money to talk about things she had told me and how I had refused. She responded:
Me, personally – I'm like you – you and I are a lot alike, as we both know. I would not ever betray a friend, ever. I don't care who it is. If that person respected me and cared about me, I would never do that for no amount of money.

Me, too, but how can you forgive Darren then?
Because I love him. Because *(I believe)* he was pushed into doing it.

He made a mistake?
You know, he was pushed into doing it, and that was the first thing he ever disrespected me with. And I just – I love this person. We have a lot in common, and I figured, you know what – I'm going to give it everything I can. I'll give 150 percent of me. I didn't go out and sell a story about him. Not one. Not one time did I ever bad-mouth him or accept money.

No, you didn't. You were very loyal.
I didn't accept one penny on any interviews that I did about this. Not one dime did I make.

I remember your mom *(Linda Lewis)* calling me when you were in jail, and she was sobbing, just sobbing, and you know *(she said),* "What can we do?" And, "It just breaks my heart." And I felt so bad, and *(during)* that time, you never said a bad word against Darren.
But it was really good on your part for being there for her because she needed somebody to be there for her, other than her husband, you know.

She just broke down, and I felt so bad for her.
She is my best friend. Yes, Darren used to be, and we are working on building that relationship up, you know, to where he can be my best friend. But Mom is like my best friend in the world, you know? She would do anything for me, and I would do anything for her.

(Tonya had an anger management class to attend that evening and wanted to end the interview to prepare for the class).
It's crazy. It's just ... it really is. I mean, yes, I have learned a lot, but it *(the anger management class)* is more like a domestic violence class, and you learn lots of different things – on how to, you know, what your list of primary feelings commonly associated with anger *(is)*.

***Tonya had mentioned to me in an earlier conversation that she was not in a violent relationship and felt the classes weren't appropriate for her particular situation.* You know what I would do if I were you, Tonya – for tonight's class – instead of going in and saying you are just not in that situation, why you don't you just sit down and write something and say ...**
Because I can't – I can't take the chance of writing something down and her saying, "This is not good enough" or "This isn't going to work" and me end up being in there for another 15 weeks.

But what if you just give it a try? Wouldn't they say that's good – that you're trying?
There is not a situation that I could write about.

What if you wrote about ...
I could write about my dog. *(She sounded very frustrated).*

What if you wrote about – if I am in this situation – if I'm married someday …
It has to be about a true thing that has happened or that is going to happen. I don't have any problems. Darren and I don't argue. We don't have any problems where we have to say, "Okay, can we set up a time so we can sit down and discuss this?" I mean, it has to be based on either what happened that night that it happened, how it went, how it did it, which I have no clue – what he said, what I said back – I don't know. Or it has to be based on something now. Well, he doesn't live with me, and we don't argue. We don't have any problems where I can actually say, "Okay, I think we need to sit down and talk about this problem."

Don't they know he is not living with you?
Yeah, but just because I'm in the class … but everyone else in the class has their husbands or boyfriends living with them, so they can easily do that.

Well, you know best. You know what to do.
I mean, if she wants me to do something, she'll tell me exactly, "Okay, how about writing a specific thing about something like this and bring it in next week." Because, I will tell her, I don't have anything to talk about because I'm not in that kind of a situation, and then she will give me something else to write about.

How much longer do you have to do these *(classes)*?
I don't know. I think I'm in the 10th or 11th week now, I think, and it's 15 weeks, and there's extra – it goes up to 26 weeks. I don't want to have to go to the extra 15 weeks or whatever it is because every single time I go, I have to pay $25.00. Plus I pay $50.00 a month probation – because I'm on probation – to the State. I had $800.00 and some odd dollars in fines to pay to the State – $100.00 a month. And it was $50.00 down just to go to the classes. It was $35.00 just to go in and see if I could get into the classes. And Monday and Wednesday evenings are the only time I can teach in the evening.

How are you making money now?
I'm not. I am flat broke.

Weren't you painting houses for awhile again?
Well, my friend paints, but he hasn't got anything right now. I mean, I haven't gotten the opportunity to do anything.

Weren't you paid at all to go …
Yeah, I was paid an appearance fee to go back and do the baseball thing
(Tonya had made an appearance at a ballgame), but that moved me into my
house. It's cost me $2,400.00 to move.

What about the TNN thing?
TNN? Well, that was three months ago.

Oh, right – you taped that a long time ago. *(It had recently aired).*
That paid my rent, my truck payment, and my rent one more time.

Do you still have debt from previous …
I don't own anything. I own nothing, and I am still paying on shit from '94.
People think I am filthy rich. If people only knew that I have to pray to God
every single day to hope that I get something that comes in by the end of
the month so that I don't have to worry about my rent and truck payment.
And right now, I am flat broke. I have like fifty bucks to my name.

Well, let's just hope to get this book published.
Yeah, and the skating video. We met with the people when we were with
the baseball team because they live a 100 miles from there, so they drove in
that night and met with us after we were done. And we talked about different kinds of videos. The first one we want to do is 'Tonya's Top Ten Greatest
Skating Hints,' and I can get some of the videos from when I was younger
and use a couple of those and a couple from the middle and then with my
Nationals title, my World title, Skate America title, Olympics, and then my
pro championships and an exhibition. And then I'm going to be teaching
on the end.

Is this a reputable company?
They work through themselves, and they have connections with WalMart.
You know WalMart right?

Yeah – huge.
Five-thousand stores and a hundred videos at $20.00 a piece for 5000
stores.

*We discussed the business aspects of publishing the book before ending
our conversation.*

(13)

Update & Reflections

*"I guess the biggest misconception is that I'm not an animal.
I am just human."*

*This interview was conducted with Tonya in January 2007 (although a
few additional questions were asked in May 2007 and inserted accordingly) with the intent of providing an update on her life.*

**What I would like to do now is provide an update of what you have
been doing since our earlier interviews and what your plans for the
future are. In the last interview, you and Darren were attempting to reconcile. Did that happen?**
No.

You did try. Remember, you went for some counseling? *(She had told me
during an informal conversation that they were going to go for counseling).* **But, you didn't move back into together?**
I don't think we even did any counseling. We had talked about doing counseling, but we never did. It is just totally gone.

**Do you blame him now for not accepting some of the responsibility for
the fight you had that night and also for selling his story to the tabloids?**
Well, it was all B.S., and I proved it.

**Yes, but at the time we last spoke, you were saying that it was not his
fault because you still loved him at the time.**
Well, it takes two to fight.

So, looking back now, you do blame him for some of what happened?
Yup.

And what about for selling his story?
All it was – was about money. That's what most people do. Everything is
always about money.

You know, Tonya, over the years, you have had so many difficult relationships with men ...
Not many – I've only had five relationships. *(She laughs).*

But they have been difficult, right?
Yeah.

And, so, have you sworn off men, or have you been through other relationships?
I was with *(Tonya didn't want his name mentioned – see below)* for almost four years.

After Darren?
Yes, but that is a very sticky situation that we have to be careful of because his parents never knew that we were together.

Well, I am not mentioning last names.
No, you can't even mention it at all.

Well, how about if I say that ...
I had a relationship with a gentleman for almost four years. That would be a good way of putting it.

All right. Are you involved in a relationship now?
No. I am happy with me.

Do you dream about marriage and kids and things like that?
I don't dream about it or anything. It would be nice to be able to have someone to share my life with. I just turned 36 in November. You know, I'm not looking, and if I don't have someone in my life, that's just – I got good friends, and that's all that really matters.

So, you, and I'm going to say this 'gentleman' because we are not going to be mentioning his name – you are still friends now?
Yes.

So it didn't end ...
It didn't end badly.

That's good. Did you live together?
Yes.

Do you ever see Jeff Gillooly?
No. *(She laughs sarcastically)*. I hope to God he rots away in prison where he belongs – you can put that in a nice way. *(She laughs)*.

Well, actually, I'm transcribing the tapes pretty much – *(as you know)* that's the whole thing of this book: the tapes are being transcribed exactly as you speak.
Yeah, okay, well, let me put it in a different way then.

We spoke about the language she used or didn't use in the book.

Do you know what he is doing now?
No, and I don't care. And I think since that time, people have seen that – I've actually – in interviews that I have done or whatever, other interviews – and what has happened in his life, I think people actually have started to, you know, think twice about what I had to say. There's a lot of people out there now that look at it and go, "Wow, maybe she really was telling the truth, and maybe we should have listened a little harder."

Has he been in prison, other than ...
I don't know about prison. I know he's been in jail, I think, for something. He beat up his wife several times – in front of the children once and once when she was holding them.

This was public knowledge?
I believe so. It was on the news. *(She laughs)*. That's how I heard about it. And I thought to myself, what goes around, comes around.

You heard about it on the news?
Yes, but I knew his wife.

She was the one who did your nails?
Yup, she used to do my nails, and I told her when I saw her and I found out they were together, I said, "You know, one of these days, he is going to do to you what he has done to me, and it may not be tomorrow or the next day or next week or next month, but it will happen."

Do you know if they are together still?
I have no idea.

Has the bitterness, has the anger – and I know you actually hated him ...
Yes.

Has that dissipated over the years? Has that gone away?
No.

You still feel the same?
Yes.

If you could see him face to face ...
Oooh. *(In disgust).*

For some reason ... what would you say to him if you saw him today?
Oh my God – what would I say?

If you could have two sentences to say to him – what would you say to him?
Ums – jeez – you know what? I really don't know. I really don't know what I would say to him if I had to see him face to face – and I say 'had to' because I don't want to see his face ever again. But I think that what he's done, not only to me, but to his wife, and being so manipulative to so many people – being able to talk his way out of things – being the *(Dr).* Jekyll and *(Mr).* Hyde that he is, he should be in jail. And that way, he could think about all the mistakes that he made. What I was going to say, too, you know, it's not just about me or her and all these other people; there are children involved now for him, and I think what he has done was way, way wrong.

I guess you are glad now that you never had children with him.
Yes, I'm glad. I mean, I've always wanted to have a child, but I don't know if that will ever happen, you know? And if it doesn't, it doesn't. If it does – great. You know what I mean? You can't predict the future, and you can't change the past, but I'm just glad that I finally am in a good place with myself, and I'm making it. I'm making it on my own. I'm doing it, despite everything else.

You cut off all ties with your birth mother.
Yes.

Did you maintain that decision, or have you been in contact with her?
I tried – oh, gosh, let's see. I tried to talk to her a few years ago. Supposedly, you know, she had quit drinking, and I heard that she was dying with cancer, and I ran into her and seen her a couple of times, and then the last time I went to see her, she had a glass of vodka and drank it right in front of me. And when I got my D.U.I., the news had reported that I had flipped my truck, or something, a whole bunch of times, and the point was, though, is I had given her my phone number, at that time, even still. And when that happened, you would think that she would care just enough to call and make sure I was okay – never got a phone call anytime – nothing.

You are referring to the car accident you had about five years ago?
In 2002 – yes, but it wasn't a car accident.

It was when you flipped your truck, which we already talked about.
I know – I didn't flip my truck. The news said that. All I did is, I pulled out of somebody's driveway, and it slipped. It died, and I went to pull over right there. I wasn't even going probably five miles an hour.

Are we talking about the accident in 2000?
No, no. This was when I got my D.U.I.

When was this?
2002.

I don't know if I have that or not, so tell me about it now, just in case.
Okay – I had put a new carburetor on my truck that day, and my friend and I had gone to another friend's house, and then my truck was cold, and I went to pull out of the driveway. The truck backfired through the carburetor and died. Once the truck dies, it does not have any power steering or brakes. So, I went to try and stop right there, and it touched the gravel on the end of the road, and it slid into the ditch. Then the tow-truck company wanted – it was an outrageous – it was like $200.00 and some odd dollars or something to pull me out of the ditch. Went to my house to get money – on the way back, we stopped at the local casino, had two drinks
...

Who's we?
My friend and his friend.

You went to the casino and had two drinks …
Right, and then came back to the truck, and his friend said, "I have a winch on the front of my work truck, and I can try and pull you out, so that way you don't have to spend all that money, and you can just pay me fifty bucks." I was like, well, hey yeah, yeah, it's fine. So, I was sitting in the truck, as he was hooked up to me with the winch trying to pull me out, and I was trying to steer out, and then the cops showed up, and I got out of the vehicle. I was talking with Linda Lewis on the phone – Mom – and then it was like for 15 minutes or so, and then the officer came over and asked me if I had been drinking, and I said, "Yes. About an hour ago, I had a couple of drinks." And so they decided that they were going to give me a field sobriety test because when they showed up, I was sitting in the front seat. And I passed all the field sobriety tests except for the 'ABC's' after they made me do it four or five times. And they wouldn't let me do it like you learn it like – *(she sings part of the 'ABC' song)* – no, you can't take a breath, you just got to do it, and by the fourth time of trying to do it, I was totally stumbling over myself, so they arrested me for D.U.I. Then, went in to the police station, they gave me the breathalyzer, and I blew one over the legal limit. So, one drink would be 0.8, and two drinks would be 1.5 or something like that, and so then I went through all that spiel, but what was interesting was the officer who took the field sobriety test tried to sell the mouthpiece on 'E-bay,' and my attorney had it stopped. Think anything happened to that officer? I doubt it. I think he got probably a slap on the wrist and said, that was not smart.

What happened to you?
I went through deferred prosecution. I went to anger – not anger management, but alcohol classes for 16 months, and went through that with flying colors.

16 months?
I think it was 16 months, something like that.

Like once a week, kind of thing?
No. I went to class – in the beginning it was twice a week, plus a couple of A.A. meetings, but I am not supposed to talk about A.A.

Okay.
Because that is a private matter with all Alcoholic's Anonymous people.

So, do you consider yourself an alcoholic?
Personally, no.

Do you still go to A.A.?
No.

Did you lose your driver's license?
I lost it for a small amount of time, and then I had a breathalyzer in my truck for a year, and, you know, lots of court costs, money costs, and everything for it.

There is a current Olympic – not the current, but ex Olympic gold medalist – a male, who was arrested for D.U.I.
There's people out there – I mean, there's even police officers that go in and drink and then drive home.

But, you know, that's not a good thing, though, to be drinking and driving?
No, absolutely not. Absolutely not.

So, your relationship with your mother now is non-existent?
Non-existent.

You always said that you loved your father, but your relationship with him was rocky, especially during the period following Olympics and Nationals.
Yes.

What is your relationship like with him now, and what is he doing?
Well, there for awhile – I don't know, I don't want to hurt his feelings because he doesn't remember anything.

What do you mean, he doesn't *(remember anything)* ...
We didn't talk for quite awhile, and then one of my father's friends got a hold of me to let me know that my father had had two heart attacks, back to back, within two days. And I went to see him at the hospital, and it was like this little three-year-old girl walking in with pigtails to see him, and at

that point in time, I just let everything go and realized, hey, I love my father. He is, you know, very naïve, but I love him, and I got to be here. He is my Dad.

You are the little three-year-old girl that ...
Um hm. He didn't remember that we hadn't spoken. So, now he comes up – when I have to go out of town, he watches my kitty. My Dad is my cat's play toy. He just adores my kitty and my cat – it is just constant play.

What is your cat's name?
Louie.

You just have the one cat now?
Yes.

How old is he?
Let's see – he was born a year ago, July, so he is ...

A year and a half, or so.
Yes.

You loved your dog, Koda, so much ...
I did.

You don't have him now?
When I moved into the house where I am now, he didn't have any place to run. I'm on a very busy road ... wild animals. He just was not safe, and I didn't want to have to keep him tied up because that is not fair. We are talking about a two hundred and some odd pound dog.

What happened to him?
The people that run a grocery store, locally, knew someone who was looking for one because he – they have one just like him, but two years older, and they have five acres and three children, so I gave him to them so he would have a good home and be able to run and play.

Were you sad?
I was sad, but I knew he was going to a good home, so that's what was important.

Do you ever see him?
No, un uh. That would be very confusing for him and me, probably. But my kitty is an indoor kitty – doesn't go outside, except in my arms, and then I held him when it snowed, and I put his paws in the snow *(she laughs)* just to see what he would do. He was kind of insulted at me – brrrr and shook his paws. *(She laughs)*.

You have formed a very loving and solid relationship with Linda Lewis and her husband, Greg. You obviously still have that relationship ...
Absolutely.

What are they doing now, and where do they live?
Well, they had to move to Texas to take care of her mother and stepfather, and, unfortunately, in the last couple of years, it has been very traumatic. She lost her sister, and she also lost her mother, who was like a grandma to me. She always called me her little angel. *(She laughs)*. So, that has been very traumatic. And her stepfather – health-wise – has not been doing very well, and it has been very difficult for them. They really want to come home. I took care of their car when they had to leave, and they came up and got it, and I got to see him. But I talk to Linda every single day on the phone at least once – sometimes twice. I just love her. I mean, she's, you know ...

She's been there for you.
Yeah– you know, if she could have been my mother – you know, she's like a mom should be – unconventional – what's that word ...

Unconditional.
Yeah– I mean, the love is always there no matter what.

No matter what – like a real mom?
Yeah, like a real mom should be. In hindsight, you look at things, and you think, oh okay, if my mother and father treated me like Linda and Greg do, then I may have been a totally different person.

When we spoke in an earlier interview, you wanted to get back to the rink teaching again, but you had physical problems, like your foot – do you remember – your car accident, your back ...
I don't even remember.

You had that car accident ...
Right.

And Koda stepped on your foot, and different things were delaying it (her coaching).
Mm hm.

Then the fight with Darren (the hubcap incident) and then what you had to go through after that. Did you go back to teaching? Do you teach now?
That was in – everything ended with him in 2000.

So, you didn't go back to teaching?
No, I didn't ... Well, let's see.

Well, I wonder what happened to your students who you were coaching prior to the hubcap (incident) ...
Well, they went to other coaches, I am sure – I believe. But, I haven't gone back to coaching. I would love to go back coaching, but the nearest rink to me is an hour away. There are new owners to the rink, I believe, so I have been letting them get used to everything before I speak to them and see if I can come back and teach.

What do you mean by getting them used to everything?
The new rink – if you got new owners, who have never run an ice rink before, they have to get used to learning how to run everything, and, you know, until you know what you are doing, it will not be a successful rink, and so ...

So you are not teaching, but it is something you hope to do?
I hope so. I hope so. I've skated a little bit, here and there, and I still love skating.

How are you physically? I heard you had gained some weight. Is it a lot of weight? Is it difficult for you to skate?
Oh, it was bad. I had pneumonia and ...

When was this?
Oh, gosh ... It would have been ... oh my God, I don't know – a year and a half ago, something like that.

So you put on some weight then?
Ah – 45 pounds.

Forty five from your normal - what was your normal ... *(weight)*?
Well, I had to go up in weight for the last fight *(pro boxing)* that I did in
Canada, and I was at 135, and then I gained 45 pounds and went up to,
like, 175.

What is your height, Tonya?
I'm 5'1."

So, this was for the boxing?
Right, this was for the boxing, and I used to usually box from 122 to 125,
and then after I got sick and was put on the medicine – I was put on
Prednisone twice, back to back, and I ballooned. I just ballooned. I mean,
within a month and a half, I had gained at least 30 or 40 pounds. I mean,
it didn't matter how much I ate, how much exercise I tried to do, but I was
so sick at the same time.

**Prednisone can put on weight. My dog was put on Prednisone, and he
...**
Well, I just ballooned, but it also stays in your system for so long. It's only
been the last six months that I've really lost a lot.

How much have you lost?
I've lost the 45 pounds.

You are down to 135 or so?
Probably – I don't weigh in. I know pants – the size of pants – how they fit
me. Oh, gosh, the other pants were really big on me, but I wear them all
the time because it doesn't really matter because I don't really care. But, I
went and bought myself a new pair of pants for Christmas and went down
two sizes, thinking ... but I could have gone three sizes.

Really?
Yeah. It was very exciting. *(She laughs)*.

So, you are really not skating now?
No. Un uh, and my breathing capacity had gotten down to 54 percent,
which, you know, 50 percent is hospitalization. And then I got on the right

medication. I had spoken with a specialist that finally didn't want to use me as a guinea pig. Here, try this and this and this and this. He actually listened to me, and I told him what I had tried and what, you know, this way and this way, and so we went ahead and tried this one, and it worked a tiny, tiny bit, but not enough, and so he says, let's put this one and this one together and see if this going to work. And it works. I take it every day, and my breathing capacity is at 65 percent, but it has been that way now for, oh, gosh, probably eight, nine months – ten months. It hasn't gotten any better than that. So, I have not been fighting.

You told me during the last interview that you were on several types of medication for pain, anxiety, depression, including Zoloft. Are you still on Zoloft?
No. Un uh.

Are you on any medication for depression?
No.

Or anxiety?
No.

Is there any truth to the rumors that you are bi-polar?
No! *(Emphatic)*.

Well, you might as well get them *(the rumors)* cleared up now, right?
Oh, wow.

So, you are not skating now, but is this something you want to do in the future?
I would love to. If someone would give me that opportunity to skate again, I would.

Do you mean to skate in a show or to skate to teach?
Both – even if it was a one-time thing for a skating show. Give me enough time to get back on the ice because I know then even more weight would come off. It is difficult, even at this weight, to be doing any triples. I mean, I can do them. The last time I skated, I skated for a week, and I was back doing my doubles and …

When was the last time you skated?
I skated in New York.

And when was that?
Oh, my gosh, that was probably five or six months ago – probably six months.

What was it in New York that you were doing?
I skated for 'Entertainment Tonight.'

Oh, yes, I remember that.
But I had only been skating for seven days, and I was already doing my doubles. And I was still heavy then, too. I have lost quite a bit more weight since that time. But, see, being on the Prednisone, it only took two weeks of Prednisone to do this to me. Each set of Prednisone, at least what I was told, can stay in your system for up to one year. So, it had to get out of my system before this medication really started kicking in and the weight would come off. I would only eat salad. I was trying to work out here at home, even though I couldn't breathe, and you know, it took its toll. It took its time to do what it is supposed to do.

Tell me about the professional boxing. How did it begin and how did it end?
It started when I did the exhibition thing against Paula Jones on 'Fox.' I think it was 'Fox' – 'Celebrity Boxing.'

How did you get involved in this?
Michael helped.

Michael Rosenberg?
Yes. He had gotten approached, or contacted, or however you want to say it, and he contacted me. And it was so great. I have always adored Michael Rosenberg, very much. And he has always been upfront and honest, and if you don't like it – tough. And so it was really wonderful being able to work with him again, and he helped me to be able to skate in that ESPN pro special. He is very intelligent. He knows what he is doing, and he's not about the money. He actually cares about me as a person. And through my pro fighting, I went through several different people of trainers and kind of like a manager – not really a manager, but kind of portraying as a manager, who

were all about themselves – about the money. "Just get in there and punch as much as you can, and don't worry about it."

Did you get hurt at all?
I broke my nose twice. The first time, it went one way, and the second time, it went back straight. *(She laughs).*

Did you win the bout with Paula Jones?
Yes.

How long did you pro box?
A couple of years. I did six pro fights, and I think it was either four or five little exhibition fights.

And what made you stop?
My health.

Your breathing problems?
Yes.

When you first started boxing – it was for celebrity events? After awhile, did you become proud of the boxing?
I did become proud of the boxing. I wanted to do something that was athletic, and I thought about racing cars – I had been offered to do that, but I thought, you know, I had never gone super fast, and it sounds like fun, but it would be breaking into a sport where there was only one, I believe, other female in drag racing, and it would have been very difficult. But in boxing, there are women boxers all over the place. So, it would have been a little more difficult, so I decided not to do that. But when I got the offer to do the boxing, I mean, I wanted to do something that was, like I said, athletic and had pride – hard work in it. Let me tell you, it was the hardest kind of work I have ever done in my entire life.

Do you think people were offering you this because of your 'tough-girl' image?
Yes, I do. And that I can bring people into the events.

And you didn't mind that?
No. I mean, it did pay the bills, and it kept me in shape.

And then after the celebrity boxing ...
I only did the one celebrity boxing, and then after that it was all professional. I have done exhibition fights since my last pro fight.

So, it is something you are proud of then?
Yeah. The exhibition fights were to make money – to pay my bills. But the
pro fighting – I mean, I was trying very hard, but boxing takes so much
energy and not just athleticism, but it takes strength, let me tell you. It was
hard, hard work. My favorite person in boxing was Ann Wolf. She looked
phenomenal. She knew how to box. All the girls I knew, we just knew how
to brawl. She was awesome.

**What did you think of the 'Skating with Celebrities' show that was so
popular last year? Would you appear on it if you were asked?**
Yeah, I probably would have, but watching it at home, I thought that it was
probably not a very smart move to do pairs because so many people got
hurt, and people could have gotten hurt ten times worse than they did. I
had done a little bit of pairs just for fun, you know, with another skater, a
long, long, time ago, and I had hurt myself a couple of times, but not serious. But I can definitely tell ... I have seen at the Olympics ... where the
girl *(a pairs skater)* got hurt. She fell right on her face. I mean, it is just scary.
And when you have people putting together – celebrity people trying to do
pairs, I just thought it was pretty risky. But if it would have been singles,
where they have to go out and do what they have to do, then it is up to
them. It is not somebody else having to rely on the other person for what
they are doing. But I watched it. I thought it was fun. I thought it was cute,
and if I was to get an offer to do something on the ice – most certainly I
would do it – just for the opportunity one more time.

Where do you live now?
I am in Washington State.

Is it a house in the country?
Yes.

So, you are away from the cities?
Yes. I love the country. I don't like driving in traffic. *(She laughs)*.

What do you do now to make money?
I do autograph signing shows and 'meet and greets.' I go to boxing events

and sign autographs. I've done a couple of events where I was like manager for the fighter, and so I would walk them into the ring. Met a lot of interesting, really nice people, and I did a second movie.

For video?
Yes, I believe it went to video.

Do you remember what it was called?
Ah … God, I'm so bad. *(She laughs).*

It wasn't porn or anything like that?
No, no, no, no, no. No, no, no, no. It was about a boxer, and I ran – oh 'Prize Fighter' is the name. And the boxer's girlfriend works in my restaurant – me and my two brothers owned a restaurant. Leon Spinks was in the movie as well. That is basically what the movie is. *(She laughs).*

Did you ever manage to pay off all your debts – the debts you owed after the outcome of the '94 Olympic scandal?
Yes, they were paid off.

Because I remember when we last spoke, you said you were still paying debts from money you had never seen.
Ah – I don't know any more, and I don't want to talk about that. I mean, the debts that were owed to the State and everything was paid off completely. And then I had donated the $50,000.00 to the Special Olympics. All that was taken care of.

Also, in one of our last interviews, you were thinking of suing one of the tabloids for the story – printing a picture of Darren that was supposedly doctored to make it look like you had beaten him up.
Right.

Did you sue?
I was not able to sue because I had very intelligent lawyers who stated that it would cost just as much to sue as I would win.

Better to stay out of it then?
Yeah. I had proved that it was all made up.

You proved that it was all made up?
Oh, yeah. The police chief brought in the picture they had taken after it *(the fight between her and Darren)* happened and the following day as well. And then the tabloid came out, and I called a press conference and showed the true picture, compared to that *(the tabloid picture)*, and there was a woman who came forward who stated that she had seen him *(Darren)* walk into an office and then come out looking like he had been beat up like Mike Tyson. *(She laughs)*. I'm serious. The picture looked like he had been beat up like Mike Tyson. So, just being able to show the people that did watch – you know, I'm not a monster – look, this is what happened.

What are your hobbies now? What do you do for fun?
Well, I like to go up in the snow …

You mean in the mountains?
Yes. I like the snow. Snow, I think, is one of God's best creations because every single snowflake is totally different. I like to go four-wheeling – not off-road, but just on the main roads – going for drives. I like to go for drives in the mountains. I like archery, and so I shoot archery here at the house. I got two different bows, and I really, really enjoy it. It's a lot of fun, and it relieves stress, and it is very – I don't know how to say – it is really difficult to do. It is challenging is what I'm trying to say.

Well, it is actually an Olympic sport, isn't it?
Oh, yeah. Chris was the person who taught me.

Who is Chris?
My ex-boyfriend – the last one. We are still really good friends. We see each other all the time. But he has beaten the Olympic Champions, and he had an opportunity to go to the Olympics in '92 or '91, or whenever it was, for archery, and the place that he shot for couldn't afford to send him, so he couldn't go. But he was an expert in archery and trap shooting.

And you do a little hunting with the archery? *(She told me this during an informal conversation).*
I do.

You said you got your buck this year *(also mentioned during the informal conversation)* **and that it was going to provide meat for the winter.**
I did. But I am concerned about talking about hunting because there are so

many people out there that are totally against it – even though it is for meat; it is not to go out and shoot something – to kill something. I don't know if I should have that in there about hunting or not.

Well, you explained it nicely in one of our previous interviews, why you do it and what you do it for, and I think it is very clear that you are an animal lover. I mean, do the animals *(you shoot)* suffer with the archery?
Pardon me?

Would it suffer at all?
Not any more than shooting it with a rifle. I mean, I got this deer at 45 yards, and it was a perfect shot, and it was dead within 50 yards.

What are your plans for the future, Tonya?
I just want to be happy. I love it that I have really good friends in my life, and, you know, someday I would like to be able to teach again, and, gosh, I don't know. It would be really nice to be able to find someone to share the rest of my life with. But I don't count on that. My friends and my kitty *(she laughs)* – my kitty is my baby. *(She laughs).*

Do you ever think about what happened in '94 or have you let it all go?
I let it go. I mean, every once in awhile, you know, when you see something on TV or something, then it brings back memories, and you just look at it and go, *(she sighs)* Hello.

Do you still believe Jeff and his acquaintances were the main players behind that attack on Nancy, or has anything new come to light since we last talked about it?
No. I know he did it. Him and his buddies did it because they wanted money.

You made a televised apology to Nancy ...
Yes.

Where the two of you appeared on air together ...
Um hm.

Do you believe it changed anything between you and her or about how the public felt about you?
I don't know that, but I do know that when I did the interview for

'Anything to Win,' it showed people that – a different side of me. I was able to, you know, just talk and not be in an interview that was just black and white, yes, no, you know, answers, questions. And I think …

Was this televised?
Yes, and I believe that it shows people a little bit difference of a show, of an opinion – I've heard it from many, many people – well, one for instance, there was a woman – she said that she really loved my skating, but she really didn't like me as a person, but after she had seen the show, she had different thoughts of that, and she wishes me well.

Did that appear on national television in the States?
I believe so. It was on GSN Network.

If you could change anything about your past life, over which you had some control, what would it be?
Not being naïve.

What do you regret the most?
Of course, being associated with people who were not good people.

What are you most proud of?
My triple Axel. I mean, no one can ever take that away from me.

Are any women doing that now in competition?
Yeah, there are a couple of girls that do it. There was one gal at the Olympics who did it, and I know there are a couple of other ones who do it. There is one young girl – I believe she is from Japan – that does it, but she was too young to go. I'm looking forward to seeing her again, and, hopefully, she will be able to achieve it as well.

So no one can ever take that away from you …
Yup.

The first U.S. woman to do it in competition.
Yes.

Now you appeared on a lot of shows – 'Entertainment Tonight,' I believe, prior to and during the last Olympics. Interviewers, I noticed, seemed to treat you almost with a reverence as opposed to the tough questions they once asked you.
Yeah.

Do you find other people now treat you kinder, more respectful?
I think people are just starting to realize that I'm human, you know? And that everyone makes mistakes, and I'm trying to go on with my life and make something good of myself once again.

There is still a certain image of you that some people have – the tough girl – sort of a public persona that has been created.
Um hm.

What do you most want people to know about who you really are? What is the biggest misconception about you?
I don't know what the biggest misconception would be, but I'm me. I like the outdoors. I like big trucks. I like Jeeps. I like the archery. I am me, and I love me, and it doesn't matter if other people love me. I used to always want to please everyone, and I realized that the only person you can please is yourself because if you can't love yourself, you can't love anyone else. And, yeah, I'm like a tomboy, but I can also be a lady. And I like to dress up every once in awhile. I just like to be me. I would rather be just normal and have a life and – people are like, "Oh my God. You are such a celebrity." No, I'm not. Just because I've been on TV doesn't mean I'm a celebrity. I'm just human. I mean, every person in this world – every single person – has something that they do good or two things that they do good. A mom is a mom, a father is a father – they got jobs that they do. It doesn't matter what they do. They do something.

And what is it that you do 'good'?
Love me and my kitty. *(She laughs).* Nowadays, what do I do good? I think I do my archery pretty good.

It's interesting that you haven't mentioned skating.
I haven't mentioned skating because I haven't done it for awhile, but skating will always be my biggest passion, and if I could ever do it again, I would.

Well, I believe that's it, unless there is anything else you want to add?
Gosh – well, you said, "What is the biggest misconception?" I guess the biggest misconception is that I'm not an animal. I am just human. There are so many people out there that make me to be this bad person. But, you know, they've got their fingers pointing out. If you're human, you should at least have one of those fingers pointing back at yourself, too. There is no one who is perfect.

Printed in the United States
117499LV00005B/82-87/P

9 781934 209806